Spanish Connections

Fol BoB,

Best reCAros,

[signature]

For Bob,

Best wishes,

[signature]

Spanish Connections

My Diplomatic Journey from
Venezuela to Equatorial Guinea

Mark L. Asquino

Library of Congress Control Number:		2023900455
ISBN:	Hardcover	978-1-6698-6182-9
	Softcover	978-1-6698-6181-2
	eBook	978-1-6698-6180-5

Print information available on the last page.

Rev. date: 01/26/2023

To order additional copies of this book, contact:
Xlibris
844-714-8691
www.Xlibris.com
Orders@Xlibris.com
848765

ENDORSEMENTS

Mark Asquino's memoirs are a little jewel. In lucid prose he paints a vivid picture of his eventful career with relevant historical and cultural background and insight into how policy is delivered at ground level. A joy to read.

John E. Herbst
U.S. Ambassador (Ret.)

Spanish Connections is an insightful and superbly crafted tour de force into the life of a veritable diplomat whose optimism and commitment to democratic values left an indelible mark where he served. Ambassador Asquino presents a masterful analysis of Equatorial Guinea's troubled history. He does so through his Spanish and many other foreign affairs connections.

Tutu Alicante
Executive Director
EG Justice

Ambassador Asquino's compelling narrative provides a unique insider's perspective of a diplomat's life through vivid accounts of remarkable personal and professional reminiscences while at the same time offering valuable insights for layman and expert alike. Anyone seeking a fuller understanding of the challenges and dynamics of the diplomatic world will be amply rewarded by Ambassador Asquino's memoirs – a must-read book!

Pedro Arbona
Lt. Colonel (Ret.)
U.S. Army

CONTENTS

DEDICATION

For Jane

ACKNOWLEDGMENTS

I COULD NOT have written this memoir without the patience and loving support of my wife, Jane, who has been there for me at every stage of this years-long project. She helped me recall events I'd forgotten and provided invaluable suggestions for revisions.

I am also deeply grateful to my good friend and graduate-school classmate, the late professor Lois Rudnick. Despite being terminally ill, Lois somehow found the energy to read an early draft of the memoir and write a detailed evaluation.

Joyce Namde, my top-flight deputy in Equatorial Guinea, and her veteran consular officer husband, Basile, jogged my memory on things that had happened there. I am especially indebted to Professor Sebastian Faber of Oberlin College, who found records in the Abraham Lincoln Brigade Archives of my long-lost uncle, Spanish Civil War veteran Albert Lahue.

My wonderful aunt, Betty Asquino, and her daughter, my cousin Cheryl, read parts of the manuscript and encouraged me to keep writing until it was done. I'm grateful to Dr. Jeffrey Ross, who gently nudged me forward when I was suffering writer's block. My diplomatic colleague Dan Whitman gave me excellent guidance and advice on how to get the memoir published. Fellow writer Baro Shalizi provided tips on marketing.

Jane's and my dear friends, Holly Kinley, Charles Mann, and Connie Deschamps, bucked up my spirits during tough stretches and made me laugh when I needed to.

Professor Janet Steele, my George Washington University colleague, persuaded me I should tell my story at a key point when the memoir's narrative was veering off in a different direction. Lt. Col. Pedro Arbona, U.S. Army (ret.), kindly shared with me his encyclopedic knowledge of Equatorial Guinea and Spain.

My good friend, photojournalist Robert Royal, allowed me to use his hanting and evocative photo of Bioko Island fot the book cover.

I am also indebted to Sara Taber and Sara Eyestone, my memoir teachers, who saw promise in the early chapters of the book.

I wish to thank the countless other friends and colleagues, too numerous to mention, who provided me with encouragement as I was writing this memoir.

Views expressed in this book are my own, and do not necessarily reflect those of the U.S. government.

Finally, I'm grateful to Chris Orleans, Christine Colborne, and the entire Xlibris editorial and production team for transforming the manuscript of *Spanish Connections* into a book.

INTRODUCTION

WHAT WAS I doing accepting the Order of the Grand Cross of Independence of the Republic of Equatorial Guinea from Africa's longest-serving dictator? That's a question I've asked myself many times since that memorable day in September 2015, one of my last as an American diplomat.

The event took place in the presidential palace's cavernous ballroom. With its dark mahogany-paneled walls, Carrara marble floors, and massive chandeliers, it hardly seemed possible that this grand Italianate room was on a small island off the coast of West Central Africa.

The ceremony began with the president draping a bright red, green, and white sash over my left shoulder. The sash bore a large enameled Maltese ross set on a gilt metal sunburst background. After bestowing the award, the president delivered brief remarks commending me for my three years of diplomatic service as U.S. ambassador to the Republic of Equatorial Guinea. This was followed by a toast with Cristal, the president's favorite, four-hundred-dollar-a-bottle French champagne.

For any ambassador, especially one like me who was about to retire, receiving the host country's highest award should have been a capstone career achievement. On a certain level, I certainly appreciated the recognition from the president for what had been three years of exceptionally challenging and often contentious diplomatic work. But there was something disquieting about accepting such an award. Then again, it was perhaps in keeping with the country's tumultuous history.

What became Spanish Guinea in West Central Africa had been ceded by Portugal to Spain in 1778. Three centuries earlier, Portuguese explorer Fernando Po, for whom its principal island was once named, had claimed this large territory for Portugal. The colony's capital, which the Spaniards christened Santa Isabel, was on the island of Fernando Po, half the size of my native Rhode Island. At the time, there was also a huge mainland portion of the colony called Rio Muni between present-day Cameroon and Gabon.

After nearly two centuries of harsh, dictatorial, colonial rule, the newly named Republic of Equatorial Guinea, now far smaller than the original concession from Portugal, was reluctantly granted independence by Generalissimo Francisco Franco in 1968. Neighboring countries that had been under Great Britain's and France's colonial rule had their independence carefully guided by democratic governments. But that was not the case for Equatorial Guinea. Its democratic constitution and parliamentary government structure were the products of a Fascist dictatorship.

The country's first president was a former minor colonial functionary named Francisco Macias Nguema, who was chosen through elections that generally were deemed free and fair by the United Nations and others. But what followed under Macias was an eleven-year reign of terror that combined the worst elements of Idi Amin's and Pol Pot's savage rule with a Hispanic dash of Franco's Spain.

In 1979, Macias was overthrown in a military coup directed by his nephew, then Lt. Col. Teodoro Obiang Nguema Mbasogo, who had served in Macias's government as one of his most brutal henchmen. Obiang has ruled the country with an iron fist ever since. And now, on short notice, he had given me this impressive-looking medal. But why?

During my first year as ambassador in Equatorial Guinea, I was constantly pushing the envelope with the government, asking it to release unjustly imprisoned regime opponents and criticizing it for the absence of free media and other basic rights for its citizens. I insisted in private and public that I was not an advocate for any political party but rather in favor of "democratic principles" that would include respecting human rights and opening political space to opposition parties. In response, regime officials made it clear that my ambassadorial tenure might be a brief one.

No, I didn't think the government was threatening to do me in. Rather, it occurred to me that I would be declared persona non grata, a term applied to an ambassador no longer welcome in the country and required to leave within a matter of days. But such was not to be my fate.

Part of the reason may have been that U.S. oil and gas companies are Equatorial Guinea's largest investors and provide the major source of the elite's immense wealth in a country where, according to reliable estimates, over 70 percent of the population lives on less than $2 a day. Perhaps, given the importance of U.S. investment, EG's government had concluded that declaring a U.S. ambassador persona non grata was not a good idea. In the end, my outspoken advocacy of democracy was tolerated, and I managed to finish my three-year assignment.

Having served as a diplomat in other countries with authoritarian leaders, including Panama, Uzbekistan, Kazakhstan, and Sudan, I took a long patient view of what constitutes success in a place like Equatorial Guinea. In short, I came to measure it in small increments.

For example, I was frequently able to gain the release of Equatoguineans who had been unfairly imprisoned by appealing to the government's image consciousness. For as much as Equatorial Guinea's rulers claimed they cared little, if at all when it came to what the rest of the world thought about them, this was far from the truth. The country paid public relations firms like Qorvis Communications in Washington DC hundreds of thousands of dollars each year to portray Equatorial Guinea's actions in the most favorable light possible.

Those and so many other thoughts went through my mind that afternoon as I stood in the ornate presidential palace ballroom. It was the only time I would ever wear that lovely medal with its accompanying silk sash. Of the many memories, both good and less so, that I have from my thirty-seven-year career in the U.S. Foreign Service, that moment remains perhaps the most unusual and haunting one. As I write this several years later, it still inspires me with an odd combination of satisfaction, pride, and ambivalence.

But I have gotten ahead of my story. How was it in the first place that I came to spend those three years as U.S. ambassador to Equatorial Guinea? Further, given my brief description of the country's unusual and brutal history, you might wonder why I would ever want to serve there. You would hardly be the first to raise this question, which I will try to answer in the coming pages.

This is a memoir about my diplomatic journey to that country. I discuss the many stops along the way that finally led to my being U.S. ambassador to Spain's only former colony in sub-Saharan Africa. It is neither a scholarly tome nor a diplomatic history, although it has elements of both. More than anything else, mine is the story of a lifelong fascination with Spain. For me, my final foreign service tour as an ambassador to Equatorial Guinea makes perfect sense. I view it as the last piece needed to complete a full circle in my personal and professional life that began in Franco's Spain. To explain that requires going back to my fascination with all things Spanish.

CHAPTER 1

A Mysterious Uncle, College, and Finally Spain

"YOU HAD AN uncle who fought and died in the Spanish Civil War," My mother told me this in hushed, conspiratorial tones as if she was sharing a state secret—something we needed to keep hidden from the Soviets. This was during the late summer of 1963, which was a time when people, indeed, worried about such things.

I was a gangly, bookish fourteen-year-old who spent hours on end reading about exotic countries in the *World Book Encyclopedia* that my parents had bought for me the previous year. The encyclopedia's deep-red-grained faux-leather covers with dark-blue lettering offered me a welcome retreat from the small confining world in which I lived. And my mother's words, for better or worse, would be the beginning of my lifelong fascination with Spain.

The latter would take me on a long, personal, and professional journey that would lead not only to my living in Spain and marrying a Spaniard but also decades later serving as the U.S. ambassador to the Republic of Equatorial Guinea. But let me return for a moment to 1963 and the beginning of this odyssey.

My mother and I were sitting on aluminum tubular-frame folding chairs with blue-and-white synthetic woven webbing in what she rather grandiloquently called the breezeway. The latter connected our gray-shingled 1950s Cape Cod house with a two-car garage that dwarfed it. My mother had a rich, romantic imagination, and reality was a constant source of disappointment for her. On this humid August afternoon, the last thing you would find was a breeze in this narrow passageway.

"His name was Charles Lahue. In those days, families took in relatives' children whose mothers had died. Grandma's brother was a widower. And I always thought Charles was just another one of my cousins who lived with us along with their widowed father. But he was actually my half brother. He told me this just before he went to Spain.

My mother was wearing a light floral print, sleeveless dress that nicely accented her natural red hair, which she wore in a tightly curled permanent. There was just a hint of perspiration on her elegant pale neck. She suddenly paused in telling her story. Her light-hazel eyes, which sometimes looked blue, were cast downward as if searching for a clear path in the brambles of an impenetrable forest.

"You see, Grandma had an illegitimate son. She was pregnant with him before she married Grandpa, but she didn't say anything until after their wedding. I think that's why Grandpa never liked Charles. And Grandma never treated him the way she did Uncle Paul and me or even our other cousins."

"But why would—" I began, only to have my mother cut me off mid-sentence.

"Well, your great-grandmother worked as a housekeeper for a rich man and his family. She went to the man's wife to ask if Grandma should tell Grandpa she was pregnant. But this lady said no because then he might break off their engagement. Grandma should say nothing, and so that's what she did."

"But wasn't that unfair to Gramps?"

"Well, yes, it certainly was," my mother said with a trace of indignation in her voice. "I think it was a terrible thing to do to him. And in a way, I also believe that's why your uncle Charles decided to leave home and go to Spain."

"But why Spain?" I asked as if on cue.

"Well, Charles told me he wanted to do something noble with his life. He said Grandma never treated him like her son, and he felt like an orphan. Charles said the world had to do something to help the Spanish Republicans who were fighting against Franco's Fascists. He kissed me and said goodbye. I never saw him again."

It was a moving story, one that I would never forget. But was there really an Uncle Charles? That's a question I've often asked myself, especially during the years that followed when I lived in Spain, first as a Fulbright university lecturer in the isolated northern city of Oviedo and later as a diplomat in Madrid.

Indeed, trying to find this elusive uncle would become something of a life-long obsession for me. My genealogical research uncovered a one-line registry entry in Providence, Rhode Island's records of the birth. It noted that my maternal grandmother had given birth to a male child whose father was listed as "unknown." But marriage records I later found revealed that this infant would have been a toddler in the year when my grandparents wed. Based on this chronology, my mother's tale of my grandmother's unconscionable deception of her soon-to-be husband didn't add up. But beyond that, all traces of my uncle disappeared after that birth registry notation. I couldn't find any census or other records documenting his life.

And then there was that other part of my mother's story. She said that after he had been killed in Spain, Charles's body was sent back to the United States for burial in New York State where his wife was living at the time. My grandparents, according to my mom, decided against attending the funeral, something she thought was a cruel, heartless thing to do.

But as I've noted above, there were no marriage or death certificates to be found for my uncle Charles in the state of New York or any other place in the United States. Nor were there archival records I could find of a Charles Lahue ever having fought for the Republicans in the Spanish Civil War. And historians of that war told me that foreign soldiers killed in Spain were buried there and never repatriated.

So what was I to believe? Was my Uncle Charles simply a figment of my mother's romantic imagination? Had she invented him to provide me with a cautionary tale about the dangers of leaving a safe, but suffocating, adult life in Rhode Island to seek foreign adventures?

I found it hard to believe that he was a complete fabrication. After all, I had discovered the birth record of this long-lost relative. At least that much was true. As a former literature professor, I sometimes wondered if my mother was like one of those "unreliable narrators" you come across in novels. I always told my students that they needed to be on guard because such a narrator might be deliberately misleading readers. Was that what my mother had done in telling me her strange, compelling story and then asking that I never share it with anyone else?

In the course of writing this memoir, I learned that, indeed, I had an uncle who went to Spain and joined the Abraham Lincoln Brigade, one of many international volunteer brigades that helped the Spanish Republican government fight against General Francisco Franco's rebellious Nationalist forces. My uncle's name was Albert, not Charles Lahue, as my mother told me.

It's beyond puzzling how she could possibly have gotten her half brother's name wrong. Further, what she told me about his dying in Spain was untrue. With help from an American professor, I found a record in the Abraham Lincoln Brigade Archives stating my Uncle Albert arrived in Spain on November 14, 1937, and had a turbulent time with a group of U.S. volunteers. In 1938, he was charged with attempting to desert. Somehow, he managed to survive the Spanish Civil War. After leaving Spain, my uncle Albert broke off all ties with his family, and I found few traces of him in the years that followed.

I knew none of this on that hot day in August. What inspired me about my mother's story was this mysterious uncle's spirit of adventure. He had been bold enough to leave home and go off to see the world. He wanted to embrace a cause bigger than himself. Someday, I thought, I'm going to do exactly the same thing. And so, I did.

In September 1975, I made my first trip to Spain and taught American literature and history on a Fulbright fellowship. After so many years of thinking about España, studying its language, and daydreaming about going there, I finally embarked on what would prove to be a life-changing journey in the final months of Generalissimo Francisco Franco's nearly four-decades-long dictatorial reign. By then, I was a graduate student in my late twenties.

So what took me so long? you might ask. I've often wondered why I hadn't simply boarded a plane bound for Madrid years earlier. Why was that so hard?

At least part of the answer is that despite my childhood vow to see the world as soon as I could, I remained firmly anchored to Rhode Island for a very long time. In retrospect, I suppose I was far less adventurous and much more cautious than I had been willing to admit to myself.

Whatever the case, instead of attending an out-of-state college as many of my high school friends did, I stayed put. In the fall of 1967, I entered Brown University in Providence, Rhode Island, just a few miles from where I'd grown up.

That said, I found attending Brown a "foreign" experience. I'd done well in the public high school I attended and had good SAT scores. But I suspected I'd been accepted by this elite Ivy League school, at least in part because of my uncle, Joe Asquino, who'd studied at Brown on the G.I. Bill after World War II. This alumni "legacy" connection undoubtedly helped me gain admission, as each year my uncle donated generously to the school. As a result, I felt rather intimidated, wondering whether I really belonged at Brown.

Not surprisingly, I found that many of my male classmates had graduated from elite New England prep schools like Choate, Deerfield Academy, and Mt. Hermon. Some had spent years living and studying overseas. Others came from affluent families. My fellow students, both male, and female seemed incredibly worldly, mature, and sophisticated to me. I asked myself, "How can I ever hope to compete academically with such classmates?" And so, for the next four years, I studied like a madman, living at home most of the time, hardly dating or getting involved in extracurricular activities.

Fortunately, I was able to make a number of good friends at Brown. Most of them came from other parts of the United States, and that was an eye-opener for me, given that Rhode Island can feel like a small parochial "island" where everybody seems to know or be related to each other. Although Brown is in Rhode Island, I came to view the university as clearly not reflecting the values of my home state.

The late 1960s, of course, was a time of enormous political, social, and cultural upheaval. At the center of everything was the war in Vietnam, which dominated and impacted the lives of so many young men of my generation. That included one of my high school classmates, who would be killed in combat barely a year after our 1967 graduation. I was among the lucky ones. As long as I remained in college and kept up my grades, I would have a student deferment from the military draft. But as the anti-war movement gained momentum on university campuses across the country, including at Brown, I found myself drawn to joining the protest movements engulfing the United States. Despite this, I steered clear of political activism for my first three years of college.

Looking back, my doing so reflected the single-mindedness I felt at that time. In many ways, it's a quality that has guided me in pursuing other goals throughout my life, including becoming an ambassador. In addition to being an overachiever, what made me so focused on my studies was the fact that my parents had not been able to attend college. As an only child growing up in a blue-collar, working-class family, I knew from an early age that they expected me to go to college. This was especially true for my father.

My dear dad Louie grew up in a poor large Italian immigrant family and had been forced to leave school after the ninth grade. As a tall, skinny, thirteen-year-old kid, he found himself learning the hazardous sheet metal and roofing trade and climbing "tripull-dekahs," as three-story tenement houses are called in Rhode Island. He would often tell me when I was growing up that it was hard, dirty work. But he'd quickly add he had been lucky to learn such a trade at a young age.

My father was incredibly determined, hardworking, and goal-oriented—all qualities I inherited from him. So not surprisingly, he became a highly successful small businessman. Good-natured, kind, and generous, Louie had strong ambitions for me as his only child. Consequently, my father was only too happy to use a large portion of the profits he made from his growing business to pay for my undergraduate tuition and expenses at Brown. That meant a lot to me and still does. But it also carried with it a deep sense of obligation.

The last thing I wanted to do was disappoint my father by foolishly wasting the opportunity he'd given me. And that made me a dutiful son. Unlike so many others of my generation during those years, I was not a rebellious soul. Rather I was only too eager to meet and surpass the expectations my parents had set for me.

In 1971, I graduated magna cum laude from Brown with an honors degree in American civilization. During my senior year, I was elected to Phi Beta Kappa, the national honor society. Perhaps I needed to excel to prove that I really did belong at Brown. Certainly, I was proud of these achievements, but now what? I had absolutely no idea what I wanted to do after graduation.

In the last year and a half of college, I began to look beyond my obsessive pursuit of a degree from Brown. After all, there was a lot going on in the world, including the tragic assassinations of Martin Luther King Jr. and Robert Kennedy. The war in Vietnam continued to rage.

Following the U.S. invasion of Cambodia in April 1970, I joined demonstrations and marches at Brown against the Nixon administration and the war in Southeast Asia. As I marched with others chanting anti-war slogans in the streets of downtown Providence, I saw FBI agents taking pictures of us from nearby rooftops. I was being surveilled along with others by law enforcement officers for exercising the right of free speech. And that angered me. In fact, the thought of it all these decades later still angers me.

Conformist that I'd been my whole life up until then, I was now vocally opposing my government and denouncing the president. In many ways, this marked the beginning of a major change in my life. Little by little, I stopped being the obedient, largely unquestioning person that I'd been brought up to be. Instead, I came to see that challenging the established order was not only important but also the right thing for me to do in Nixon's America.

As graduation approached, the one thing I knew for sure was that I didn't want to be drafted into the U.S. military. This was due in large part to my increasing opposition to the Vietnam War. Fortunately, I'd drawn a high number in the 1969 military draft lottery and was never required to report for military service.

In the end, like so many others who had excelled academically in college during the tumultuous 1960s, I took the line of least resistance. I simply postponed having to make a decision about my future by applying to PhD graduate programs at a number of universities, including Brown.

I applied for full fellowships, as I wanted to be financially independent from my parents.

Although I was accepted by other prestigious universities, only Brown offered me financial assistance. It was hard to turn down a full tuition waiver plus a generous monthly stipend from my alma mater. And so here I was once again deciding to stay in Rhode Island. But I decided it was time to indulge my wanderlust.

Midway through my PhD studies, I spent a summer in Winchester, England, working as a volunteer excavator at a Roman-era archaeological site. That was my first overseas experience, and I found it deeply satisfying despite the fact it was and remains the hardest work I've ever done in my life! And as a graduate student, I matured on a personal level as well, entering into a wondrous, romantic relationship with a dear classmate from my undergraduate years.

But I was still stuck in Rhode Island. And even worse, I was pursuing a career goal I increasingly began to question. As a PhD candidate, I designed and taught my own course and came to the sad realization that teaching was not for me. I found it grueling and tedious, and I hated standing in front of a group of undergraduates. More and more, I asked myself if I really wanted to spend the rest of my life doing something I clearly didn't like.

Just as I came toward the end of completing my PhD dissertation, I discovered a remarkable opportunity. One of my Brown graduate-school classmates had just won a Fulbright grant to teach American Studies courses as a junior lecturer at a Spanish university. As we talked, all I could think about was that I wanted to do the same thing. At the time, I'd never even heard of the U.S. government's Fulbright fellowship program.

I certainly knew something about Senator J. William Fulbright, an Arkansas Democrat. As chairman of the Senate Foreign Relations Committee in the 1960s, he held televised hearings on U.S. military involvement in Vietnam. Based on testimony to his committee,

Fulbright went from being a staunch supporter of President Johnson's war policies to one of his most eloquent and effective critics.

With a bit of research, I learned that after World War II, Fulbright had introduced a bill in the U.S. Senate to create a new overseas exchange program in the fields of education and science. The purpose of the program, which eventually came to bear his name, was to "promote international goodwill." In the years immediately following the carnage of global warfare, Fulbright believed that educational exchange programs between foreign countries and the United States would foster mutual understanding among the nations of the world. This, in turn, might help to prevent future wars.

By 1974, when I applied for a grant, Fulbright fellowships were known throughout the world as the U.S. government's premier exchange program. In Europe, where the program began, there were American Studies fellowships in Spain, France, Germany, and Italy for U.S. junior lecturers who had not completed their PhDs. After eight straight years at Brown, I saw the program as offering me the chance of a lifetime. Finally, I would live and work in Spain!

In the spring of 1975, after what seemed like an endless wait, I finally received a letter from the Fulbright Foreign Scholarship Board. It offered me a fellowship to teach American Studies at a Spanish university. I would later learn that I had been assigned to the University of Oviedo in northwest Spain, where my graduate-school friend had been teaching for the previous two years.

I was elated and immediately accepted. I was even happier with the coincidence that I would be teaching at the same university as my classmate. But what I didn't know at the time was that it was due to a complete fluke that I received the grant at all. I learned this several years later when I was doing educational exchange work as a diplomat at the U.S. embassy in Madrid.

Someone I knew at the U.S.-Spanish Fulbright Commission in Madrid told me one day in the early 1980s that he had been on the 1975 selection committee reviewing fellowship applicants. He explained that all the American Studies lectureships for that year had been decided. Letters had gone out offering the fellowships to those who had been chosen. He chuckled and said, "Unfortunately, Mark, you weren't one of them!"

Dumbfounded I replied, "What do you mean? You know as well as I do that I got the fellowship!" He explained that one of those initially selected for a lectureship had turned it down. Although I was on the list of alternates for a grant, I was not at the top.

He continued that just as the committee was about to choose the person heading the list for the vacant fellowship, someone piped up and said, "Hey, wait a minute! We don't have any Hispanic grantees this year."

Another committee member chimed in, "Well, how about this Asquino guy? He has a Spanish name. Why don't we choose him? He's from the same graduate program as the lecturer we now have in Oviedo. Let's offer the lectureship to Asquino."

And so it was, quite belatedly, that I received the letter offering me "a Fulbright," as the grants are known. I was blithely unaware that my getting the fellowship was completely due to last-minute "political correctness" by the selection committee.

Now, I'm not Hispanic, neither have I ever claimed to be. Although Asquino is an Italian name, I am frequently asked if it's Spanish, and I always say it's not. But had it not been for someone turning down the opportunity to go to Spain at the last minute and then the selection committee's desire to give it to "a Hispanic," I never would have gone off to teach at the University of Oviedo. For that matter, I would also not be writing this particular memoir.

So in mid-September 1975, my parents drove me to Boston's Logan Airport to board an Iberia flight to Madrid. My Spanish adventure was about to begin, but it had anything but an auspicious start.

My mom and dad accompanied me to the Iberia Airlines ticket counter. We saw dozens of noisy protestors waving placards and loudly denouncing the U.S. government's support for the Franco regime. They were particularly incensed about the death sentences just handed down by a Spanish military tribunal against alleged terrorists—three members of El Frente Revolucionario Anti-Fascista y Patriota (FRAP)) and two from Basque Hearth and Homeland (ETA). All five had been convicted of killing Spanish policemen the previous spring.

The convicted men were subsequently executed by firing squad on September 27, 1975, which set off protests against Franco in both Europe and the United States. Following their execution, a new leftist terrorist group, Grupos de Resistencia Primero de Octubre,(GRAPO) would kill four more policemen on October 1 as retaliation against the Franco regime. Years later, I would return to Spain as a diplomat assigned to be director of the U.S. embassy's Cultural Center in Madrid. In one of life's ironic twists, this same center had been bombed by GRAPO in the late 1970s. GRAPO would fire an anti-tank rocket at the U.S. embassy during my 1982–86 diplomatic tour in Madrid. However, I'm once again getting ahead of my story.

Upon seeing the protestors at the airport, my mother became livid. She strode to them and said in a scolding voice, "You stop that right now! My son is going to Spain. I don't want anyone protesting against him or Spain. Do you understand?"

The demonstrators were momentarily taken aback and fell silent. Who was this furious middle-aged woman wagging her finger at them? Rising to her full five feet six inches in height, my mother could be quite formidable when angry—or even when not. After a few minutes, the protesters resumed their chants, oblivious to my mother's scowling glances.

I presented my ticket at the counter, checked my bags, and soon was happily on the plane heading to Madrid. But not so fast. About an hour into the flight, when we were a good way out over the Atlantic, my fellow passengers and I noticed the aircraft was losing altitude. Not a good sign on a trans-Atlantic flight, I thought. There was also an acrid smell permeating the cabin. That was even worse. After what seemed like a long while, the captain spoke calmly over the intercom, announcing there was a "technical problem" with the aircraft. Rather than returning to Boston, he said we would be going to JFK Airport in New York to address the issue.

At this point in my life, I'd made all of two previous flights. Neither of my parents had ever boarded an aircraft. Growing up, I thought my parents' fear of flying made perfect sense. Finding myself in this situation, I was plenty scared. Frightened out of my wits, to be precise.

As the plane was making its approach to JFK, I spotted fire trucks near the runway. My seatmate was an attractive young woman with whom I'd spoken briefly. Seeing how terrified I was, she reached over and gently took my hand without saying anything. The landing was fine, after which the Iberia staff herded us off to a business-class lounge where we were provided unlimited drinks on the airline's tab. I must admit I needed more than one after that experience.

But no amount of alcohol could blunt my reaction upon hearing that Iberia was repairing whatever was wrong with the plane and that we were expected to board the same aircraft once it was fixed.

"There's no way I'm going to get on that damn plane again," I announced loudly to no one in particular.

By this time, the young woman who had been my seatmate was becoming something of my travel companion. She told me in soothing tones there was nothing to fear. After several more drinks and her increasingly amorous gestures, I managed to persuade myself that I was going to Spain that night, come hell, high water, or even a broken aircraft.

I resumed my seat next to the young lady, who was becoming more attractive by the moment, and we headed off again for Madrid. The flight proved to be uneventful although I should actually qualify that. One thing led to another and the young woman and I began passionately making out until she finally got tired and fell asleep in my lap. I figured if I was going to die, this was a pretty good way to go!

But having gotten through the evening and entered Spanish airspace, I decided I might survive after all. Upon landing and entering the airport terminal, the young woman and I gave each other one last long embrace. She was headed to Andalusia on vacation, and I had a week of Fulbright orientation sessions in Madrid. We exchanged contact information, saying that we must spend time together again. Of course, we never did.

Back then, the Spanish-American Fulbright commission had its offices on an upper floor of the imposing National Library (Biblioteca

Nacional) near Plaza Colon in the center of Madrid. As I climbed the stone library's grand stairway with its carved facade leading to heavy wooden doors, I passed statues honoring Spanish kings and writers, including Cervantes.

It was a heady and fraught time to be in Spain. Although none of us knew it during our orientation, Franco would be dead in a matter of months. Following my orientation week in Madrid, I took a six-hour train ride to Oviedo in the northwest province of Asturias. The journey wound through the dramatic Cantabrian mountains and picturesque green valleys of Spain's coal mining region. As we entered Asturias, I saw "horreos," traditional round stone structures with red tile roofs that are used to store dried corn.

When I arrived in Oviedo in the fall of 1975, the city still had scars from the 1936–39 Spanish Civil War. I saw bullet holes that remained in the facades of government buildings in the city center. Perhaps, I thought, they had been left by the Franco regime as a reminder of the fierce fighting in the Republican stronghold of Oviedo, which had continued right up to the end of that war.

My assignment was at the University of Oviedo's Faculty of Literature and Letters. Its classrooms were housed in a rather drab 1960s-era two-story building. But what really impressed me was a statue in its courtyard. It was of the seated figure of a renowned eighteenth-century Spanish monk and scholar named Benito Jerónimo Feijóo, who was born in Oviedo. His grim stone scowl surveyed all those entering the faculty. He seemed to be saying, "This is a serious place of learning!"

As the Fulbright lecturer in the Department of English Literature and Letters, I taught two survey courses on American literature and one on American history. And I have to say, like undergraduates everywhere, studying was not the chief priority for many of them.

As noted earlier, teaching did not inspire me, but the Fulbright grant had been my ticket to Spain.

What I did enjoy as a teacher was that my best students possessed an openness and curiosity about American literature and history that I found immensely refreshing after having taught freshmen at Brown. I decided that teaching here was different and interesting. But it also exhausted me as I struggled with preparations for three survey courses with thirty to forty students in them.

I began teaching prior to Franco's death during the first few weeks of October and November 1975. My British and German colleagues at the faculty warned me that we all had student "spies" in our classes. These were young people paid by the police to report anything "subversive" or critical of the regime uttered by teachers. That bothered me, but I soon learned that the spies were easy to spot. They tended to be the most amiable, but least diligent, students in each course. They deliberately failed year after year to stay on the government's payroll. The whole spy situation would have been funny had it not felt so creepy.

With Franco's death on November 20, 1975, the University of Oviedo, along with all other Spanish institutions of higher education, was closed for several weeks. My British colleague and I decided to continue classes in our homes to keep our courses on schedule. The sessions were voluntary, and not all of my students came. Some who initially did decide to stop telling me it was "too dangerous." Indeed, the immediate days and weeks after Franco's passing were tense because of enhanced security everywhere. Spain's future direction remained unclear.

At some point, my colleague told me that he was ceasing to offer classes at home. This surprised me, but he explained he'd gotten word that the local police knew about it and were unhappy with our continuing to teach. They regarded what we were doing as "disrespectful" during the period of national mourning for Franco. He continued that he'd been told in no uncertain terms that "something unfortunate" might happen to us if we continued to teach.

That was a shock in my young life as it was hard not to take such a warning seriously. Clearly, living in Spain was rather different than I'd imagined. In these turbulent times, the U.S. embassy and Fulbright Commission were hundreds of miles away in Madrid. I was on my own, and there was little either could do to help me in this situation. With great reluctance, I stopped my classes as well.

But despite this tense atmosphere, when the university reopened, I was impressed with how students who had never openly discussed politics now wanted to do so all the time both inside and outside of the classroom. Political change was in the air, and Franco's old guard was beginning to retreat.

This made the remainder of my year in Oviedo lively and memorable as Spain moved ever so slowly toward democracy. But at the same time, I realized this transition would be a long and difficult one opposed by those who continued to mourn the passing of the dictatorship.

It was toward the end of my time in Spain that I became romantically involved with an undergraduate student from another department. Spending time with her, her family, and her friends, none of whom spoke any English, did wonders for my still-halting Spanish. It also allowed me to immerse myself in Spanish culture and history.

Over the years, I've wondered whether I fell in love with a Spaniard, Spain, or both and why I seemed incapable of distinguishing between the two. The consequences of the former would eventually lead to an exceptionally unhappy marriage and divorce.

During that year in Spain, I came to know young U.S. Information Agency (USIA) officers at our embassy in Madrid. USIA had an interesting history. Founded in 1953 at the height of the Cold War by President Eisenhower, with the slogan "Telling America's story to the world," USIA was viewed by some as a propaganda agency dedicated to countering the international influence of the Soviet Union and to a lesser extent China. Indeed, during the Cold War years, much of its activities— which employed educational exchanges, cultural presentations, and information dissemination—were aimed at promoting a positive image of America overseas in response to "Communist propaganda."

But for me, this was a narrow and mistaken perspective. The term "public diplomacy" was first used in the 1960s by former U.S. diplomat Edmund Guillon. It was developed in part to distance overseas governmental information, cultural, and educational activities from the term "propaganda." Until 1999, when USIA was dismantled, it played a key role in advancing U.S. foreign policy goals through both public diplomacy and also what came to be known as soft power. The latter term, coined by Professor Joseph Nye in 1990, maintained that the United States benefited most when it employed persuasion and attraction to its culture and educational institutions, rather than relying on "hard power" military and economic coercion to achieve those goals.

After the fall of the Berlin Wall and the dissolution of the Soviet Union, politicians like Senator Jesse Helms and others, mostly in the Republican Party, claimed there was no longer "a need" for the USIA. They argued that as we had "won" the Cold War, it was time to rid the U.S. government of such "wasteful relics."

In my view, nothing could have been further from the truth. USIA was no more a Cold War relic than NATO. Both had a continuing role to play in addressing new, post-Cold War challenges. But in October 1999, the Clinton administration, after much vacillation, unwisely bowed to Helms's political pressure. Secretary of State Madeleine Albright oversaw what was called the "consolidation"' of USIA and another "Cold War" organization, the Arms Control and Disarmament Agency (ACDA), into the U.S. Department of State.

As a result, the United States lost the expertise of these highly specialized, nimble organizations, both of which had people with skills lacking in the State Department. What we unilaterally gave up as a country was much of our capacity to counter disinformation by foreign adversaries and the specialized knowledge of experts at ACDA to address the threat of nuclear proliferation.

Once again, I've considerably digressed. Turning back to 1975–76, the USIA ably led the U.S. government's international people-to-people or public diplomacy. It was in early 1976 that the officers I'd met at the Fulbright Commission asked if I would help them set up programs for American speakers at the University of Oviedo. I told them I would be more than happy to do so, never imagining this would turn out to be the first step toward a lifelong career. When I shared my ambivalence about pursuing an academic career, they encouraged me to take the foreign service test to become a USIA officer. I was intrigued by the thought of pursuing a career in diplomacy rather than teaching, especially after having spent such an exciting and politically transformative year in Spain.

CHAPTER 2

Back to Grim Reality

AFTER THE EXCITING year I'd spent in Spain, it was hard returning to Brown and the confines of Rhode Island in the summer of 1976. One of the greatest difficulties was resuming work on my PhD dissertation, about a third of which I'd written before leaving the United States.

I had brought along research materials to Oviedo with the notion that I would somehow find time to work on my PhD during my fellowship year. What a wildly unrealistic idea that was! First of all, although I'd done preparations for my classes during the months prior to departing the United States, I had no idea how time-consuming teaching three survey courses at a Spanish university would be.

As it turned out, much of what I prepared was nearly useless once I got in the classroom and realized how limited my students' English was. So, I wound up having to start over, often putting together teaching plans on the fly literally hours before I gave classes.

And then, there was the challenge of settling into life in a remote Spanish city in the final days of the Franco regime. Filled with the romance of what it would be like to teach in Spain, I had little understanding of what living overseas entailed. This was all the more so in a country whose language I could barely speak.

Eight years had passed since I'd last studied Spanish. After fulfilling Brown's undergraduate foreign-language requirement, I had cavalierly decided that it was time to move on to more "intriguing" subjects. So despite my lifelong fascination with Spain, I closed my Spanish textbook for the last time in 1968 without giving any thought to why the language might be useful to know in the future. Little did I realize at the time that Spanish would not only become my second language but also form the basis for much of my personal life and career in the foreign service.

Once I received the fellowship to Spain, though, it became clear I had to relearn Spanish pronto. The first thing I did was sign up for a Spanish evening course at nearby Providence College in the summer of 1975. I enrolled as an "auditor," or someone not seeking credit, and much to my delight, I learned I would not have to pay anything for sitting in on the classes. Credit or not, I studied once again like a madman. But sad to say, after so many years away from Spanish, the classes barely breathed life into my atrophied language skills.

In my experience, forced language immersion is a wonderful but terrifying thing. That was how I felt during my first weeks in Spain. I found that my British and German colleagues at the University of Oviedo, who had spent years living and working in Spain, were fully fluent in Spanish. In contrast, I struggled to use my basic Spanish in daily chores that ranged from grocery shopping to trying to persuade my grumpy non-English-speaking landlord to fix things in the apartment.

Because of my teaching load, I had no time for a Spanish tutor, so learning Spanish was a catch-as-catch-can experience. This often resulted in hilarious, albeit deeply embarrassing, experiences.

For example, there was no washing machine in my apartment. I asked the wife of the building's *portero* (doorman) to do my laundry, for which I would pay her. She readily agreed, and this worked out reasonably well enough until one day I realized I was virtually without anything to wear.

So, I went to her apartment and knocked on the door, hoping to get the laundry back I'd left many days before. When no one answered, I hammered more forcefully. Much to my surprise, the woman's sleepy-eyed teenage daughter, dressed only in skimpy underwear, answered the door with a startled, upset look. Flustered, I immediately tried to say to her in my broken Spanish that I was so sorry if I had embarrassed her.

But as speakers of Spanish know all too well, *embarazar* is what is called "un falso amigo," or "false friend" in the language. While it may sound like "to embarrass" to a neophyte Spanish speaker such as I was, it literally means "to be pregnant." And so, what I had said to the young lady was "I'm so sorry to have impregnated you!" Of course, much to my astonishment, she immediately slammed the door in my face, leaving me to ponder what it was I'd said that would make her so angry.

When I arrived home that evening, my still- dirty laundry was piled up in a heap in front of my apartment door. The following day, the portero, with a disgusted look on his face, told me to find someone else to do my washing and stay away from his daughter. I later found out my blunder. Because of such linguistic misadventures, I found little time to pursue PhD.research and academic writing.

There was also the less-than-scintillating subject of my PhD dissertation entitled "Criticism in the Balance: The Literary Anthologist as Critic and Promoter in Nineteenth-Century America." Why, you might ask, would anyone choose such a subject, let alone spend years of his youth researching and writing a long-winded unpublished four-hundred-page tome that no one would ever read?

Graduate students often choose obscure PhD dissertation topics to fulfill their department's requirement to make an "original contribution" to existing scholarship. In my case, not a whole lot of previous PhD candidates had devoted themselves to delving into the musty long-forgotten world of nineteenth-century literary anthologies and some of the shady characters who produced them. But beyond that, I was fully aware that the job market was going to be a tough one. What could I do to distinguish myself from the hordes of other would-be professors of American literature?

What I came upon was a growing subfield of scholarship focused on the history of U.S. publishing. Although it was not something that truly appealed to me, I rationalized that if I wrote a dissertation on the publishing and "marketing" of American literature, this would distinguish me from other new PhDs. Perhaps I might teach a course about the history of publishing as well as classes on American literature.

As it turned out, my assumption was sadly wrong. Applying for academic jobs in 1976, I found there was virtually no interest from universities in my "unique" specialty. On the positive side, there was a lesson to be learned in all of this. As they say at commencements, follow your passion and rely on your intuition.

Instead, I moved forward step by step up the steep PhD incline. I reached the "summit" and successfully completed my dissertation in the winter of 1977, a year and a half after returning from Spain.

In doing dissertation research, I would occasionally come upon some bizarre little story or startling fact, usually gleaned from an archival letter, about one of my long-forgotten, oddball, literary anthologists. But those moments were few and far in between. Having finished what remains an unpublished dissertation, I stepped forward at age twenty-nine in the spring of 1978 to accept my degree and become Dr. Mark L. Asquino. In that proud moment, I felt like someone with near-zero employment prospects.

Fortunately, a couple of years earlier, I'd taken the advice of the USIA officers I'd met as a Fulbright lecturer in Spain. In the fall of 1976, I sat down to take the written foreign service examination offered at the federal building in downtown Providence. In an irony not lost on me at that time, I'd protested the U.S. government's war in Vietnam in front of that same building just six years earlier.

When I filled out the test application, I requested to be considered for entry into the USIA rather than the Department of State. Back in those days, candidates for both State and USIA took the same current events/general knowledge test during its first two-hour portion. It was much like the graduate record exam. After a short break, State candidates took another test focused on economics and politics. Those of us aspiring to be USIA officers were tested on what we knew about U.S. history, literature, and culture—all areas that played to my strengths.

I've always been reasonably good at standardized tests as long as they don't include numbers. Fortunately for me, the USIA exam was blessedly math-free. Largely for that reason, I was able to pass with a decent score.

No one has ever said that getting into the U.S. Foreign Service is fast or easy. In the spring of 1977, having passed the written test, I went to Boston for a two-hour interview with three veteran USIA foreign service officers from the agency's Bureau of Examiners. Before entering the interview room, I met other candidates outside who told me not to be too disappointed if I didn't pass the oral exam. They confided that this was their third or fourth try, which required them to pass the written test again each time to get to the orals. This was not exactly encouraging, and I wondered if I'd be willing to start the process again if I flunked the oral exam.

Not surprisingly for those years, when I entered the examination room, I saw that my panel consisted entirely of middle-aged white men. After a few pleasantries, they presented me with a series of ever more dire diplomatic scenarios, asking me in each case how I would respond and why I thought such action would be effective or appropriate. It was hard to figure out what the "right answer" might be, but I tried to come up with what seemed reasonable. Having finished this part of the interview, they moved on to ask a number of probing questions about my time as a Fulbright lecturer in Spain. Finally, I had about ten minutes to tell them what it was about my education and experience that qualified me for a career in the foreign service.

After the exam ended, I left the room, sat down, and felt completely deflated. I was quite sure I'd failed the test miserably. All three examiners had been adept at keeping stern expressions throughout my two-hour ordeal. They told me they would briefly confer and inform me shortly of their verdict on my performance. After about fifteen minutes of waiting in agony, the large wooden door to the examination room slowly creaked and then swung open. One of the examiners, a short bald gent with the same inscrutable expression, beckoned me to enter. But then came the surprise as all three of the examiners smiled and said, "Congratulations! You passed the interview!"

I felt like I'd just won the lottery.

I'm going to be a USIA officer! I thought.

But before I could exhale and do a jig, the head of the panel added, "But this is not an offer of employment."

"Huh?" I mumbled to myself. Having been on an emotional roller coaster I thought had just stopped, I was now headed up another dizzying slope.

Responding to my confused look, he explained that before qualifying for a job offer, I would have to undergo a security background check and then pass a health examination. If I got through both of these, my name would be placed on a rank-order roster with others who had also passed the entrance examinations.

The examiners cautioned that this whole process could take up to two years. In fact, if I had not been high enough on the roster within that time to get a job offer, that was it. I would have to start the whole process over again.

Whoosh! There went that sure-thing opportunity.

While I felt great jubilation for having somehow managed to get through the oral interview, I can't say that I was filled with confidence that I would ever actually become a foreign service officer. With the chances of finding a teaching job not all that great, I decided to pursue other employment possibilities as I slogged through the tedious long USIA employment process. But nothing came of these attempts.

Then, out of the blue, I lucked into something. During the late spring of 1978, I was perusing the English Department's bulletin board to see if there were any new university teaching or administrative jobs. It was then that I saw a flyer for postdoctoral fellowships at New York University. It had the intriguing title of "Careers in Business for Humanities PhDs." The program was sponsored by the National Endowment for the Humanities and a number of major U.S. corporations. It was a pilot project meant to take the writing, analytical, and presentation skills of unemployed humanities PhDs and find ways to apply them to jobs in the world of business.

My immediate reaction was "What a great idea! Where do I sign up?"

But my heart sank when I saw that the date for submitting an application for the fellowship was just a day away. Undaunted, I scribbled down the information from the flyer and headed home to my small apartment. It was mid-afternoon, and if I was to get my application in and postmarked that day, I'd need to do it right away. I sat down at my portable gray Smith-Corona electric typewriter. I banged out a two-page essay on why New York University should give me a summer fellowship to study at its Stern School of Business. I'd never taken a business course in my life and knew next to nothing about what a "career in business" actually might be like or why I would be good at it.

My essay focused on how I'd grown up watching and learning from my father what it took to run a small sheet metal and roofing business. I noted that I had worked with him during summers when I was in high school.

There was little time for revision. I put the essay and a résumé in a big manila envelope and drove to the nearest post office. The clerk there was about to close the shop. But he kindly stopped long enough to let me in and then attach special-delivery stamps on the envelope, assuring me my application would arrive in New York the next day.

I figured I had little chance of getting the fellowship. After all, I'd been turned down for literally hundreds of jobs in academia for which I was actually qualified. When the letter from NYU arrived, I was prepared to accept yet another "Thank you very much for your application, but we regret" reply. It took me a while to process that this was different.

I was one of a select group of applicants who would be interviewed in New York City for a Careers in Business fellowship. Back then, all I owned were a few scruffy-looking sports coats that I wore when I taught. I bought a summer-weight, serious-looking three-piece suit and a couple of nice silk ties to go along with it. A week after getting the invitation letter, I dressed up in my new finery, got on the Amtrak train from Providence's old Union Station to NYC, and settled for the bumpy four-hour ride. Emerging into the confusing Penn Station, I found a cab and went to NYU's Stern School of Business, which was in the financial district near Wall Street.

When I arrived for my interview, there were several other applicants in the waiting room scheduled before me. Sitting there, I heard them discussing business jobs they'd had before entering PhD programs. As someone with no business experience, how could I ever compete with such people? It brought back memories of my first days as an undergraduate at Brown.

When it was my turn, I went into a well-appointed large office with a pleasant view of the historic Trinity Church across the street. My interviewers were a young woman who was a vice dean of admissions at Stern and an older male business professor. They cordially asked me to take a seat on a large brown leather couch as they settled into overstuffed wing chairs. A highly polished mahogany coffee table separated us, with the *Wall Street Journal* and various other business publications nicely arranged on top.

Unlike my two-hour foreign service grilling, the interview was more of a friendly chat about what I'd written in my essay and an exploration of what might interest me as a business career were I to be accepted. During past teaching and university administration interviews, I'd always been rather tense and often wound up overselling myself. But this time around, I was extremely relaxed. After all, I didn't have much to sell! Of course, I made the best case I could for getting the fellowship. The interview lasted only thirty minutes. My interviewers seemed pleased as they bade me farewell and called in the next candidate.

The only thing that occurred to me afterward was not whether I'd gotten the fellowship but what a good time I was having in New York. I had a few hours to walk around the city before heading back to Providence. I enjoyed the free trip and decided not to feel too badly when I inevitably would get yet another rejection letter.

But that was not what happened. A few weeks later, I indeed received a letter from NYU, but rather than beginning with the usual polite "get lost!" opening, it congratulated me for winning a Careers in Business fellowship. The letter noted that of the five hundred PhDs who applied for the program, I was one of fifty chosen to participate in the prestigious pilot project. It occurred to me that perhaps in the future I should only pursue things for which I was utterly unqualified.

The all-expense-paid fellowship consisted of six weeks of graduate-level classes in accounting, marketing, management, and statistics that were the equivalent of what was taught during the first semester of NYU's MBA degree course. In addition, we would attend special lectures on business and meet with top-flight executives at major corporations. At the end of the fellowship, the Stern School would arrange entry-level management-position interviews for us.

My fellow students were an impressive, albeit curious, lot. One fellow had been an original member of the Sha Na Na retro rock band. He earned a PhD in English at Columbia and was ready to move on. A woman in the class had done modeling and yearned to become a fashion industry executive. Others expressed interest in investment banking. But on that opening day of class, I was clueless about what I might do.

One of the fascinating things about the fellowship was getting to meet leading Fortune 500 executives who talked to us about what had drawn them to their extremely lucrative business careers. We usually went to their opulent, mid-town offices, which had discrete, soft lighting, expensive artwork, and plush furnishings. Once there, we looked out at the breathtaking views of the Manhattan skyline that were a perk of having upper-floor corner suites.

I remember on one such occasion listening intently as a venture capitalist described in almost-loving terms the excitement he felt every time he prepared for and closed on some high-risk financial deal. I was struck by the fact that he spoke with the same passion about mergers and buy-outs that I once felt for the writings of Hawthorne and Melville. It occurred to me that I was unlikely to find similar satisfaction were I ever to enter the world of business. The reality of that sobering thought was soon to take a concrete form.

Toward the end of our studies, NYU began arranging interviews. My dormitory roommate was very much focused on a career in corporate banking and soon was successfully interviewing with the likes of Chase Manhattan and Citibank. As I still had trouble balancing the meager resources in my checking account, banking was clearly not a career option for me. I've always been quite a gregarious soul who enjoys talking to people, so the placement office decided marketing and sales were something at which I might do well.

Accordingly, they asked if I would be interested in interviewing with the Maidenform Bra Company, a well-established manufacturer of women's undergarments. I paused for a moment, thinking about all of my academic friends. I could imagine them asking me to describe the Maidenform bra "training program." I politely demurred.

"Well, what about insurance? Now that's something that might work for you!"

While hardly filling me with joy, selling insurance seemed better and easier to explain to my friends than becoming a bra tycoon, so I said, "Sure, why not?"

A couple of weeks later, I took the noisy suburban PATH commuter train from Manhattan to Newark, New Jersey. There, I had an interview with the Prudential Insurance Company. In preparing, I learned that Prudential was founded in Newark more than a century earlier as The Widows and Orphans Friendly Society. As insurance companies went, Prudential held a certain prestige. I was about to visit its corporate headquarters in Newark, which appealed to the historian in me.

But as the cab from the PATH station made its way through heavy early-afternoon traffic, I saw a city still scarred from the July 1968 race riots. More than a decade later, we passed burnt-out buildings and the continuing blight of inner-city poverty and inequality. And then, suddenly, the imposing Prudential Tower emerged in the distance as if occupying some enchanted island. The whole experience seemed surreal, and I hadn't even had the interview yet.

Once inside the impressive headquarters, I was taken to the top-floor executive suites. There, I had several interviews with various corporate vice presidents. They described their work and what made Prudential different from other insurance corporations. They spoke of how the company invested in the poor communities where it worked and had minority employment programs. The men and women I spoke to were polished and well-educated. They reminded me of some of my Brown classmates. All encouraged me to apply for a corporate position, noting that my soon-to-be-completed NYU business studies suited me well for a career at Prudential. Once again, I thought, "You're on the verge of getting something for which you have virtually no qualifications. What the hell are you doing in this place?"

My last interview was several floors down with the retail sales director. His office was neither as large nor well-appointed as the ones I had just visited. He was an overweight middle-aged man with thinning hair whose suit seemed at least one size too small. His stomach bulged in his shirt, straining against the middle buttons. His tie looked like it was made of polyester. Glancing at my résumé, he began in a thick New Jersey accent, "So Asquino, I see ya got all these degrees. Went to an Ivy League school, right? Ya even published articles. Looks pretty good on papah. But let me tell ya somethin'. None of it means a goddam' thing when it comes ta sellin' insurance. Lemme esplain ta ya why."

He then spoke at length about growing up poor in Newark. His family couldn't afford to send him to college. Right out of high school, he got a job with Prudential going door-to-door, selling basic life insurance policies in some of the city's roughest neighborhoods.

He was good at it, he said and wound up supervising others doing the same work. Gradually, he rose up the corporate hierarchy's sales division. Given his lack of education, it was clear he'd never get any higher than his present job. But all in all, he'd done extremely well, lived in the suburbs, and made a good salary. He then turned and said something that startled me, and which I've never forgotten.

"So here's da deal, kid. Ya gotta want one thing: money! Is it all ya think about? Because all that stuff ya just heard upstairs is a buncha crapola. Know what I mean? Insurance is about money. The more ya sell, the more ya make. An' ya gotta try ta pay out as liddle of it as ya can. So that's what I'm askin' ya. Do ya love money? Yes or no? Because if ya don't, this ain't the right kinda bizness for ya." He stared at me intently, waiting for an answer.

"Well, yes. I . . . you know . . . uh . . . sure, money's really important. So I suppose I do love money."

He nodded but looked at me skeptically as I left his office.

As I went back on the PATH train to New York, I knew one thing for sure. Neither insurance nor any other business was right for me. Money wasn't what drove or made me happy, and it never would. I didn't want to spend the rest of my life constantly looking at the bottom line. I owed the man I'd just seen an enormous debt of gratitude for his bluntness.

That was my last business interview. I never followed up with Prudential. When the NYU program finished, I packed up my few possessions and headed back to Providence. It had been a wonderful summer. Unfortunately, Careers in Business was not for me.

But not long after I got back home and started to teach a university extension course, which barely paid for my rent, I got a phone call that would change my life.

CHAPTER 3

Welcome to USICA!

(And an Unforgettable Tale of Sex, Madness, and Murder)

AFTER I PASSED both the USIA written and oral exams in early 1977, I successfully completed the background security investigation and was declared healthy enough to enter the foreign service. My name then went on the rank-ordered hiring roster, where I would be eligible for a position during the next two years. This meant that I had a "chance" of obtaining a foreign service entry level job, but as I was not at the top of the list, it was far from guaranteed I would get an offer.

Unbeknownst to me, just about the time that I was applying for the NYU fellowship, President Jimmy Carter decided to reorganize and change the name of USIA. On April 1, 1978, it officially became the United States International Communication Agency (USICA). In the process, the president also got rid of the slogan, "Telling America's story to the world," which graced the main entrance of the USIA headquarters building at the iconic Washington DC address of 1776 Pennsylvania Avenue.

For President Carter, diplomats should not be "telling" foreign audiences about the United States. He wanted them to engage in two-way communication and dialogue. Carter was also a strong advocate of "public diplomacy." As I noted earlier, the latter term is attributed to Edmund Gullion, a career diplomat, who in 1965 began using it in reference to the curriculum of the new Edward R. Murrow Center at Tufts University. In a pamphlet published by the Murrow Center, public diplomacy was defined as follows:

> The influence of public attitudes on the formation
> and execution of foreign policies. It encompasses

dimensions of international relations beyond traditional diplomacy . . . [including] the cultivation by governments of public opinion in other countries; the interaction of private groups and interests in one country with those of another . . . (and) the transnational flow of information and ideas.

In practical terms, what this meant was using information, educational exchanges, and cultural outreach programs to reach foreign public audiences. It was something that USIA had been doing since its founding in 1953. But it had done so in programs jointly administered by the Department of State.

After World War II, the State Department created an Office of International Information and Cultural Affairs (OIC). This was before USIA was founded as an independent agency. The new organization's primary mission back then was to expand international information programming, including the use of radio broadcasting as a way of countering Soviet Cold War propaganda. But in an odd twist, USIA officers were also charged with overseeing education and cultural exchange activities overseas with the State Department continuing to administer the programs, including the Fulbright Fellowships in Washington. In 1959, President Eisenhower made this permanent by replacing the OIC with the Bureau of Educational and Cultural Relations (CU) in the Department of State.

This division of overseas programming and domestic administration between two distinct foreign affairs agencies was always awkward. The rationale was that education and culture should remain at the Department of State and be kept separate from the USIA, which, as I've written earlier, many viewed as little more than a propaganda agency. But Carter disagreed. Much to the regret of many talented veteran cultural officers in the Department of State, he folded CU into the USICA in 1978.

Somehow, I was unaware of this major change, still believing I remained on the "USIA roster." But in September of 1978, shortly after my return from New York, I received a phone call from a woman who congratulated me for having been selected for the next USICA entry-level officer class scheduled in Washington for late October. USICA? My first reaction was to tell her that there must be some mistake. I never applied for a job with any such organization.

I was saved from considerable embarrassment when the woman explained that what had been the USIA was now a brand-new organization called the USICA. While not sure exactly what any of this meant, I gladly accepted the offer. I felt greatly relieved to find out subsequently it was an expanded version of what had been the USIA.

I drove to my parents' nearby house and was sure that they would be absolutely overjoyed with my good news. For my father, who had worked as a Department of the Navy civilian employee in Boston during World War II, it was just great that I would be working for the U.S. government. But it was not so for my mother, who immediately said, "What a terrible thing! You'll spend the rest of your life flying around the world on dangerous assignments. We'll be constantly worried and hardly ever get to see you!"

Looking at me with a fiercely disapproving expression, she then added, "So this is how you treat your father and me after we spent all of that money on your Brown education. Instead of taking a sensible job, you're going to run off and be a diplomatic courier!"

I was dumbstruck. It wasn't as if my mother hadn't been aware of my taking the foreign service exam or had forgotten our discussions about the possibility of my working for the USIA. Apparently, none of this had registered. All she focused on was that I was leaving Rhode Island forever to take what she regarded as a foolish, dangerous job.

I began by trying to explain that I was not going to be a "diplomatic courier." Rather, as a diplomat, my work would entail taking assignments of three to four years in different foreign countries doing press, educational and cultural work. I assured her that from time to time I would also work in Washington. But none of this seemed to matter. She was dead set against my joining the "foreign legion," as she sarcastically called the USICA.

Now, it needs to be said that my mother, although a highly intelligent woman, drew much of her understanding of the wider world from the romantic images supplied to her by Hollywood. In this case, as I would later learn, she'd seen a 1952 movie called *Diplomatic Courier*. Starring Tyrone Power and Patricia Neal, the film's noir plot revolved around two American diplomatic couriers who are sent by the Department of State on a risky overseas mission during the Cold War. Early on, one of the men is murdered, and his body is tossed off a speeding train somewhere in Europe. The other courier escapes but is pursued throughout the continent by hired killers. Along the way, he meets seductive foreign women who turn out to be deadly Soviet agents.

Little wonder that my mother so vehemently opposed my entering the foreign service!

It took a while, including considerable persuasion from my father, for my mom to accept that there was nothing she could say or do that would sway me from accepting the USICA job. But even years later, after I was fully launched on a career, she would sometimes complain bitterly to friends that her only child had abandoned her to join the foreign legion.

So it was that in late October 1978, I boarded a plane in Providence and flew to Washington DC to begin the USICA training. My mother had been right about one thing: I would never again live in Rhode Island.

I was just a few months shy of my thirtieth birthday and incredibly happy that I had finally begun a well-paying job. I had no idea at the time that this would be the beginning of an amazing thirty-seven-year odyssey taking me to nine countries in Latin America, Europe, Central Asia, and Africa.

The composition of my USICA entry-level class very much reflected the U.S. Foreign Service of the late 1970s. It was overwhelmingly male. It had no African Americans or Hispanics and included just three women in a class of fifteen all-white recruits. My group had several other people with PhDs, a librarian, an attorney, a one-time Peace Corps country director, three journalists, a high school teacher, and others who'd previously worked either in business or government. We ranged in age from those in their early twenties to "old-timers" who had either passed their fortieth birthday or were close to doing so. At twenty-nine, I fell in the mid-range of both age and experience.

It was an exciting time to enter this new agency. President Carter recently named John Reinhardt, a USIA career diplomat, to lead thd USICA. Reinhardt was the first black U.S. ambassador to Nigeria and held a PhD in American literature from the University of Wisconsin. He was an assistant secretary for public affairs at State. He served as a key adviser on Africa for Secretary Henry Kissinger. In becoming the first director of the USICA, Reinhardt was very much "on message" in terms of the direction President Carter wanted the new agency to take. Years later, Reinhardt said in an interview,

> "USIA's focus was always fundamentally one way. Its mission was to tell others about our society. In contrast, the International Communication Agency has two-way communication as a fundamental principle. Our activities and programs as a whole should be designed to learn as well as inform, and to inform as well as learn.[1]"

This all sounded good to us, but there were some immediate problems with the new agency, starting with its name. Having been around by 1978 for a quarter century, the USIA was well-known in government circles as well as overseas, where it ran libraries and cultural centers. In a sense it had a brand name that the USICA lacked. It was immediately noted that ICA sounded a lot like an all-too-clever transposition of the CIA. This was not good for an agency whose predecessor had allegedly been associated with the murky world of propaganda, if not espionage.

Accordingly, all of us with the new agency became the butt of endless CIA jokes, especially from our State Department entry-level colleagues, so much so, in fact, that several wags in my class had T-shirts printed up for all of us that said on the back:

---

[1] Quoted from "John E. Reinhardt, first career diplomat to lead USIA, dies at 95," The Washington Post, February 24, 2016. Accessed online, July 9, 2019.

ICA: Lies not Spies.
We're the other guys!

It was immediately communicated to us by the mid-level officer who had the unenviable job of guiding and mentoring the rambunctious group we were in that such humor by aspiring foreign service officers was neither appropriate nor appreciated.

In late 1978, the world was approaching what would soon be an information technology revolution that would change forever how all of us lived and worked. But it would not be until 1981, during my second overseas assignment to Panama, that I learned on my own how to use the lone state-of-the-art Wang desktop computer terminal that had just been installed, with much fanfare, in one of our offices.

Unfortunately, during our USICA training, some of the "tradecraft" we learned drew on soon-to-be-obsolete technology. For example, we were taught how to use bulky 16mm projectors that the Victor Animatograph Corporation had first begun manufacturing back in 1923. They would soon be replaced by 3/4 video cassette players or recorders, which seemed very much in the avant-garde back then. Within a few years, they too would go the way of eight-track audio cassettes—yet another short-lived innovation.

Part of our orientation was attending joint training with new State officers in their A-100 course, as their standard training was called. This course included classes on political and economic issues, which became part of our training as well. I recall one session during which a State Department policy expert condemned Vietnam's recent invasion of Cambodia to remove the brutal Pol Pot regime. He told us that whatever we thought of the latter, U.S. policy opposed Pol Pot's overthrow. The official line was that the Communist Vietnamese invasion as of Cambodia was part of a plan to establish Vietnam's hegemony throughout Southeast Asia.

Outspoken academic that I still was, I found this outrageous. In my view, getting rid of the genocidal Khmer Rouge regime in so-called Kampuchea, as Pol Pot and his henchmen called Cambodia, was the morally correct thing to do, no matter who had done so. When no one else raised a hand, I stood up and forcefully made this point, much to the surprise and seeming annoyance of both my State Department A-100 classmates and the instructor.

The lecturer told me in that I had better learn how to follow U.S. foreign policy or "You'll never make it as a foreign service officer, young man!"

Now, this was quite a put-down. I'm sure others would have kept quiet. Still, I stood my ground and said defiantly, "Well, U.S. foreign policy should not be based on hypocrisy!"

Over time, I learned to be more diplomatic when I disagreed with something. As a foreign service officer, I frequently had to advocate in public for U.S. foreign policies with which I personally disagreed. This, of course, comes with the job, and I recognized that with time the incensed State Department official was largely correct.

But there was one A-100 policy session that left me utterly speechless. It was the story of a grisly 1971 episode in which one foreign service officer stabbed to death his colleague with a pair of scissors in an embassy chancery or main building and then hid the body. This was a story none of us would ever forget because it had all the elements of a lurid, bloody crime novel set in a far-off country.

As the story we were told went, in August 1971, the murder had unfolded in the island capital of the Republic of Equatorial Guinea, a wretchedly poor, tiny Spanish-speaking country in West Central Africa that was ruled by a mad dictator named Francisco Macias. As I sat in the A-100 course listening to this tale of murder and mayhem, I thought to myself, "What a dreadful place! I'm never going there, that's for sure. So you can cross that one off the list of my future assignments!"

Ironically, among the USICA and State officers sitting in that class, I would be the only one, as far as I know, to serve in Equatorial Guinea. In fact, decades later, I would actively seek a posting there as an ambassador, and when I received the assignment, I would be absolutely delighted.

So how and why did that happen? I will answer that question in due course.

First, because the murder has shaped so many perceptions about Equatorial Guinea among generations of foreign service officers, I need to provide some details.

The tale I heard that day in late 1978 was bizarre. What happened, in a U.S. embassy, of all places, involving two Department of State diplomats is a lurid story of sex, madness, and murder. In many ways, it's the State Department's version of the 1984 classic film *Nightmare on Elm Street*. However, the murder in Equatorial Guinea is a real-life account of horror. Here are the basic facts of what happened.

On August 30, 1971, Alfred Erdos—the middle-aged principal officer (or chargé d'affaires, as it's called in foreign service lingo) at the U.S. embassy in Equatorial Guinea (EG)—stabbed to death his administrative assistant, Donald Leahy. Based on a subsequent autopsy of the dead man done in the U.S., there were allegations the two men were having a homosexual affair, as spermatozoa were found in Leahy's throat. The murder weapon was a pair of standard-issue U.S. government scissors. The crime occurred inside a rented villa, which served as the embassy, and Mr. Leahy's body was found in an unused office.

On the day of the murder, Erdos had been making wild accusations on the embassy radio about a Soviet invasion of the country. A foreign service officer at the nearby U.S. consulate in Douala, Cameroon, was asked by the acting chief of mission at the U.S. embassy in Yaoundé to investigate the strange broadcast. The Douala-based officer immediately took a charter flight to Equatorial Guinea, where he discovered the grisly crime on that same day. At the time, Erdos's and Leahy's families were living with them in the capital city of Malabo, then called Santa Isabel.

As with any murder mystery, these are the basic facts. Since then, those knowledgeable about the killing have agreed upon them. Beyond those facts, things become murky. There are decidedly different views and interpretations of the exact circumstances and motive for Erdos's brutal stabbing of his assistant, the embassy's only other American employee. Throughout the decades since the murder, the facts themselves have been embellished and distorted with each retelling of the story to new classes of foreign service officers.

For example, in the version my classmates and I heard, the two men's families had not accompanied them to Equatorial Guinea. Living alone in an isolated and hostile place, the diplomats began a homosexual relationship. Told by his younger lover, Mr. Leahy, that he no longer wanted to continue their affair, Mr. Erdos killed him in a fit of sexually driven rage. We were told, erroneously as it turned out, that Erdos put Leahy's body in a large orange diplomatic pouch and hid it in the embassy's air-conditioned communications vault. Erdos pretended for the next several days that nothing had happened to Leahy. It was only when questions arose at the U.S. consulate in Douala about Mr. Leahy's whereabouts that the crime was uncovered.

Obviously, there is little factually correct about the story I heard as part of my foreign service orientation. Leahy was a year older than Erdos, and their families had accompanied them to the post. While there is evidence that Leahy performed oral sex on Erdos on the day of the murder, it was most likely nonconsensual, as there is no evidence the two were involved in a homosexual relationship. Neither was it likely that the motive for the murder was sexual but rather because of paranoia. Erdos did not put Leahy's body in a diplomatic pouch, neither did he hide it for days in the embassy vault while pretending his colleague was still alive. In fact, the crime was discovered on the same day it occurred.

Over the years, I've asked foreign service colleagues what they were told about the murder. I found that most had also heard a wildly embellished version of the event. This has led me to wonder over the years how and why the Erdos-Leahy story has morphed into a macabre foreign service urban legend about Equatorial Guinea. Why, exactly, does it continue to be part of the orientation for each new generation of foreign service officers? Furthermore, if it is a cautionary tale, what exactly is the moral of the story? Before I try to answer these questions, let me explain why the new nation of Equatorial Guinea was important to the United States back when the murder took place.

In the lead-up to Equatorial Guinea's independence in 1968, outgoing president Lyndon Johnson recognized that establishing a strong relationship with this former Spanish colonial possession was essential to protect U.S. security interests in West Africa. Equatorial Guinea is in a strategic position in the Gulf of Guinea and has excellent ports.

In a September 1968 State Department memorandum, the assistant secretary of state for Africa wrote that the new country would be important beyond its small size due to this geo-strategic location. He continued that despite what he called "ideological radicalism" in EG's independence movement, a clear reference to Communist influence, the prospects were good for "the development of responsible, moderate leadership."[2]

Francisco Macias, whom I've noted earlier had been a minor bureaucrat in the Spanish colonial administration, had just been elected the new country's first president in UN-supervised polling. Even before the 1968 elections, Macias had demonstrated mental instability, which would only get worse. Following a failed March 1969 coup staged by his foreign minister, Macias descended into full-blown paranoia and uncontrollable violence. On the night of the coup, the foreign minister was allegedly thrown from a presidential palace window, possibly by Macias himself. Denied medical attention, the foreign minister died soon after.

Macias used the coup to begin a reign of terror against his people that has often been compared to that of Idi Amin and Pol Pot. By 1970, Washington had no illusions about EG's president. He was described in reporting cables as erratic, vindictive, and most likely mentally disturbed. By that time, he had imprisoned, tortured, and murdered thousands of those he accused of opposing his brutal and erratic one-man rule. Many believed him to be mad. Despite these assessments, during the subsequent Nixon and Ford administrations, the United States continued to do all it could to maintain its relationship with the Macias regime as a way to counterbalance the perceived spread of Communism in Africa.[3]

---

[2] Joseph Palmer to the Undersecretary, "Memorandum for the President: Recognition of Equatorial Guinea, Establishment of an Embassy, and Accreditation of Ambassador," September 16, 1968. U.S. National Archives.

[3] In addition to my primary source research, I am greatly indebted to Geoffrey Jensen for his comprehensive analysis of the Macias regime in "Tyranny, Communism and U.S. Policy in Equatorial Guinea, 1968–1979." Oxford University Press, "Diplomatic History," May 16, 2019 (https://doi.org/10.1093/dh/dhz20) Accessed on July 18, 2019. See also my article, "Murder in Equatorial Guinea: A Foreign Service Urban Legend", in *American Diplomacy,* September 2019.

Given Equatorial Guinea's small size, the State Department decided against having a resident ambassador stationed in the capital of Santa Isabel. Instead, it sent a principal officer (or chargé d'affaires) as the head of the embassy in the former Spanish colony. The ambassador in a neighboring country was the non-resident chief of mission in EG, and he or she supervised the principal officer there. In 1971, the principal officer at the U.S. embassy in Santa Isabel reported to the U.S. ambassador to Cameroon.

In early 1971, the Department of State was looking for a new principal officer to take on the increasingly difficult assignment in EG. There were reports that the screams of political prisoners being tortured to death at one of Macias's detention centers across the street from the U.S. principal officer's residence could be heard day and night. Western diplomats confined to the island of Fernando Po were not allowed to leave the capital without permission, and they could not even use the city's nearby beaches.

When the Department of State approached Alfred Erdos about the job, he had been in the foreign service for twenty years. The U.S. ambassador to Cameroon knew Erdos casually. He had a generally good impression of him. Recent supervisors used adjectives that included *cool*, *capable*, and *unflappable* to describe Erdos. However, following the murder, investigators found that Erdos was known as a strict disciplinarian who had bullied and mistreated subordinates during his previous postings.

Erdos arrived in the capital of Santa Isabel in April, accompanied by his wife and their two-year-old son. The only other Americans at the embassy were Donald Leahy and his Ecuadorian wife. Leahy's title was administrative assistant. This two-officer post had just three Equatoguinean local employees, all of whom had been imprisoned by the Macias regime at the time of the murder. Leahy not only did administrative work but also was the "communicator." The latter's responsibilities included transmitting sensitive, encrypted reporting telegrams, or "cables" as they're known in the foreign service. He also maintained the embassy's radio transmission equipment. Because of poor phone service in EG in 1971, this radio provided the only reliable outside link to other embassies.

Erdos complained shortly after arriving in Santa Isabel that Leahy was a below-average employee lacking the varied skills needed for the job. He asked that his assistant be transferred and a more experienced administrative officer be sent in his place. Despite indications that there was tension between the two men over work issues, a State Department embassy inspection report, written just a month before the murder, concluded that Erdos and Leahy had a good personal relationship.

During his first few months at the embassy, Erdos sent a number of reporting cables to the State Department and the U.S. embassy in Yaoundé on political and economic developments in EG. In the weeks immediately leading up to the murder, Deputy Chief of Mission Lannon Walker—his immediate supervisor at the U.S. embassy in Yaoundé, Cameroon—found something unprofessional about the alarmist tone of these reports.[4]

Beginning on August 20, Erdos's cables became more erratic. In a series of immediate messages to Washington, he claimed the political situation in the capital was veering out of control with mass arrests taking place on a regular basis. About this time, Erdos also became convinced that EG's government had turned against the United States, in general, and him personally.[5]

On August 30, Erdos prepared a long cable detailing what he claimed was a Soviet plot that was being orchestrated against the United States. He wrote that he had been targeted for death by the plotters. Among the latter were not only members of the EG government but also Soviet agents, including the embassy's locally employed staff and most significantly his administrative assistant, Dan Leahy.

When Leahy refused to encrypt and send this message, Erdos forced him into the communications vault and locked its thick metal door behind him. He then made Leahy, who was a much smaller man, sit

---

[4] Asquino-Walker telephone conversation, July 22, 2019. I am deeply indebted to Ambassador Lannon Walker for this and other insights he provided me about the Erdos-Leahy episode.

[5] Hoffacker, "Murder in an Embassy, Part I," p. 5.

down in a chair. Erdos bound his assistant with an electrical cord and proceeded to interrogate him about the "plot."

Although Leahy denied the accusations against him and others, Erdos was convinced more than ever of his assistant's role in the conspiracy. He decided to call for help via the vault's radio. But fearing that the U.S. consul in nearby Douala, Cameroon, was also a conspirator, he contacted the U.S. embassy in Ghana and said the following,

> "I am not losing my mind. I am locked in the vault with my admin officer who is a communist agent and part of a massive plot against the United States. The U.S. will be accused shortly in a large showing at the UN and I fear for my life. I feel assured that if I leave the vault, I will be killed. We have been misdirected and all or any reports from here are not to be believed.
>
> All local employees [i.e., of the U.S. embassy in EG] are part of the plot and have placed electronic devices in the homes. I am extremely worried about my wife and son who are alone at home. Watson and Obiang [EG government officials] are also suspected as part of the massive plot against the U.S. I am in complete control of my faculties. And I realize how dramatic this sounds, but this is the way things are. Please rush help immediately."

The transmission was overheard by U.S. embassy officers in Yaoundé, Cameroon. Shortly afterward, Leahy was able to free himself from his bonds, but as he tried to leave the vault, Erdos stabbed him several times with a pair of scissors. Nevertheless, Leahy managed to escape and ran to the main door of the building. Erdos caught up with him, stabbing him repeatedly. The wounds were apparently superficial, but one of the blows nicked Leahy's jugular vein. This caused him quickly to bleed to death. Erdos then dragged his colleague's lifeless body to a nearby empty office.

The Douala consular officer was dispatched by U.S. Embassy Yaoundé to travel immediately to the embassy in Santa Isabel. But when he arrived there in the early evening, Erdos refused to let his colleague inside. Later, though, Erdos talked to his wife and allowed her to enter the embassy. When he finally came out of the building with her, Erdos said to the Doula consular officer, "I lost my cool. I killed Don."

Fearing arrest by EG authorities, Erdos asked foreign diplomatic colleagues assembled outside the embassy if one of them would provide him and his family with refuge. The Nigerian ambassador agreed and drove them to his home. Leahy's body remained overnight in the embassy.

The next day, Lannon Walker, then the acting chief of mission at the U.S. embassy in Cameroon, arrived in EG with another officer. After negotiations with the Macias regime, they departed on a flight to Douala with Erdos, Leahy's remains (which had been preserved in improvised cold storage), and the two men's family members. Erdos was subsequently transported from Cameroon on an official U.S. aircraft in the custody of an embassy security officer, and he was served with a legal summons at Dulles Airport in Washington. He was immediately taken to George Washington University Hospital for psychiatric observation. Erdos was subsequently released on bond after being formally indicted for first-degree murder. He pleaded not guilty, with his attorneys mounting an insanity defense. The prosecution later reduced the charge to second-degree murder.

The judge sentenced Erdos to a maximum sentence of ten years. An appeal of the verdict was rejected by an appeals court, and Erdos was released on parole in 1976 after serving a little over three years of his sentence. He reportedly never expressed remorse about Leahy's death either during the trial or afterward. Erdos died of a heart attack in California in 1983.

Why is it that to this very day new foreign service officers are told some version of this gruesome story? An important moral of the tale is that diplomats and other American citizens who commit crimes in overseas diplomatic facilities, leased or otherwise, will be prosecuted under U.S. law. The Erdos case established this legal precedent.

Arguably, telling the story is a dramatic way of illustrating this legal reality to all new foreign service officers.

The fact that the Erdos-Leahy murder took place on a remote foreign island with few embassy staff members, and lacking basic medical resources also reinforces another important lesson for new diplomats about to serve for the first time overseas. This aspect of the story certainly was a cautionary tale for me as I would come to serve at more than one small isolated post with poor medical facilities. What I learned from the grisly tale is that it is especially important as a supervisor to monitor the health, both physical and mental, of staff in such places.

It's been decades since the building where the murder occurred served as our embassy. We now have a modern diplomatic compound that I was honored to inaugurate as ambassador to Equatorial Guinea in 2013. The Macias regime is also long gone. Despite all this, anytime I mention to diplomatic colleagues that I served as ambassador in Equatorial Guinea, they look at me rather strangely. I don't need to ask why because they are undoubtedly thinking about the Erdos-Leahy murder story and wondering, "Why would you ever have wanted to go to that godforsaken place? You must have been crazy!"

In fairness, as I've said, that was exactly my own reaction as a brand-new foreign service officer on first hearing about this strange little country. Why did I end up going there?

Once again, I've gotten ahead of my story. Clearly, Equatorial Guinea is at the very end of my overseas diplomatic journey. It's time to return to how it all began.

CHAPTER 4

Starting at the Bottom

WITHIN THE FIRST months of training, all new foreign service officers are given a list of possible overseas assignments from which they have to make high-, medium-, and low-preference bids. Although it's been more than forty years since I first saw the bid list for my fifteen-member USICA entry-level class, I still vividly remember all of the posts offered to us.

In the top tier were the plum European assignments: Rome and Lisbon. Almost everyone bid on them—and why not? I sure did! Another European post, Warsaw, was also on the list but less sought after due to Poland's then being under Communist rule. You also had to learn Polish, a very hard one-country language, so I decided Warsaw would not be high on my list. Other popular places included Egypt, Japan, and Kenya. Latin America also offered several desirable assignments: Mexico, Ecuador, the Dominican Republic, and Guatemala. And finally, there were the less popular countries on the list: Sierra Leone, Sri Lanka, India (Calcutta), South Korea, and El Salvador, where a civil war was raging.

Latin America appealed to me for many reasons. First of all, I'd never been to the region, and accordingly as a Spanish speaker, it intrigued me. Second, given my mother's fierce opposition to my foreign service career, it seemed like a good idea to start off somewhere not too far away from the United States. This would allow me to get back to Rhode Island for frequent visits. And, last but not least, my relationship was becoming more serious with the young Spanish woman I'd first met when I was a Fulbright lecturer. As she spoke no English at the time, I reasoned that should we decide to marry, being in a Spanish-language country would be a good choice. In my youthful naivete, I incorrectly thought a Spaniard would be delighted to live anywhere in Latin Americas. Foolish me.

I didn't expect to get either Rome or Lisbon, as the foreign service assignment officer who would decide postings for our class seemed to favor others. Still, I was hopeful that I would have a chance to snag one of my preferred Latin American bids for Ecuador or Mexico.

"Flag day" is when foreign assignments are officially announced, and it is a celebratory occasion, especially for those who get a top bid. Alas, I was not to be in that select group or even close as it turned out. I'd put El Salvador toward the bottom of my list, but that was where I wound up being assigned. Welcome to the foreign service! What troubled me most was how I was going to explain to my parents, soon-to-be-Spanish fiancée, and her folks that I was headed for a war-torn country. But I resigned myself to the assignment.

At the time, unlike the Department of State, the USICA sent new officers on an initial twelve-to-fifteen-month "training tour," not a two-or three-year assignment. At least my time in El Salvador would be brief. The rationale for a short training assignment was that you would learn not only public diplomacy skills but also have the opportunity to do rotational work in the State Department's consular political-economic and administrative sections. This would provide exposure to the full range of what foreign service officers did. In theory, it was a great idea, but in practice, as would be the case for me, it didn't work out that way. This was because it all depended on who your boss was for that first training assignment.

Well before flag day, they told us that once we received our assignments, we could not cancel them. For this reason, I began to prepare for my tour in El Salvador's capital of San Salvador. However, the more I read about the deteriorating political and security situation in the country, the more I questioned the wisdom of doing a training tour there.

As for my work in other embassy sections, the public affairs officer (PAO) was silent when I asked how my rotation would proceed. It turned out that I was not high on the PAO's list of concerns, as I would learn subsequently. Suffering from serious health problems, he would soon leave San Salvador on a medical evacuation or "medevac" back to the United States. It appeared neither he nor anyone else had the vaguest idea about what I'd do in San Salvador.

Based on this, I decided I would make a case to the assignments officer that El Salvador was not a suitable place for me to begin my foreign service career. I would do this on what I thought were sound professional grounds. Although we were about the same age, the woman who oversaw assignments was already a tenured officer with several overseas assignments to her credit. She was slight, dark-haired and had a crisp voice. While she enjoyed a generally good reputation in the USICA, some viewed her as difficult, noting she could be mercurial and inflexible. I shared the latter view based on my few dealings with her but was not deterred.

I made an appointment and after entering my assignment officer's dimly-lit office, I sat down in an uncomfortable wooden chair. I put my carefully researched, written arguments on the edge of her desk. Looking at my notes from time to time, I proceeded to tell her why El Salvador made no sense as a training assignment for me. She listened quietly, and then there was a long pause. Staring at me with her dark eyes, she said in an even tone that I was completely out of order. As an untenured officer, I was not allowed to reject an assignment. Doing so, she said firmly, was unheard of and would be grounds for my immediate termination. There was a finality in her voice despite its low controlled tone.

At this point, I think she expected me to apologize meekly, agree I had been wrong even to propose such a thing, and then skulk out the door. But I'm a stubborn soul, and that was not at all how I reacted. I insisted the assignment made no sense whatsoever. I said I was prepared to appeal, if necessary, all the way up to the USICA's director.

"All right. Suit yourself," she said curtly. "You're making an enormous mistake that you'll come to regret."

Having said that, she added she'd report my decision to her superiors.

It was clear to me the meeting (and perhaps my career) was now over. I left her office feeling downhearted, wondering if I'd done the right thing. Of course, there was no turning back.

Weeks passed without hearing anything from my assignments officer. When I called her for an update, all she'd say before hanging up was "No, nothing new. Your case is still under review. I'll let you know if there's any change."

Finally, I received word that she wanted to see me. Arriving at her office, I tentatively knocked on her door, expecting the worst. She told me to come in and then wordlessly motioned for me to sit down in the same uncomfortable chair. Wasting no time, she said, "Your assignment's been canceled."

For a moment, I wasn't quite sure what to make of that. Was this the sort of bureaucratic language USICA used to tell people they'd been fired? But no, she quickly added that I would be reassigned. She then added coldly that this had nothing to do with what I'd said during our last meeting. "You'd be sorely mistaken to think otherwise."

She explained that the embassy's security office in El Salvador had decided the country's worsening urban violence in the capital and guerilla warfare in the countryside warranted canceling any new additions to the staff. Obviously, this included my training tour, which was "over complement," meaning it was not a required position.

I had a choice, she told me. I could either go to a position at the U.S. consulate general in Calcutta, India, the only unassigned post from my class's bids list, or do my training tour instead at the U.S. embassy in Caracas, Venezuela. Before I could blurt out, "Caracas!" she said I should think over my choice carefully and let her know the following day.

In retrospect, Calcutta might have been an excellent first assignment. It is one of the oldest U.S. consular missions anywhere in the world, going all the way back to 1792. And the city with its bustling commercial port, fascinating history, and rich cultural offerings would have opened up a whole new world for me. But back then, all I thought of was the "black hole of Calcutta," an expression my mother often used, probably from some film she'd seen, to refer to a dreadful locale. And that led me to conclude, "I'm never going there!" Of course, I could have done some research, which is always a great antidote for woeful ignorance, but I didn't. What a dumbbell I was!

I called my assignments officer the first thing the following morning and said I was delighted to accept the assignment in Venezuela. After I got off the phone, my only thought was "I beat the system!" I was elated that I would be going to a prosperous country in the Caribbean, which was one of Latin America's oldest democracies. I had visions of sipping margaritas by a poolside during my time off. On top of that, it was close to the United States and a Spanish-speaking post. What could be better?

Little could I have imagined just how wrong I was.

The Life of a JOT: Venezuela

New USICA officers were called JOTs, which stood for *junior officer trainees*. The dictionary defines a *jot* as "a little bit," and that was exactly how I felt on my first overseas tour. When you've been in the foreign service for a few years, you quickly learn that in considering an assignment, the most important thing is not the country you're bidding on but rather the reputation of those for whom you'll be working. In short, what you want is a "good post," one with supervisors who provide meaningful work, and fair evaluations, and who can serve as future mentors willing to help with your career.

Sad to say the public affairs section at U.S. Embassy Caracas was completely lacking in such officers. The previous PAO had recently left the country and retired from the foreign service. He apparently had been unhappy in Venezuela and decided it was time to call it quits. There were a number of reasons for this, as I would soon learn.

Venezuelans are proud of the fact that Simon Bolivar, the best-known leader of South America's successful revolution against Spain's colonial rule in the early nineteenth century, was one of their own. But shortly after independence, the country became dominated by *caudillos*. These were dictators from the upper class whom Bolivar came to oppose. Because of his principled opposition, he was subsequently forced into exile from Venezuela and died a broken man in neighboring Colombia. In the decades that followed, Venezuela languished into becoming something of a backwater, overshadowed by the achievements of Mexico, Brazil, and Argentina, which were viewed as the region's richest, dominant countries.

However, starting in the twentieth century, Venezuela began to emerge as one of the world's major oil producers. In 1958, President Marcos Perez Jimenez, who ruled as a military dictator, was overthrown, which led to a stable democratic government for the coming decades. In 1960, Venezuela became a founding member of the Organization of Petroleum Exporting Countries (OPEC), which would play a decisive role in the global economy starting in the 1970s.

All this might have led Venezuelans to celebrate their increasing economic and political prominence in Latin America. Instead, they continued to suffer from an inferiority complex, feeling slighted not only by their neighbors but also by the United States and Europe, which they saw as only focused on exploiting their country's natural resources. Part of this sense of a lack of appreciation was cultural. Unlike Mexico, Peru, and many other countries in the region, Venezuela lacks a rich indigenous history or a culturally vibrant, literate society, such as that of Colombia.

All of these made Venezuelans, especially Caraqueños, as residents of the capital city are called, sometimes haughty and difficult people. Following a brief Spanish brush-up course at the Department of State's Foreign Service Institute, I arrived in Caracas in April 1979 and became aware of just what a status-driven place Venezuela was. At embassy receptions, Venezuelan guests would abruptly break off conversations with me as soon as they learned of my lowly diplomatic status. I was also unprepared for the stratospheric cost of living in Caracas, and this was a challenge as I tried to make ends meet on my JOT starting salary of $17,000. The 1973 Arab oil boycott and the 1979 Iranian Revolution resulted in OPEC's complete dominance of world oil prices, which had soared by the late 1970s. This made Venezuela one of the world's most expensive countries in which to live.

Although the embassy provided me with a housing allowance, it hardly was adequate for a single first-tour officer to cover an apartment rental in one of the city's nicer neighborhoods. After months of searching, I finally took a small two-bedroom place on a busy street.

Even that was beyond my allowance. Eating out, except in very modest places, was virtually impossible. All of this made me nostalgic at times for my life as a Junior Fulbright lecturer in Spain. There, I'd been able to live well, including having a much nicer apartment than the one I had in Caracas.

And then there was my work as a JOT. In general, the embassy had a tough time attracting first-rate officers to serve in Venezuela. It was an expensive city, even for those who were seniors. Affordable housing was scarce, as was reasonably priced domestic help. The country lacked the sort of history and cultural attractions that made other less expensive places in Latin America far more desirable. In addition, the Caraqueños had a reputation among foreign service officers for being exceptionally arrogant. What all this meant was that there was not a great crush of officers vying for the vacant PAO position at the U.S. embassy. In fact, months passed without a qualified bidder.

The ambassador eventually became so exasperated with the vacancy that he insisted USICA appoint the information officer (IO), who focused just on press issues, to become PAO. When I arrived in Caracas, the former IO and now PAO had been at his new job for just a few months. But in my first few days in the office, virtually everyone pulled me aside and said they couldn't stand the guy. They told me the new PAO was a former Merchant Marine seaman who often still acted as if he was browbeating and threatening crew members on some rusty freighter in the middle of the ocean. He had the habit of yelling at everyone who worked for him, both Americans and Venezuelans. He frequently swore; told crude, sexist jokes; drank too much; and cheated on his wife, who had remained behind in the United States. In short, the PAO was something less than the perfect diplomatic role model for a JOT learning the ropes!

The former PAO had been the one who had requested a JOT, and his successor really was at a loss for what to do with me, starting with where I would sit. There was no vacant office, so I was relegated to a dusty storage room where supplies had been pushed to one side to create a tiny space for a desk. For the first few months, I alternated between the press and cultural sections of the public affairs shop, doing mostly menial tasks that no one else was willing to take on.

The ambassador, William Luers, was a veteran diplomat who served previously in the Soviet Union. He would later become ambassador to Czechoslovakia. Standing at six feet six inches, Luers had a commanding presence. He was also a forceful, no-nonsense leader. Some found him intimidating, but he was someone who could effectively engage with Venezuela's overbearing government officials and social elite. He also had a passion for culture, especially contemporary American art and literature. He insisted on having weekly meetings with the PAO and his staff to discuss our work.

As the new PAO had little strategic vision in his heavy-handed management of the public affairs section and precious little background in culture, our sessions with the ambassador were not pleasant ones. Luers wanted to know how much cultural and educational programming we were doing and if it was having any impact on our audiences. Unfortunately, the cultural affairs officer (CAO), an extremely vain former local TV news anchor, was nearly as clueless about cultural programming as the PAO. In addition, the CAO could barely speak a word of Spanish. One of us would always have to translate on the rare occasions when he met Venezuelans.

Consequently, the ambassador was not very happy with the public affairs section and made his displeasure with us known whenever we met. Usually, the PAO, CAO, new information officer (IO), and assistant officers took such criticism silently. But one day, I spoke up on a project I'd been given, defending my work and that of others. I then told the ambassador that I thought he was being "extremely unfair" to us. Ominously, Luers looked at me sternly and said nothing in reply. I once again had a sinking feeling that I'd made a career-ending faux pas by not controlling my tongue.

In fact, after the meeting, my USICA colleagues told me I most likely would be on the next flight out of the country. But that's not how things turned out. At a reception that night at his residence, Ambassador Luers motioned for me from across the room to come to talk with him. My only thought was, "How many hours will I have to pack?"

Instead, he said, "I liked what you had to say today. You should speak up more often."

That was the beginning of my close relationship with the ambassador. When he learned I had a PhD in American Studies, he put me in charge of a major visiting writers' series he was organizing.

While a political officer in Moscow, the ambassador had met and come to know many leading American writers who were visiting Russia. In Caracas, he invited such luminaries as John Cheever, Edward Albee and William Styron to come to Venezuela and stay at the ambassadorial residence. As someone who had until very recently been teaching American literature, I found it an amazing opportunity to arrange programs for these writers. The new IO, an accomplished although unhappy officer, taught me how to write press releases and set up high-level visits with sometimes-demanding authors.

In addition, the ambassador asked that I prepare speeches for him, as he liked to address audiences at universities and elsewhere. Again, this was a new skill that the IO helped me learn.

Although the PAO refused to let me do work in other embassy sections or spend time at the embassy's branch post in the oil-hub city of Maracaibo, my fourteen months in Caracas passed quickly. I was very happy to be doing substantive work because of the ambassador's intervention and support.

Midway through my tour in Caracas, my Spanish fiancée, Pilar, as I will call her, and I were married in Oviedo, Spain, where I had been a Fulbright lecturer. Still afraid of flying, my parents mustered the courage to take a flight across the Atlantic and attend our wedding. Pilar and I went to Barajas Airport outside of Madrid to meet them. Pilar had previously come to Rhode Island before I entered the foreign service and met my parents there. They were pleased to see her again, and my mother was delighted I was marrying "a nice Catholic girl."

All things considered, the wedding in the university chapel went well enough. My parents got along with Pilar's folks and happily returned to the United States shortly after the ceremony.

Honeymoons are supposed to be among the happiest interludes in your life, but that's not always the case. Pilar and I spent ours in

Barcelona, Mallorca, and Ibiza. It proved to be a time of disagreements between us, often over small things. Our less-than-idyllic honeymoon foreshadowed larger problems on the near horizons of our married life.

Pilar had previously visited me in Caracas, so she was familiar with my noisy, cramped apartment and its odd mix of furniture I'd bought from departing officers. During those first few months, she seemed to adjust well, studying English at Caracas's binational cultural center. She also did volunteer work at makeshift schools in the sprawling slums known as *ranchitos* in the hillsides surrounding Caracas.

Like me, Pilar was distressed by the deep poverty we both saw. As a volunteer in the slums, she witnessed on a daily basis the appalling misery of its dwellers in what was then one of South America's richest nations. She was deeply disturbed by the conditions she saw. Despite its democratic institutions, Venezuela was a country dominated by two institutional political parties controlled by members of the wealthy upper class who alternated power.

Despite Venezuela's enormous oil wealth, these politicians did little to improve living conditions for most of their countrymen. While the rich few lived in ostentatious luxury, millions of other Venezuelans, especially those in the slums, endured poverty and squalor. Two decades later, all this would lead to Hugo Chavez's populist Bolivarian Revolution, which swept the selfish elite from power.

Pilar was openly critical of the tremendous inequalities she saw in Venezuela, which I fully understood. I had never experienced similar economic disparities in my life, certainly not in Spain. But it went deeper than this. Pilar became increasingly scornful of Latin America, in general, ridiculing its people with a sort of Spanish postcolonial elitism that I found disturbing.

In those days, I was an uncritical admirer of all things Spanish, and her condescending views of Latin America surprised me. How could my new wife, who was so generous, react with such venom toward an entire continent? It was the beginning of differences between us that would become even greater during the coming years. However, at the time I dismissed such worries, attributing them to the challenges and stress of her living for the first time outside of Spain.

Panama or How I Learned to Love the Canal

As I neared the end of my training tour in Caracas, I began to bid on my next assignment. I wanted to stay in Latin America, believing that Pilar's dislike for the region would pass. This time around, I considered not only the appeal of the countries but also the reputation of those for whom I would be working. Based on this, my preferences were for postings in Mexico, Ecuador, Peru, and Uruguay. Once again, I wound up getting my last place bid: Panama.

However, the good thing about the U.S. embassy in Panama was that the PAO had an excellent reputation. The not-so-good news was that I found myself once again in a less-than-ideal work situation. The reasons were somewhat complicated.

In the years leading up to the 1977 Panama Canal Treaty and during the years immediately following its signing, there had been a need for two press officers at the embassy in Panama City. The negotiations attracted worldwide media attention, which required a great deal of embassy press work. By 1980, things had gone back to normal at what was a rather small diplomatic mission. There was barely enough work for one press officer. Despite this, rather than lose the assistant press attaché position I bid on, the PAO left it on the books. As I would soon learn, no one ever wants to downsize staff in the foreign service!

No sooner had I arrived in Panama than I learned that I was really not going to be doing much press work. Instead, the CAO informed me I would be the "program officer." Now, as it turned out, the duties of this position were vague. Much like my initial work in Caracas, I was assigned to whatever it was that neither the CAO nor IO wanted to do.

This included running speaker and other information programs on watershed management and deforestation. Having grown up in Rhode Island, not exactly known as an agricultural powerhouse, these were subjects about which I knew next to nothing. But they were ones of importance in maintaining Panama's fragile biodiversity which depended on the operation of the canal and the generation of hydroelectric power. I was fortunate that Panama City hosts the Smithsonian Tropical Research Institute (STRI), a world-class organization. Its staff of scientists and administrators kindly took me under their wing. They taught me the basics of watershed management, soil erosion, and deforestation. It was because of them that I became environmentally aware.

I also arrived in Panama with no experience supervising local employees. Despite this, the PAO put me in charge of the USIA in-house print shop, run by two Panamanian employees who didn't get along with each other. Interestingly enough, before becoming an officer, the PAO was a foreign service printing specialist who worked for years producing press and cultural materials at major USIA regional production centers in the Philippines and elsewhere. I knew even less about printing than I did about watershed management.

One Saturday morning, the PAO showed me the basics of how a printing press works. This was something I needed to know to supervise the production of our materials by the shop. That too turned out to be a highly valuable experience.

The senior printer was one of the most hardworking, versatile, and talented people I would supervise in my career. His subordinate was just the opposite. Getting the two of them to work together productively provided lessons that would serve me in my future posts. Best of all, rather than my dingy storage room or nook in Caracas, I had a nice second-floor office near the printing press with a lovely view of the Bay of Panama!

I also learned about ballet during this assignment. Panama City had a struggling national ballet company that performed in the beautiful, although run-down, Casco Viejo, the city's historic district. Some of the buildings date back to when the French were trying to build the first canal across the isthmus in the late nineteenth century.

With their ornate iron balconies and delicate grillwork, they lent a New Orleans ambiance to the district. And the old quarter's National Theater was magnificent. Inaugurated in 1908 and built on the site of an eighteenth-century Spanish monastery, the theater boasted striking Neo-Baroque architecture. Its Italianate interior gave it the aura of faded grandeur from a long-gone past when world-acclaimed artists performed on its stage. Needless to say, I loved the place!

MARK L. ASQUINO

As neither of my colleagues was interested, I started working with the ballet company, arranging for American choreographers to assist it during year-long residencies. I also set up visits for leading U.S. ballet soloists to come to Panama. The soloists performed and also conducted masterclasses for company members.

Panama was far less expensive than Venezuela, and Pilar and I found a spacious apartment overlooking the Pacific Ocean. The U.S. military still had bases in Panama City, which gave us access to their commissaries, clubs, and movie theaters. Beyond that, Panama is a beautiful country, and we were able to visit colonial-era ruins and beaches on both its Pacific and Atlantic coasts. Life was good, or so I thought.

Despite all these positive things, my marriage was starting to spiral downward. My wife belonged to a women's organization called Las Damas Diplomaticas (The Diplomatic Ladies), most of whose members were married to senior Latin American diplomats, including ambassadors. Pilar complained bitterly about how these women enjoyed luxuries that were far beyond her reach. Increasingly, nothing that we had seemed to please her. When I would resist buying things we couldn't afford, she would angrily call me a *tacaño*, Spanish slang for "miser." Further, Pilar constantly berated Panamanians as ill-educated, rude, and dirty.

One day she was at a local market with the CAO's wife, an elegant tall blonde from the Peruvian upper class. Pilar was an equally tall, elegant, and striking brunette. When Panamanian fishmongers began taunting these foreign-looking women as "gringas," the two let loose with a tirade in their native Spanish that I would have loved to have heard. I can only imagine the shocked look on the fishermen's faces when they learned neither was American.

While the incident was hilarious, it elicited deep rancor in Pilar toward Panama that darkened our remaining time in the country. While I was delighted with all the new things I was learning, my wife saw only the downsides of being married to a still-junior American diplomat who, in her view, had limited future prospects.

At the end of my two-year tour in Panama City, I was once again looking for a new overseas assignment. This time, aware of my wife's unhappiness in Latin America, I bid on mostly European posts, including Spain. I was turned down for the assistant press and assistant cultural affairs officer openings at the U.S. embassy in Madrid. But one day, my assignments officer called and asked if I was interested in being director of the U.S. Cultural Center in Madrid, a position that had unexpectedly become open. I jumped at the opportunity, and a few hours later, he called back to say I had the job.

"Wow," I thought, "I'm finally getting an assignment I really want!" My wife was also delighted that we would be returning to Spain. Professionally, it seemed ideal, as the new PAO, McKinney Russell, was regarded as one of USIA's best senior officers. Little did I know at the time that going to Madrid would eventually involve my working with our embassy in Equatorial Guinea. Yes, the "awful place" where the grisly murder occurred. Despite the "cautionary tale," I came to have a very different view of the country during my tour in Madrid.

What serendipity! It all seemed absolutely perfect but proved far from being so.

CHAPTER 5

Back to Spain

T HE SPAIN THAT Pilar and I returned to in the summer
of 1982 was a dramatically different country from the one
I'd departed six years earlier. The reason requires some historical
background.

From October 1, 1936, when he proclaimed himself as head of
state shortly after the start of the Spanish Civil War, until his death on
November 20, 1975, Generalissimo Francisco Franco wielded absolute
power over his countrymen. Adopting the title of *caudillo* (the equivalent
of "dictator" in English), Franco ruled Spain during this entire time as a
one-party state through his Fascist Falange party, which supported the
so-called National Movement.

Staunchly anti-Communist, Franco was ideologically, but not
militarily, allied with Hitler and Mussolini during World War II. As a
result, he managed to keep Spain out of direct involvement in the war by
declaring his country "neutral." Nevertheless, Franco's Spain emerged
from World War II as an international pariah state condemned and
isolated by the international community because of its covert support
for the wartime Axis powers. Consequently, Spain was excluded from
the Marshall Plan for Europe's reconstruction, something Spaniards
had never forgotten. It was also not admitted to the United Nations
until 1955.

In 1947, the Francoist regime promulgated the law of succession,
returning the country to monarchy again but only after Franco's death.
The law declared the caudillo as head of state for life and gave him the
sole right to choose who would become his successor as king. In 1969,
he chose the thirty-year-old prince Juan Carlos of Bourbon as the royal
heir apparent. The young prince, educated in Spain and seemingly

subservient to the Francoist regime, was viewed by many as weak and malleable.

Franco's plan was to transfer real power to Admiral Luis Carrero Blanco, a hard-line regime insider. The latter was named prime minister in June 1973 at a time when the old caudillo's health had begun to decline. In this succession scenario, Juan Carlos would ascend the throne as little more than a figurehead monarch, with Prime Minister Carrero Blanco entrusted with carrying on the Francoist dictatorship.

But this all changed on December 20, 1973. Just six months after assuming his powerful new post, the sixty-nine-year-old Carrero Blanco was assassinated in Madrid by the Basque terrorist group ETA. He was replaced as prime minister by Carlos Arias Navarro, another Francoist stalwart. After Franco's death, many were disappointed, but not surprised, when the newly crowned King Juan Carlos I left Arias Navarro in place.

Initially, it appeared that Prime Minister Arias Navarro would fulfill Franco's plan, and he clearly indicated he had no desire to bring real democracy to Spain. Instead, he proposed a "democracy Spanish style," keeping in place Franco-era institutions and laws with only minor cosmetic changes. He thought Juan Carlos would play a largely ceremonial role as head of state.

However, Arias Navarro and other Francoists underestimated the young king. Much to their surprise and that of the international community, King Juan Carlos I turned out to be a democratic reformer who had no intention of merely being a figurehead. One of his chief allies in leading Spain's transition to democracy was Adolfo Suarez, who served as minister secretary general of Franco's National Movement. Despite this, Suarez, a nationalist and political centrist, was a skilled dealmaker. He outmaneuvered Arias Navarro and the old guard in the months after Franco's death by soliciting support from a disparate array of allies spanning the political spectrum.

Gradually, they stripped power from the Franco holdovers and managed to persuade the powerful military to remain on the sidelines. In July 1976, the king named Suarez as the new prime minister. The Cortes—Spain's Franco-era parliament, which had largely been a rubber stamp assembly—became a true legislative body that worked with Suarez to develop the "law for political reform." The latter was approved by the Spanish public in a 1976 referendum. General elections followed in 1977, with Suarez's Democratic Centrist Union (UCD) party winning at the polls. But having fallen short of an absolute majority, Suarez was forced to govern with his party sharing power as part of a political coalition. This democratically elected government helped craft a new constitution that was approved by Spaniards in a late-summer 1976 referendum.

I had been in Spain during much of this amazing transition. In early 1976, the newly crowned King Juan Carlos I, Queen Sofia, and their three young children (Elena, Cristina, and Felipe) visited Oviedo, the capital of the northwestern region of Asturias, where I taught. The new king's son, Felipe, was his royal heir. He held the title of the prince of Asturias, much as the male heir to the British throne is the prince of Wales. For this reason, it made sense that one of Juan Carlos's first domestic trips as monarch would be to Oviedo.

Standing with Pilar, my then-girlfriend, in the throng of well-wishers who greeted the royal family, I remember thinking how very young this new king seemed. Indeed, he was just eleven years older than me. Yet I thought, here he was, having been thrust into a succession snake pit.

Dressed in a dark tailored suit, the handsome tall thin young king spoke from the balcony of Oviedo's ornate *ayuntamiento* (city hall). This large edifice was built in the early seventeenth century. It dominated the main square of the historic section of the city, not far from the university. After being heavily damaged by Francoist troops in their deadly siege of Oviedo during the Civil War, the ayuntamiento was restored and enlarged in 1939.

As he began to speak, the king seemed unsure of himself. His remarks were brief and decidedly uninspiring. There was something slightly awkward about his Spanish, even to my foreigner's ears. Afterward, Pilar explained that the king's Spanish was not quite native. Juan Carlos was born in Rome in 1938. During the Spanish Civil War, his father, who would later renounce his claim to the throne, took the royal family into exile in Italy, and they later moved to other places in Europe. When he was ten years old, Juan Carlos was sent to Spain, where he was groomed to be Franco's successor.

Although he'd spoken Spanish since that young age, it was not the king's first language. As a result, Spaniards often poked fun at his less-than-perfect accent and inflections. Even worse, they made cruel jokes about him as someone who was dim-witted. After he was crowned, many called him Juan Carlos El Breve (The Brief), convinced he would not last long.

I heard all of this during my Fulbright year in Spain. Although being encouraged by the nation's first tentative moves toward democracy when I left Oviedo in the summer of 1976, I still wondered if Juan Carlos's critics were right. Happily, along with so many others, I was mistaken. This young monarch would continue to play a decisive, historical role in moving Spain from dictatorship to democracy. The king would soon prove he was not the dolt many of his countrymen thought him to be.

In August 1982, when Pilar and I arrived in Madrid for my four-year diplomatic assignment, Spain seemed to be on a firm path toward establishing itself as a constitutional monarchy. But there had already been one serious challenge to its fledgling democracy. It would be once again up to the king to stop those who sought to turn back the clock in Spain.

On February 23, 1981, Lt. Col. Antonio Tejero and two hundred heavily armed fellow members of the para-military "Guardia Civil" (Civil Guard) stormed the Congress of Deputies, as the Francoist Cortes had been renamed. The entire assembly and senior members of the UCD government were present, including Prime Minister Suarez, and all were taken hostage at gunpoint. Tejero called on the country's military and citizens to rise up in revolt and support his coup so that "order" could be restored to Spain.

Initially, a number of military units throughout key parts of the country seemed to support Tejero and his plotters. However, King Juan Carlos saved the day. Appearing on national television in his full-dress military uniform as commander in chief of the armed forces, he ordered Spain's armed forces to oppose the coup. After a brief period of uncertainty, pro-Tejero military forces returned to their barracks. Democracy would be preserved through the bold assertion by the king of his authority and that of the elected civilian government. This was the turning point leading to the coup's collapse.

Tejero and his followers surrendered and were arrested the following day. King Juan Carlos was acclaimed as a hero and became a revered figure in Spain. But in 2014, with his popularity in sharp decline and in the midst of personal scandals, the king abdicated the throne in favor of his son Felipe. Juan Carlos would eventually be forced to leave Spain and go into exile, which was a sad end to his reign.

However, in 1981, the king played a key role in helping Spain survive a close-call threat to its democracy. In the summer of 1982, with the coup attempt beginning to fade, Spain was filled with youthful optimism and hope for the future, especially in Madrid. La Movida Madrileña, a brash countercultural movement, was flourishing in the country's capital. It soon spread to other major cities. The provocative films of director Pedro Almodóvar would come to exemplify the artistic freedom, sexual bravado, and often wild antics of La Movida. The movement also found expression in art, music, theater, and fashion. As the newly arrived young director of the U.S. cultural center and its Washington Irving Library, I could hardly have had better timing in taking on this post. It would prove to be one of my favorite foreign service jobs—far more fun actually than being an ambassador!

The political landscape was also changing in Spain during my first few months in Madrid. Adolfo Suarez's coalition government began to unravel by early 1981. He stepped down as prime minister and was replaced by Leopoldo Calvo-Sotelo, a dull sixty-something-year-old politician who seemed completely out of step with everything happening around him. In the summer of 1982, Calvo Sotelo called for new parliamentary elections in October.

That proved to be a fatal misjudgment by his UCD party. The Spanish Socialist Party (PSOE), led by the charismatic forty-year-old Felipe González Marquez, won a resounding electoral victory that fall, which ushered in generational political change. Pilar and I were there for the election and transition. The PSOE had been in clandestine opposition during the Franco years and ran slightly behind the UCD in the first post-Franco democratic elections. Unlike the UCD, none of the Socialist Party's leading members had been tainted by Francoism. In the October elections, the UCD won just a handful of parliamentary seats and ceased being a major political party.

Gonzalez's PSOE was dominated by youthful supporters who enthusiastically embraced the "new" Spain. In many ways, La Movida now became a political movement as well.

From the perspective of U.S. foreign policy and my taking up duties at the U.S. Cultural Center, the PSOE victory presented challenges. The young Socialists, led by González, deeply distrusted the United States and not without good cause.

During the height of the Cold War, the United States helped the Franco regime break out of its international isolation. In September 1953, the Eisenhower administration signed executive agreements with Spain that provided economic and military aid to Franco's dictatorship. In return, the United States was permitted to build military bases and, as a bulwark against the Soviet Union, allowed to station U.S. troops throughout the country. The military facilities included Torrejón Air Force Base outside of Madrid, Naval Station Rota and Móron Air Base in the south, and Zaragoza Air Base in the north.

While not a formal defense alliance, U.S. military support to Franco allowed him to strengthen his armed forces and provided an economic lifeline to consolidate power against those who opposed his dictatorship. The agreements also provided Franco's Spain with a degree of political legitimacy. For example, in 1959, President Eisenhower, a World War II hero, visited Madrid and stood side by side with a dictator whose sympathies had been with Hitler and Mussolini.

During Calvo-Sotelo's UCD-led government, Spain took its first steps toward full membership in NATO. But the PSOE ran on a platform promising, if it won, to pull the country out of NATO. It also called for the closing of U.S. military bases on Spanish territory and the withdrawal of all American armed forces from the country.

During my four-year tour in Madrid, young Spaniards would often ask me how my country, the most powerful democracy in the post–World War II period, could have embraced and shored up a Fascist dictatorship. Throughout the Franco dictatorship, there was no free press, opposition political parties, or independent trade unions. They would note how the regime repressed those in the Basque country and Catalonia, refusing to grant these regions any autonomy and systematically cracking down on their languages, history, and culture.

Of course, all of this was true. But as an "official American," a role I was slowly getting used to, I was required to defend U.S. foreign policy. I countered that U.S. support for Franco had to be viewed within the context of Cold War politics. I argued that America's bringing Spain out of political isolation in the 1950s had positive consequences, including encouraging Franco to liberalize Spain's economy. This, in turn, led to the creation of a middle class and an economic boom from 1959 to 1974, which came to be known as El Milagro Español (The Spanish Miracle). Finally, I said that pressure from the U.S. and other Western democracies forced the Franco government to become less repressive and authoritarian, especially in the later years of his rule.

My arguments were factual, but I was well aware of the contradictions, inconsistencies, and outright hypocrisy of post–World War II America's foreign policy. It was impossible to paper over or deny this history.

As the director of the U.S. Cultural Center, a large part of my job was to address what was perceived to be the post-Franco legacy of anti-Americanism in Spain. But it seemed to me that the roots of the friction between our two countries went far further back in time than the Franco era.

When I first went to Spain in 1975, I became a great fan of zarzuela, a uniquely Spanish light-opera genre consisting of music, dance, and spoken dialogue that dates back in its modern form to mid-nineteenth-century Madrid. One of the most famous short zarzuelas is the 1898 *Gigantes y Cabezudos* (*Giants and Big Heads*). Its opening scene depicts weary Spanish soldiers crossing a bridge with their hometown of Zaragoza in the distance. As they approach the city, they sing bitterly of their defeat in Cuba during the Spanish-American War. Although this is largely a comic work, there is nothing amusing about the soldiers' song or their sadness over Spain's loss of Cuba to the rising United States.

For most Americans, the war was a brief conflict in which the United States emerged victorious. If we remember anything, it's about Teddy Roosevelt and the Rough Riders charging up San Juan Hill. But as I learned more about Spain, it seemed to me that there was a lingering, historical sense of tragic loss among Spaniards because of that brutal short war. They viewed it very differently than we do. And this led to feelings of bitterness toward my country that were never far from the surface. In a way, it helped to shape the Spanish view of the United States as an aggressive young nation using its military might to dominate others.

The challenge I faced as center director was how to convey through our library collection, speaker programs, concerts, exhibits, English teaching, films, and other outreach activities that there are a great number of nuances in both U.S. society and history. American culture is far richer and more diverse than the Hollywood images many Spaniards knew. It was these challenges that I found so fascinating and difficult during the two years I spent as center director before moving to another embassy job.

The cultural center was in the Chamberí district of Madrid, a neighborhood not far from the country's flagship, Complutense University. Working-class Chamberi offered affordable student housing, cheap restaurants, and picturesque old bars where they could congregate.

Upon arriving at Madrid's Barajas Airport, my wife and I were met by a young USIA officer who had been running the center for about a year. He'd been unhappy as a center director, and his departure created the immediate opening and my getting the job. He was allowed to break his assignment and leave Spain a year early because he'd volunteered for a hardship assignment.

The outgoing center director was accompanied at the airport by a somewhat distinguished-looking older American with a high forehead and receding hairline, whom I'll call Frederick, who had no formal connection to the embassy or the U.S. government. While being met on arrival by your predecessor is normal in the foreign service, it was strange to be greeted as well by this non-official American. As Pilar and I were driven in an embassy car from the airport to Madrid, the center director explained that Frederick had lived in Spain for decades and possessed an encyclopedic knowledge of its art and cultural scene. He added that his American friend would be "indispensable" to my running the cultural center.

Although I was still relatively new to diplomacy, this seemed like an odd thing for anyone to say. Why would I need this total stranger to help me run the center? In fact, my first management challenge would be dealing with Frederick, who seemed to have a great deal to say about how I should do my new job.

Running the cultural center would prove to be unlike anything I'd ever done previously in my brief professional life. Shortly after starting the job, I remember greeting the blue-uniformed local-hire Spanish security guards, who sat at a desk as I entered the center. As I walked to the stairway leading to my second-floor office, I almost tripped over a loose floor tile. "Someone should fix that!" I said to myself. Then, I had a shock of recognition. As the director, I was that "someone." No one was likely to fix the tile unless I did something about it. If I failed to act, it was quite possible that one of our patrons would trip, fall down, and get hurt—and it would be my fault.

I was now in charge of an organization with ten local employees and responsible for the well-being of hundreds of people, many of them studying English, who came to the U.S. Cultural Center every day. As I've mentioned, the center had been bombed a few years earlier by a terrorist group, so security was also a weighty responsibility. Fortunately, that attack occurred after hours, although a night-time guard had been seriously injured. But there was no guarantee another attack would not happen when the center was crowded with people.

During the time I was the director, we received a number of bomb threats by telephone, often with the message that an explosive device would detonate in fifteen or twenty minutes. More often than not, when this happened, I decided to evacuate the center and inform other occupants of the building. Our guards, with assistance from the embassy, would then do a thorough search of the premises for any suspicious objects.

For the first time in my life, I found myself spending considerable time addressing safety and security problems in the building while also overseeing a budget and supervising a large staff. When there were complaints, they came directly to me, as I had no deputy. As a thirty-three-year-old, I was entrusted with running a library, art gallery, and entertainment venue all rolled into one. This was incredibly exciting but also rather daunting, at least at first.

Little by little, I settled into my new duties. I consulted with my local employee library director about new acquisitions while setting up film series and musical events with Josefina, my highly efficient Spanish cultural assistant. I also chose American speakers on a wide range of topics.

But my early days as a center director were not without problems. I soon learned from my staff that Frederick had taken full charge of selecting the mostly American artists resident in Spain who exhibited their work in our gallery. Although in an unpaid role as the center's "artistic adviser." Frederick, some believed, was remunerated under the table by those who sought a show at the center. I was never able to substantiate such rumors, but I found them disturbing. I would also hear that Frederick called the shots at the U.S. Cultural Center, as one person told me. Within weeks, the issue of who was running the place came to a head. Without informing me, Frederick showed up one day and handed Josefina a list of artists for upcoming exhibits.

When Josefina told me that this had been the way things were done by my predecessor, I asked her to set up a meeting with Frederick for the following day. I began the discussion by thanking him for his list of suggested artists, adding that I'd be happy to review it and make selections. I then said that I would be the one making decisions on exhibits in the future and that I intended to run the center in a more hands-on manner than my predecessorhad done.

I thought I'd delivered this message quite diplomatically, but Frederick clearly didn't take it that way and became agitated. He said he couldn't believe I was so "ungrateful." After all, I didn't know anything about the art scene in Spain, and he'd been more than generous in offering me his "help." But if this was the way I was going to react, then he was done with the center. Abruptly standing to leave, he adjusted his somewhat threadbare, but still elegant blazer. "You have no idea how influential I am in Madrid's cultural circles!" he thundered. Looking at me with an ominous expression, he warned, "Just wait and see. I'll ruin you as center director!" He then unceremoniously stomped out the door.

That was the last time I would see Frederick at the center during my time there, although we would occasionally run into each other at cultural events elsewhere and exchange chilly greetings. Josefina, who sat in a small reception area outside my office, heard the entire exchange and spread the word quickly among the rest of the center's staff about what had happened. It was clear they were extremely happy when they learned Frederick would no longer be a near-daily presence at the center. Although being threatened so early in a new job was somewhat unsettling, I took it in stride. I soon developed an extensive network of contacts, including some wonderful artists, and I was delighted not to be encumbered by the center's erstwhile artistic adviser.

I realized over time that my predecessor at the center with little Foreign Service experience had been made director of a large complex operation. Even worse, the previous public affairs officer (PAO) viewed the U.S. Cultural Center as something of an orphan on the "wrong" side of town. He seldom spent time there and didn't want to know anything about the headaches of running the center. He put the least experienced member of his staff there to sink or swim. This led my predecessor to turn to Frederick for help.

Fortunately for me, I previously lived in Spain. I was comfortable with its culture, was fluent in Spanish, and, most importantly, was on my third USIA tour. In addition, McKinney Russell, the new PAO, took a keen interest in the center.

Not surprisingly, my second management challenge at the center also involved, albeit indirectly, issues with art shows at the center. Josefina, who'd worked at the center for years, and I went through the list of American artists Frederick had left, and with her help, I chose some he'd already contacted, but also reached out to new people who were not in his circle of acquaintances. This breathed new life into the exhibit program. Artists throughout the country learned they didn't need a special contact at the center and began to send examples of their work to Josefina and me.

Since I'd never set up an art exhibit, I asked the Spanish staffer who physically arranged the shows to come to my office. He was a mid-fifty-year-old chain-smoking, tall, gruff man who said little when I first met him. On subsequent occasions, he seemed to want to avoid me. When I began our meeting by asking for his advice on the best way to stage an upcoming show, he said nothing. He finally broke the silence by telling me that in the past Frederick had simply ordered him around and never asked for his input. Furthermore, he said I was the first center director in a long time to treat him as anything other than a manual laborer with no creative ideas. I was to learn that this Spaniard, who'd worked for decades at the center, once had his own office, which he used to design exhibit layouts. A proud, sensitive man, he was unceremoniously moved out of this space years earlier and relegated to a dark corner of the center's basement.

It turned out that the Hispanic-North American Cultural Association (ACHNA), the center's English teaching contractor, had been taking over space for its operations. This included the previous office of the exhibits specialist, which had become a classroom. ACHNA, I would learn, had an interesting history.

In the early 1960s, it had been formed as a U.S.-Spanish friendship society. Many of its members were now middle-aged American women who, years earlier, as university exchange students, had met and married Spaniards. They subsequently remained in the country, and some were never able to complete their college education. With their children now grown up, they decided to try their hand at teaching English. Although such Americans lacked formal English teaching training, ACHNA hired them because the demand to learn the language was exploding in Spain. In return for rent-free classroom space at the cultural center, ACHNA gave part of the English teaching proceeds to support center programming. For many years, this had been a mutually beneficial relationship.

By the time I arrived at the center in 1982, ACHNA had become one of the most successful English teaching businesses in Madrid. It now employed young Americans with English-as-a-second-language teaching credentials who often clashed with the untrained women teachers. ACHNA was run by professional Spanish business managers who had little connection with the United States.

What surprised me most was that ACHNA continued to pay no rent at the center, devoting only limited funding to our programming. This gave it an enormous advantage over competitors. Despite this, ACHNA's management often acted as if the cultural center was its tenant rather than the other way around. They would complain to me that noise from our programs disrupted classroom teaching.

As with Frederick, it was inevitable that I would need to address this situation sooner rather than later. Accordingly, after talking with the exhibits specialist, one of my first acts was to take back a classroom from ACHNA so that he had much-needed space to do his job. This employee soon transformed the former classroom into a meticulously ordered workshop. Artists with upcoming shows would meet him there and work collaboratively on exhibit layout and lighting. Even more striking was how this older Spaniard went from being one of the most unhappy, sullen people on my staff to becoming a productive, cheerful employee.

ACHNA was furious with me for taking away "their space." They vigorously argued that they needed it as well as other center areas for their expanding English language enrollment. My previous experience as a Fulbright lecturer made me sympathetic to the importance of English teaching in Spain. But my job was to run the cultural center, not expand ACHNA's English language program. I suggested to its managers that the time had come for ACHNA to rent a nearby commercial space. Not surprisingly, this didn't go down well.

My next step was to formalize the center's agreement with ACHNA, putting in writing for the first time the amount, which I significantly increased, they would provide us each year for programming in lieu of rent. This was the final straw for ACHNA. Its directors went over my head and complained to PAO Russell. But I consulted him in advance, and he backed me. ACHNA grumbled a great deal but agreed to the new conditions.

As I've noted, my first two years in Spain as a center director were among the most enjoyable ones of my entire foreign service career. Now firmly at its administrative helm, I went about making programmatic changes. For example, when our long-serving Spanish library director retired, I hired a Belgian-Spanish dual national who held a PhD in library science degree from a U.S. university, and she modernized our library operations.

The center sponsored well-attended American film series that showcased the work of classic American directors like John Huston and genres ranging from film noir to science fiction. It had been years since the center had held regular concerts. I was told this was due to the poor acoustics of our multipurpose room. One day, I asked the wife of one of my USIA colleagues to come to the center. She was a professional musician. She informed me that while the hall's acoustics were not perfect, they were certainly good enough for musical events. What followed were frequent piano recitals that drew appreciative audiences.

We also began to program more ambitious concerts, scheduling groups that USIA sent on tours to nearby European countries. One of the most memorable was the program we hosted with New Grass Revival, an American progressive bluegrass band that performed at the center as part of a USIA-sponsored tour in May 1984. New Grass was well-known for its unorthodox and innovative approach to bluegrass music. Its performances combined elements of rock and roll, jazz, and blues. The band gave a bluegrass dimension to music by artists as diverse as Jerry Lee Lewis and Bob Marley.

The two concerts that New Grass Revival performed at the cultural center were among the most successful events there during my time as a director. On successive nights, the group performed to standing-room-only audiences who were enthralled by New Grass's innovative music. They called for, and the group obliged, with repeated encores at the end of each show.

Our exhibits were also raising the center's profile. Perry Oliver, an American graphic artist who lived in the south of Spain, won rave reviews for his solo print show. Yolanda del Riego, a dual Spanish American national who lived for many years in the United States, mounted an exhibit of fabric art that fascinated Spanish audiences because of its striking originality. Both became close friends whom I frequently saw after their shows.

Another noteworthy exhibit was Spanish Photographs 1973–1983 by American photojournalist Robert Royal. Bob had been working for *Time* magazine and had lived in Spain since the late 1960s. His show at the cultural center brilliantly documented Spain's transition from dictatorship to democracy. It featured photos of the leaders of Spain's La Movida cultural revolution in film and fashion.

Although Spain's democracy in 1984 was less than a decade old, Bob's magnificent photo exhibit demonstrated just how far the country had come in moving from its repressive past. But one photo in the exhibit seemingly had no connection at all with the transition, the world of entertainment, or anything else that was obvious.

The shot featured a tropical landscape with palm trees and an imposing volcano in the background. I asked Bob about it, wondering if it had been shot in Spain's Canary Islands. But Bob said no. It was a photo he took in Malabo, Equatorial Guinea. He went there on assignment to cover the historic 1979 visit to the former Spanish colony by King Juan Carlos and Queen Sofia. Suddenly, I remembered hearing about this infamous nation years before as a new USICA officer. I quickly put that memory and the photo out of my mind. But within a matter of months, the bizarre little place would reemerge, this time in my work.

While I was literally having the time of my professional life as cultural center director, my marriage was going into free fall. Difficulties began soon after Pilar and I arrived in Madrid. As in Venezuela and Panama, I was given a modest housing allowance and expected to find my own apartment with some assistance from the embassy's management section. But when the management officer learned that I was married to a Spaniard, help went out the window.

My wife had spent her entire life in Oviedo, a small provincial city hundreds of miles from Spain's bustling capital. She'd never lived in

Madrid, and she hardly knew the city much better than I did. But here we were, with a limited budget, trying to navigate the city's difficult real estate rental market. Much of this burden unfairly fell on Pilar as I was getting settled into my new job. We were initially living in a hotel, and Pilar went out every day to look at apartments. As the weeks went by, we both grew increasingly frustrated with how few rentals were available that would be affordable on my allotment.

But much to her credit, Pilar finally found a pleasant, albeit small, two-bedroom apartment that was fully furnished with charming Castilian-style furniture, thick rugs, and heavily lined curtains. After some negotiation with us, the owners significantly lowered the rent.

Pilar initially loved our new digs but soon began complaining about how small it was. We'd become friendly with a senior American officer at the embassy who was also married to a Spaniard. They would sometimes invite us to their gracious Old World apartment with its huge high-ceilinged rooms and stunning views of Madrid's Casa de Campo Park. Of course, my wife wanted to know why we couldn't live in such a grand style. My attempts to explain that my embassy colleague had spent two decades in the foreign service while I was just starting made little impact. The notion that one gradually moves up the diplomatic ladder to bigger and better things didn't sit well with Pilar. I remember once when we were walking in the Casa de Campo neighborhood where our friends lived. Pilar turned to me and said in Spanish, "!Debería haber casado con un caballero rico del estilo antiguo [I should have married a rich, old-fashioned Spanish gentleman]!"

I took this as a joke. After all, I simply couldn't imagine that my wife of just a few years could possibly be serious as we had what I thought was quite a nice life together. As it turned out, she was absolutely determined to find a rich old Spanish gentleman to replace me. In fact, that's exactly what she did!

The other irritant in our marriage concerned Pilar's increasingly disdainful view of Americans. This became apparent when she began working at the embassy. As we were not planning to have children, and Pilar now spoke fluent English, I thought she would enjoy working. When a job opened in the embassy's commercial section for a Spanish employee, I persuaded the commercial officer that my wife would be ideal for the position. After an interview, which went well, Pilar took the job although with some reluctance. She later told me that as a diplomat's wife, she thought working was far beneath her station in life.

Despite that, for the first year or so, things seemed to be fine with her embassy job. But one day, a fuming Pilar came home from the office. When I asked her what was wrong, she said her American boss had told her and other Spanish employees that if the González government made good on its electoral promise to pull Spain out of NATO and shut down U.S. bases, the United States should immediately break off diplomatic relations with the country. What was the point of having an embassy here if the Spanish were going to treat us in this way? Of course, this was an incredibly stupid thing to say. And when the officer's comments somehow wound up in the Spanish press, the embassy arranged for his early departure from Spain.

Pilar never showed any interest in giving up her Spanish nationality and becoming a U.S. citizen. What her American supervisor said epitomized everything she thought was wrong with Americans and the United States, whose government just happened to be paying her salary. She held nothing back in sharing what she thought on this particular evening and many future occasions, "You're a bunch of overgrown babies who have no culture whatsoever! Your country has no business telling the rest of the world, especially us Spaniards, what to do. I'm sick of Americans, and that includes you!"

Well, that was quite a revelation to me. No matter how much I tried to address her revulsion for my country and apparently me as well, nothing would change Pilar's mind. As a result, things rapidly went downhill in our marriage. She all but stopped coming to most center and embassy events. If I wanted to entertain at home, I did so myself with outside help, and Pilar made sure she was somewhere else. On those rare occasions when she did attend something at the center, she would criticize the program or exhibit as "shallow" or "a total waste of time."

It became increasingly hard for us to be together. She asked me to sleep in the guest bedroom, and I saw less and less of her at home. When

Pilar would return after being away for days on end, she would tell me she had been staying with a female friend from Asturias, who was now living in Madrid. While I found that somewhat difficult to believe, I initially gave her the benefit of the doubt.

In a way, it didn't matter all that much to me. Given the nature of my work, I was out late most evenings, either attending my own programs or cultural events elsewhere. Madrid is a vibrant late-night city, and I greatly enjoyed that part of living there, especially in those exciting years. Increasingly, I started to spend more time with two American friends, Marcia and Mary. Both were attractive young women who had lived and worked in Spain for years. Marcia was married, and Mary was in a relationship, so romance was not what brought us together. Rather, we were each going through difficult times in our lives, and the three of us shared a great passion for all things Spanish.

We often attended cultural events together, celebrated one another's birthdays, and went barhopping until the wee hours of the morning. The three of us became inseparable, which inevitably raised eyebrows when we ran into my embassy colleagues. The friendship the three of us shared was something I cherished and came to rely on. They very much helped me through a challenging period in my life when my marriage was crumbling.

Those were not the only big changes in my life. In the summer of 1984, PAO McKinney Russell asked me to move from the U.S. Cultural Center job and become head of the quickly expanding International Visitors Program (IV). Taking the IV job would mean I'd have to work at the U.S. embassy in the staid, upscale part of Madrid, not something that appealed to me. I was told that a new American officer was about to arrive in Madrid who had originally been assigned the IV slot. Still, McKinney preferred that I take the position. I agreed, not really having a choice in the matter. I packed up the things in my office and said goodbye to my staff and the U.S. Cultural Center.

The IV program provided a three- to four-week professional program of visits to various cities in the United States for grantees. It was intended for upwardly bound young Spaniards. Coordinated with private U.S. program agencies contracted by USIA, the IV grants include three or four stops throughout the country where grantees would meet with U.S. counterparts in government, business, academia, and the arts.

Perhaps my most memorable IV program involved a group of rising Socialist politicians. They were deeply skeptical about the United States and just the sort of young Spaniards we hoped to reach. Based on a request from the group, I was able to arrange a meeting for them to meet with former president Jimmy Carter in Plains, Georgia. Such high-level meetings with grantees were rare. Fortunately for me, I knew a Georgia state senator who was a personal friend of Carter. When I contacted the state senator, he said he'd be happy to arrange a visit with the former president. This was one of those strokes of incredibly good luck and serendipity that I've sometimes had as a foreign service officer.

President Carter was greatly admired by those in Spain's Socialist Party as someone who had not just spoken about democracy but actively promoted it as a cornerstone of U.S. foreign policy in countries throughout the world. They respected him for his unwavering promotion and defense of human rights, especially in Central America and Cuba. Not surprisingly, they detested his successor, Ronald Reagan, for ending this policy.

Former president Carter met with the young Socialists for over an hour in the small building he uses as a study at his farm in Plains, Georgia. He had no staff in the meeting and dispensed with interpretation, using his serviceable Spanish to speak directly to them. The grantees later told me they discussed a wide range of international issues with Carter but mostly wanted to talk about his work in protecting human rights.

When they returned to Spain, the Socialists said it was amazing that a former U.S. president would take the time to meet with a group of relatively low-ranking foreign politicians. That he did so at his home and made an effort to speak with them in their own language was even more surprising.

Years later, as the deputy chief of mission at the U.S. embassy in Khartoum, Sudan, I was included in a small lunch honoring Carter and his wife, Rosalyn. They were on their way to Juba to monitor South Sudan's 2010 independence referendum. As I told him the story about the Spanish IVs' visit to Plains, the former president listened attentively, remaining silent. But when I finished, he looked at me and broke into one of his broad trademark smiles. Carter didn't utter a word, but that wasn't necessary.

While still in the IV job, I received a call one day at work from a woman named Kateri Ruddy, who said she was a U.S. ambassador's wife. It was a terrible connection, and I didn't hear where her husband was serving. Mrs. Ruddy said she was at a small embassy without a USIA officer, and as there was no one else to run the post's IV program, she volunteered to do so. But she was having a particularly difficult time. Mrs. Ruddy continued that she understood I was in charge of a large IV program, adding she was sure that I could help her. I said that beyond offering general advice, there was not much more I could do for her. Perhaps, I suggested, she might talk with someone in the IV program in Washington.

Mrs. Ruddy said, "No, I don't think you quite understand, Mr. Asquino. You see, I'm calling from the U.S. embassy in Malabo, Equatorial Guinea. As you may know, it's a former Spanish colony. The only way for our IV grantees to travel to the United States is via Madrid on Iberia Airlines, where they stay overnight and then get on a TWA or Pan American flight to the United States the next day."

Equatorial Guinea? Ah yes, that was the country where I vowed never to serve. What did any of this have to do with me and my running the IV program in Spain? Mrs. Ruddy must have sensed my hesitation because she explained that following the 1979 military coup in EG, people there had hoped conditions would improve under the new Obiang government. He promised democracy and an end to his uncle's tyranny.

Sadly, six years later, Obiang turned out to be just another dictator. In sending promising young Equatoguineans to the United States through the IV program, the U.S. embassy in Malabo hoped to prepare a new generation for a much-hoped-for future transition to democracy in the country.

I listened sympathetically, thinking about my own time in Spain during the final days of the Franco dictatorship and the country's

MARK L. ASQUINO

near-miraculous emergence as a democracy. Nothing was impossible, I mused, but I still didn't understand how I could help Mrs. Ruddy.

She continued that her main problem was that the U.S. embassy in Malabo had to give the Equatoguinean grantees a cash advance to pay for their hotel and expenses while passing through Madrid. Because of the conditions in EG, many IVs literally took the money and ran once they arrived in Spain. They never showed up at the hotel or boarded the U.S.-bound plane the next day.

She wondered if I would be willing to take over the financial administration of the Madrid portion of Malabo's IV program. She would send fiscal data for us to cover the cost of hotel lodgings and meals. She thought perhaps I could work with EG's embassy in Madrid to make sure the grantees actually went to the hotel on arrival and on the following day took the flight to the United States.

It was a persuasive pitch, and I didn't want to turn the ambassador's wife down. I told her that, in principle, I'd help. Before making a final commitment, I needed to talk with someone at EG's embassy in Madrid. I added that airport transportation was something we could not provide for the EG IVs, but I'd figure out a way to address the problem.

After many calls, my assistant Paloma reached someone at EG's Madrid embassy, and she was told a diplomat would meet with me to discuss the issue. About a week later, a young Equatoguinean diplomat came to my office. He was not exactly what I'd been expecting. Tall, skinny, and disheveled, he wore a worn, ill-fitting dark suit. I immediately noticed a large hole in the wrinkled jacket. I'd seen lots of foreign diplomats in Madrid, but none looked quite as shabby as this poor fellow.

I thanked the young Equatoguinean for coming by, asked him to sit down, and began describing in Spanish the problem of his country's disappearing IVs. I could tell he was having a hard time following what I was saying. I thought it was due to my heavy American accent. Soon, though, it became clear this was not the problem. The young man asked in broken Spanish if we could speak in French.

French? This floored me. Here was a diplomat from a former Spanish colony posted to Madrid who lacked fluency in Spanish. How could that be? And why was the guy so badly dressed as a representative of his country?

Decades later, when I became ambassador to Equatorial Guinea, it would make more sense to me. Many members of President Obiang's Fang tribe lived in small villages around the city of Mongomo on the mainland. This region is near the border of French-speaking Gabon, and the president himself came from a nearby poor village. The first language of tribal members was Fang, followed by French, and only then Spanish.

The young diplomat was most likely a poorly educated relative of someone in government. He'd been given a patronage job for which he had virtually no qualifications, including fluency in Spanish. The shoddily dressed fellow was probably a very junior member of EG's delegation to Madrid, which included far more polished, professional diplomats. He'd been sent to meet me because EG's embassy surmised I was relatively junior, and the matter I wished to discuss was of no great importance to their country.

Of course, I knew none of this at the time. I told the young man I had a good comprehension of French, but my speaking ability was poor. I proposed that I would speak in Spanish very slowly and that he could reply in French at a comparable snail's pace. This worked out, and I was able to convey the issue to him, noting having IV grantees staying in Spain was not good for either the United States or EG.

The diplomat said he would talk with his supervisor to see if EG's embassy could provide the transportation the IVs would need to get to and from the airport. The United States would pay for their hotel and meals. A couple of days later, he came by my office again. Greatly pleased with himself, he said his embassy would work with us on transporting the EG IV grantees. Paloma addressed the details, and I called Malabo to let Mrs. Roddy know the good news.

On a certain level, I found it extremely distasteful to make such a request to a foreign country whose president was a long-serving dictator. But on the positive side, if the arrangement worked, as it subsequently did, EG's IV grantees would travel to the United States and benefit from their time there. When they returned, we hoped they would contribute to EG's future. That was certainly in the U.S. government's interest.

For EG, providing transportation to and monitoring the movements of the grantees while in Madrid prevented them from seeking political asylum in Spain. Clearly, I was helping the dictator's representatives in Madrid avoid an embarrassing situation. All things considered, was this a win-win situation for both sides?

Some thirty years later, as U.S. ambassador to Equatorial Guinea, I would be faced with similar moral quandaries on a near-daily basis as I engaged in difficult negotiations with the Obiang government. Balancing a respective country's interests with sometimes-unsavory people on the other side of the table is what diplomats do all the time. That was the case for me not only in EG but also during many other postings prior to Malabo.

My final year in Spain was, in many ways, one of the most turbulent in my life. It started on an August weekend during the summer of 1985. Pilar had taken our car on a Friday evening without telling me, only to return home late Sunday. Madrid is miserably hot in the summer, which is why many residents flee to beachside resorts for their month-long vacation. On that particularly scorching weekend, most of my friends were out of town, and I decided to walk to a nearby public swimming pool.

I was reading a novel entitled *Te Trataré Como a Una Reina* (*I Will Treat You Like a Queen*) by Rosa Montero, a leading Spanish writer. The story is set in late 1950s Havana, and much of the action takes place at the city's famous Tropicana Hotel nightclub. The book has a film-noir quality about it. The plot is full of jealousy, doomed romantic relations, and political tension in the run-up to Castro's takeover of Cuba.

Montero's female protagonist says at one point that to live without passion in your life is not living at all. As I thought about that, sitting on a damp towel in a shaded grassy plot of grass near the pool, it occurred to me there was really no passion in my own life. At that time, all I felt was emptiness. My marriage would soon be over. The excitement I'd experienced as a director of the cultural center had been replaced by meaningful but less interesting work at the embassy. I cared deeply about my friends, especially Marcia and Mary, but ours were hardly what you'd call passionate relationships. My skinny rump felt cold as the towel's wetness began to seep into my bathing suit.

Rightly or wrongly, I decided on the spot that my wife must have taken the car to go off and meet a lover. Returning to the novel, I thought about its main character, a sad, fading musician nearing the end of his once-promising career at the fabled Tropicana. I suddenly felt his mounting anger and a deep sense of having been deceived and wronged.

So I decided that I would confront Pilar when she returned, accusing her of having an affair and taking our car to carry out one of her romantic trysts. For some reason, the purloined car, an old Ford Mustang, seemed to annoy me even more than what I took to be Pilar's perfidy. No sooner had she entered our apartment than I spoke to her in a cascade of overwrought Spanish, voicing my suspicions that she was having an affair.

Pilar listened expressionlessly. There was an uncomfortable silence after I'd finished. Much to my surprise, she didn't deny my accusations. Instead, she came up, gently hugged me, and said softly that she could no longer fulfill the role of being my wife. It was time, she told me, to find someone else to take her place. She then quietly picked up her overnight bag and walked to the bedroom we no longer shared, closing the door behind her.

I stood there speechless. Having expected heated arguments, denials, tears, and anger, none of those things happened. So, this is the way a marriage —no, I thought, my marriage—ends after six years. There was a cold finality to that moment that I've never forgotten. I considered what Pilar had said. She was right, I concluded. It was time to move on.

Several months later, I was at the wedding reception of a Spanish journalist whom I knew. There I met one of his friends, a Catalan woman who was a well-known television personality. Carmen, as I will call her, covered culture and entertainment as a reporter and an on-air commentator for Spanish National Television in Madrid. She had short spiky bleached-blonde hair. She wore heavy makeup and dressed flamboyantly. Carmen said she was a radical feminist, and during our brief conversation, she shared her far-left political views with me.

We were immediately attracted to each other. Ours, to say the least, was an unlikely romance. On one occasion, Carmen said to me, "Given how I look, I don't know how you have the guts to walk down the street next to me."

I countered, "And I'll never understand how you're willing to be seen in public with an American diplomat wearing a conservative pinstriped suit."

Despite our extreme differences, which often led to titanic shouting matches, Carmen and I became extremely close during a relationship that would last for several years. I'd been longing for passion in my life, and I definitely found more than I had bargained for in Carmen.

As my time in Spain was coming to an end, a family crisis forced me to return to the United States. In late January 1986, my uncle Joe, one of my father's brothers, called me from Rhode Island. He said that my mother was gravely ill and refused to eat. He urged me to return as soon as possible, saying my father was at his wit's end.

My mother's health, both physical and mental, had long been a concern for my father and me. Never robust, Eleanor suffered from ulcers, insomnia, and migraine headaches. Despite what were real illnesses, she was also a hypochondriac who frequently saw doctors. My mom was also highly neurotic and overly fearful, especially when it came to my well-being. She suffered from depression, which she refused to acknowledge, much less seek medical help to address.

In the late 1960s, her father, whom she dearly loved, died at age eighty after a long painful struggle with cancer. The passing of my grandad, a lively, funny, and delightful man, was also a great loss for me. Eleanor went into a deep depression after his death. For reasons that remained unclear, she decided she too would soon die of cancer. As a result, my mom stopped going out or seeing her limited circle of acquaintances. Despite pleas from my father and me, she refused to get medical help or explain why she clung to such an irrational fear.

During this time, I was a junior at Brown. One lovely spring morning before going to classes, I looked in to say goodbye to my mom, who, uncharacteristically, was still in bed. It soon became apparent she was not just sleeping but unresponsive as I tried to wake her. I then noticed on her nightstand a clear brown plastic bottle for prescription sleeping pills. It was empty. I frantically called my father, who rushed home from work. We carried my mom to the car and raced to a nearby hospital's emergency room. Thankfully, the doctors were able to save her life, but they later told us she had been very near death.

I was deeply traumatized by this harrowing event. I often thought I could just as easily have left the house that morning without saying goodbye. Had I done so, she would have died. It was never clear to my dad or me if Eleanor deliberately tried to take her life. And if so, why?

After my mom returned home, my father and I gently tried to get her to talk about what had happened. But Eleanor accused us of being responsible for her hospitalization. She said angrily, "You men were no help after I lost my father. I took those pills because I couldn't sleep. You'll never understand me. I just wish I'd had a daughter instead of a son!"

The Spanish have an expression: "!Me arrojó un balde de agua fria [I had a bucket of cold water dumped over me]!" That was more or less how I felt on hearing my mother's words. Eleanor and I had been exceptionally close. It started when I was born on January 4, which just happened to be her birthday. As a child, I developed serious asthma, and Eleanor became obsessively protective, fearing she would lose her only child. I was encouraged to think I was far more like her than my dad.

On the surface, that certainly was true. Louie was a dark, handsome man with the curly raven-black hair and olive skin of a southern Italian. In contrast, with my blue eyes, freckled skin, and brown hair, I inherited my mother's northern European looks. My father had remarkable dexterity and spatial depth skills he used in his work as a tinsmith and roofer. I was utterly devoid of such abilities, much like my mom. Like her, I gravitated toward academics, and she inspired in me a deep love of learning and especially literature, for which I will always be grateful. As I grew into young adulthood, I became, for better or worse, my mother's best and only friend.

In the years that followed, I began to realize how much I was like my father. We were both workaholics, which unfortunately made him largely absent during much of my childhood. We both loved a good laugh and were pragmatists. Most importantly, I benefited from the sense of self-confidence Louie instilled in me. Unlike my mother, who constantly put limits on herself and me as a child, my father was an optimist and risk-taker who started his own business. He encouraged me to set my sights high and told me I could achieve anything I wanted in life if I worked hard enough.

Considering my mother's history, I took seriously the urgent call from my Uncle Joe. It would be the second health crisis I was about to face with my mom. Before boarding the flight to the United States on January 28, 1986, I decided it was better not to let my parents know I was coming home. I knew they would discourage me from doing so. While waiting for a commuter flight to Providence from New York's LaGuardia Airport, I glanced at an overhead television screen.

It was late afternoon, and to my horror, I saw repeated footage of the *Challenger* spacecraft rising majestically into the clear blue Florida sky and then bursting into flames. Minutes later, it exploded in mid-flight. The commentary couldn't have been more somber or grimmer. What a tragic time, I thought, to be back in America. This national tragedy made me feel even more apprehensive as I boarded the flight to Providence, where I would soon be dealing with my mother's illness.

I took a cab for the thirty-minute ride from Rhode Island's T.F. Green Airport to my parents' house. It was already dark and cold when I arrived. My father, seventy-three at the time, had retired and sold his business several years earlier. The expression on his face as he opened the outer storm door conveyed both surprise and relief. "Mark, I'm so glad you're home! Your mother's not well at all."

I'd last seen my parents the previous summer when I made a quick trip home. They both seemed reasonably well then. As usual, my mother complained about a variety of ills, both real and imagined, but none of them seemed serious. However, Eleanor developed abdominal pains the following fall and went to see a doctor. After doing a routine examination and finding nothing, he said he wanted her to enter the hospital for a series of diagnostic tests. While my father encouraged her to do so, Eleanor said absolutely not. She had an irrational fear of hospitals and refused to get a second opinion. Instead, she shut herself inside the house and fell into a deep depression, telling my father she would soon die.

Fearing another overdose episode, Louie kept strict control over her sleeping pills. At some point, my mother decided to stop eating. Except for some occasional yogurt and water, she touched none of the food my father prepared and refused to get out of bed. It had been like this during the week before I arrived home.

Although I knew none of this when I entered my mother's bedroom, which was dark due to the shades and drapes being drawn, I tried to prepare myself for what I knew would be a shock in seeing her.

It was much worse than I'd imagined.

In the dull light from a table lamp, I saw my mom's pale face that was drawn and deeply wrinkled, her lively green eyes clouded, and her hair dirty and matted. I also saw the outline of her shrunken frame under the covers. The air in the room was stale and felt thick. For just a moment, I felt the strong urge to flee.

When I greeted her and said I'd come home after hearing she was ill, my mom stared at me and then said in a low, hoarse voice, "You shouldn't have come. I'm fine. Why don't you go back home to your wife and job?"

I answered that I was there to help, adding, "I hope, Mom, that you'll let Dad and me find medical care for you. I'm not leaving until you get better."

At this point, Eleanor pulled herself up in the bed, balancing uncomfortably on her bony elbows. Her slack thin arms suddenly became visible. There was anger in her voice. "You've made the worst mistake in your life by coming here!"

It was hard for me to sleep that night, despite the exhausting long journey I'd just made. Tossing and turning, I kept thinking, "Am I doing the right thing in forcing my mom to live if she is so determined to die?" Of course, I knew that I was. All that I had to do was look at my father's worried face to know that was true. After decades of what had never been a particularly happy marriage, he was still in love with Eleanor. He had no idea how to save her. I was his last hope.

By early 1986, I'd lived outside the United States for almost eight years. All of the family doctors in my hometown had either retired or died. The last doctor who my mother had seen refused to speak with me. Finally, his receptionist said that as Eleanor had refused to follow his advice, she was no longer his patient. I asked friends and relatives for advice but got nowhere.

At one point, I looked into having her committed to a private residential mental care hospital, desperately thinking this might be the only way to save her life. Finally, a graduate-school friend told me about a gerontologist who was on the faculty of Brown's relatively new school of medicine. For once in my life, the Brown connection worked, helping me get past her secretary and directly in touch with the doctor. She agreed to see me in her office at Brown the next day, where I provided background on Eleanor's deteriorating condition. She told me we needed to act immediately. She would arrange for my mom's emergency hospitalization in the coming days.

I conveyed this to my father and agreed it would be better for us to take my mom to the hospital rather than call an ambulance. When the time came, we told Eleanor we had made arrangements for her to go to the hospital. Although she initially protested, she finally agreed.

My mother spent the next two weeks hospitalized. She was initially admitted to an intensive care unit as her electrolytes were dangerously low. The gerontologist and her other physicians also feared Eleanor's lack of nutrition potentially damaged her internal organs. Rather than have a psychiatrist see my mom, the physician I'd chosen would sit down and speak with her casually, asking Eleanor about her life. Her questions were non-threatening. At first, my mother remained silent, but she gradually warmed up to the good doctor. The conversations helped her find medications to lower my mother's anxiety.

During the entire time, my father was at my mother's side. This continued when she went into rehabilitation for several more weeks after leaving the hospital. Louie and I also became closer as I developed a deep appreciation for his devotion to my mom. After nearly six weeks in Rhode Island, I knew it was safe for me to return to Spain. Eleanor was clearly on her way to recovery, but the road would be a long one. I said goodbye to both of them. As I left the rehabilitation center, my father took me aside. Looking at me gratefully, he said, "Thank you for coming home. I don't know what I would have done if you hadn't." We hugged each other.

It had been an especially torturous month and a half for me. I was happy to be going home, but doing so was bittersweet. Shortly after arriving in Rhode Island, I called my wife once or twice to let her know how my mother was doing. However, she never called me or expressed interest in Eleanor's health, so I stopped reaching out.

Before I left Rhode Island, I called Pilar. She told me not to expect her at the airport. The Mustang was not running well. Taking a cab to our apartment, I entered and found the musty, closed-up quality you'd expect after being away on a long vacation. Pilar returned late in the afternoon of the following day. She invited me out for a drink. We walked to a neighborhood bar. She asked a couple of questions about my mother's health. I inquired after her parents.

Under the informal arrangement we had, neither of us spoke of the significant other now in our lives. I continued to see Carmen in my remaining months in Spain. Her job as an entertainment reporter gave her access to unlimited cultural events we both enjoyed, and we spent time in her beautiful native Catalonia.

A couple of months after my return, I told Pilar I wanted a divorce. She voiced no objections. We spoke of how we would divide up our possessions. And yes, I got the Mustang, although I first asked if she wanted it. Instead, Pilar told me she needed $10,000 immediately for the down payment on a Madrid apartment. When I said it would take me time to come up with the money, she became angry and once again called me a tacaño. That was the only disagreeable moment in our divorce discussions. Getting such a large transfer of funds to Spain from a U.S. bank was a challenge, but I was finally able to do so.

With help from Carmen, I had spoken with an attorney about starting the legal proceedings. As Pilar and I had been married in Spain, it was not difficult to get a divorce there. Neither of us contested it, there

MARK L. ASQUINO

were no children involved, and we agreed on a division of property, so we were able to get the equivalent of no-fault divorce. We filed legal papers in June, and the final divorce decree came through in September, shortly after I returned alone to Washington.

By the spring of 1986, PAO McKinney Russell had left Madrid. He became a mentor who provided me with much-needed instruction on the finer points of diplomacy. McKinney was replaced by Bob Earle, a highly skilled officer and Ed McBride was the new CAO. They asked if I might be interested in staying on for an additional year.

Normally, four years was the maximum that officers spent on an overseas tour. I was sorely tempted by their offer but decided it was time for me to return to the United States for a Washington assignment. In large part, I was still concerned about my mother's recovery, and I wanted to be able to spend time in Rhode Island with her and my father. Beyond that, I just needed to close this Spanish chapter in my life, although I found it a hard thing to do.

CHAPTER 6

To Bucharest via Washington

THERE IS AN old adage in the foreign service: the real hardship assignments are all in Washington DC. That may seem counterintuitive, but there is a fair amount of truth to the saying.

Foreign service officers and their families are provided either free housing overseas or given an allotment to rent on the local market. Once they return to the United States, they are on their own to find accommodations in what are expensive housing markets in metropolitan Washington. In addition, Uncle Sam pays the cost of all pre-college schooling for the children of foreign service officers posted abroad. It picks up the expenses for many of those youngsters to attend elite U.S. prep schools that their parents normally could not afford. When you return for a Washington assignment, that benefit also ends.

As a U.S. diplomat overseas, you are "somebody." Even as a junior officer, you have quite a bit of prestige in most countries. You are often invited to cultural and other events in the host country simply due to your diplomatic status. But once you return to the United States, unless you are a senior official at State, you're just another faceless government employee struggling to get by financially.

With that said, from a career perspective, State Department officers benefit from and are required to return from time to time to serve domestic tours. That's because without working in DC, it's extremely hard for them to climb State's career ladder and be promoted. The most coveted domestic positions are in regional and policy-oriented bureaus or in offices that directly support the work of the secretary of state and senior officers. If you enter the State Department as a Foreign Service officer, you must return to headquarters after your second or third overseas tour. Washington is where you'll "make your bones," so to speak. It's the place to establish yourself as an up-and-coming officer, and where you'll make the crucial contacts needed to advance your career.

While I was overseas, President Ronald Reagan changed my agency's name back to the original USIA. Unlike domestic assignments at the State Department, working at the USIA headquarters in DC was not at all career enhancing., .

For USIA foreign service officers, the action and the place where you could make your professional mark were definitely abroad. There, you got to run cultural and educational programs or do press work that was vital to the operation of embassies. Headquarters was a backwater organization. As a small independent foreign affairs agency, the USIA had little political visibility. Unlike the secretary of state, who serves as the first among cabinet equals during meetings with the president, the USIA director was a nobody in the government.

As I would soon learn, USIA officers in DC essentially provided domestic support for the agency's overseas operations. It was rare that you could do anything to make yourself stand out, and most promotions came from overseas tours. In my case, I returned to headquarters in the summer of 1986 and was assigned a "bottom of the totem pole" job. That was due to yet another one of the time-worn foreign service sayings: "After you've been given a plum assignment, expect to wind up with a real lemon of a posting next time around."

A four-year assignment in Madrid was regarded as a plum. I wasn't even given a chance to turn down the lemon they gave me at headquarters. Several months before my departure from Madrid, I received an email informing me that I was a "leading candidate" to serve as a watch officer at the USIA Operations Center.

Well, that was curious because I'd never bid on the job. Plain and simple, I wound up with a one-year assignment at the USIA Operations Center because very few people wanted to work there. It was staffed twenty-four hours a day and required that all watch officers spend time on the deadly boring midnight to 8:00 a.m. shift.

In truth, the USIA really had little need for such a center. Anytime there was a crisis overseas, like an attack on an embassy, violent overthrow of a government, or natural disaster, it was the State Department Operations Center that took center stage. Watch officers at State were the ones who monitored world events; woke up senior officials, including the secretary of state, in the middle of the night if needed; and set up and staffed task forces to deal with emergencies. They got face time with senior officers who could help advance their careers. As a result, the jobs at all levels in the State Department's Operations Center were sought after.

In contrast, we handled a few urgent situations. Occasionally, an international visitor's family would need to contact a grantee in the United States. If a U.S. speaker didn't show up for an embassy program, we would find out what had happened. Most of the time, USIA watch officers did tedious, mundane work. We served as a round-the-clock, step-and-fetch-it service for the USIA's front office. And that was actually what sometimes made my 1986–87 tour on the job amusing. The reason was largely due to the USIA director.

President Reagan named Charles Z. Wick as head of the USIA in 1981, and he would serve in this position throughout the president's two terms. Loud, brash, and a self-promoter, Wick had been an entertainment lawyer, a talent scout, a successful California businessman, and a small-time film producer. He became a fundraiser for Reagan's successful campaigns for governor and the presidency, and in the process, Nancy Reagan and Mary Jane Wick became close friends.

After his appointment, Wick was widely ridiculed by many as a buffoon who produced such forgettable films as *Snow White and the Three Stooges*. But as USIA's longest-serving director, Wick launched the first U.S. government global satellite television network called WorldNet. It allowed us to have live programs with leading U.S.-based experts and a boon to the USIA's overseas programming. Although initially skeptical of the value of educational exchange programs like the Fulbright fellowship, Wick to his great credit, changed his mind and markedly increased their funding. During his tenure, the USIA's overall budget nearly doubled. That allowed us to increase every aspect of our press, culture, and education operations.

But as a staunch, anti-Communist conservative, Director Wick had a dark side. It was reported that he kept an "enemies list" of people he viewed as opposing President Reagan. Among others, Walter Cronkite and Coretta Scott King were barred from participating in USIA programs. Wick also taped without their knowledge a number of his telephone calls with prominent people. Although not illegal in the District of Columbia, his taping when it became known, was an embarrassment to the Reagan administration. Fortunately, for watch officers, our encounters with the director were of a decidedly more jovial nature.

The running joke at the USIA Operations Center was that Director Wick knew by heart only one agency telephone number. Unfortunately, it happened to be ours. He would frequently call the center at all hours with strange requests. For example, according to one story, late one night, the watch officer on duty received a call from the director. The electricity was apparently out in Wick's house. He wanted to know if the watch officer could help him. The fellow on duty replied, "Mr. Director, are the lights out as well in your neighborhood?"

"How the hell should I know?" Wick barked.

The watch officer diplomatically suggested that the director might check by looking out his window. Sure enough, it turned out the problem was just in the Wick residence. The watch officer then told the director how to reset the circuit breakers in the house's fuse box.

I was on duty alone one summer, Sunday morning when the phone rang. It was an operator for a service called MARSAT which, for a hefty price, allowed those on the high seas to make phone calls. I was connected to Wick, who said he was on a friend's yacht somewhere in the middle of the Mediterranean. Apparently, he had met actor Kirk Douglas a few days earlier when both were passing through the Rome airport. They agreed to set up a subsequent meeting in Rome. Unfortunately, said the director, he lost the name of Douglas's hotel and needed my help contacting him.

"Here's what I want you to do," he began. "Get in touch with the White House switchboard. Tell them you're calling on my behalf and that I need to contact Kirk Douglas. Call me back with his number."

I paused, wondering why the director couldn't call the White House himself. But suggesting this did not seem like a good idea, so I said, "Yes, Mr. Director. Right away!"

After I hung up, I thought to myself, how the hell will the White House know where Kirk Douglas is staying in Rome? The operator is going to think I'm a crank caller or, worse, someone who's absolutely nuts.

But I dutifully called the White House switchboard operator, told her who I was, and repeated the director's request. She listened and then said, "Just a moment, sir." before putting me on hold.

As I waited, I fully expected the next person on the line would be an irate Secret Service officer.

But no, instead, I heard an odd ringtone sound, and then someone picked up on the other end.

"Hello, this is Kirk." The distinctive voice was unmistakably that of the famous actor.

I choked up. "Well, Mr. Douglas, uh . . . my name is Mark Asquino, um . . . I'm a watch officer at the USIA Operations Center in Washington." I then told him why I was calling.

"Charlie Wick!" Douglas said in an annoyed voice. "Just tell him to call me here."

"Well, you see, Mr. Douglas, I can't do that because I placed this call through the White House. I don't know where you're staying."

Douglas then shouted to his wife, "Hey, Anne, what's the telephone number of this place? Some guy wants it for goddamned Charlie Wick!"

Kirk Douglas's wife came to the phone and kindly gave me the hotel's name, telephone number, and room extension.

I called the director, who was pleased with the information. He then went on at length about how wonderful MARSAT was. All I could think of was the cost to the U.S. government and how to explain it to my boss the next day.

Who would ever have thought Ronald Reagan kept track of his Hollywood buddies when they traveled just in case he might want to chat with them? I can only imagine the look on Kirk Douglas's face when he got me on the line rather than Reagan after the operator said, "This is a call from the White House, sir."

My assignment as a watch officer passed by relatively quickly. On the plus side, the job included premium pay for after-hours and weekend work, which I appreciated. Doing the night shifts allowed me time during the day to look for and eventually purchase an apartment in Washington. Best of all, after that tedious assignment, my reward was becoming a country affairs officer for France, Spain, and Portugal from 1987 to 1989 in the USIA's European regional bureau.

Back then, there were about a dozen of us working as desk officers, as the jobs were called. We covered Western and Eastern Europe. We worked closely with the public affairs officers at our embassies, tracking their requests for speakers, exhibits, and films needed for programming. We argued on their behalf for more resources and provided them and other USIA officers with administrative assistance.

I thoroughly enjoyed the three years I spent at the USIA working on France, Spain, and Portugal. What was there not to like? First of all, as a desk officer, I made official visits to all three countries at least once a year and occasionally more. In each, I would consult with the PAO and other USIA officers, and often be included in embassy receptions and get tickets for cultural events. I usually tacked on vacation time at the end of the consultations.

The sorts of issues that came up in my job could be delightfully amusing. For example, one day, a group of women from the Mount Vernon Ladies Association came to see me. In the mid-nineteenth century, the association's founders raised money to purchase George Washington's residence from one of his descendants and began its restoration. Unlike other national monuments overseen by states or the federal government, Mount Vernon is owned by this nonprofit association.

In our meeting, the women told me that the embassy of France in Washington had asked if their association would be willing to loan the key to the Bastille displayed at Mount Vernon for France's celebration of the 1989 bicentennial of the French Revolution. The French government wished to borrow the key to the main door of the infamous Bastille prison and put it on exhibit.

The key's history is fascinating. It was given to George Washington by French General the Marquis de Lafayette in 1790. Lafayette had been awarded the key for his part in storming the prison during the French Revolution, which fell on July 14, 1789. The French general had earlier played a major role in helping the United States achieve its independence from Great Britain. In recognition of the influence of the American Revolution on France's overthrow of its monarchy, Lafayette presented the key to Washington. In its original case, the key has been displayed at Mount Vernon for almost two hundred years.

The Mount Vernon ladies told me they were perplexed by the request. Their association never loaned anything from Mount Vernon for an exhibit, either domestic or international. Still, they said it would be a great honor to have the key as a centerpiece of the bicentennial of the French Revolution celebrations in Paris. However, they had no idea how such a loan to the French government could be safely and securely made. They were turning to me, they added, because the Department of State told them I would know how to arrange this.

Well, truth be told, I was every bit as clueless as they were, but in my most authoritative-sounding voice, I promised that I would get back to them. Fortunately, I had friends at the Smithsonian Museum of History, who sent me the standard contract they used to make international loans of priceless artifacts. In a subsequent meeting, I gave the ladies the multi-paged form, which their lawyers, in turn, studied and finally approved.

By then, I'd been in contact with my USIA colleagues in Paris, who were in direct discussion of the loan with officials at the French Ministry of Culture on insurance, length of the loan, and other technical matters. A date was set for the air shipment of the historic key to Paris. I heaved a sigh of relief. But then, it looked like the whole arduous process might collapse.

When I met with the ladies from Mount Vernon to discuss the sort of packaging that the Smithsonian had recommended for shipment, they said this would not be a problem. They had already ordered a special plexiglass container for the solid-iron key, which weighed a bit over a pound. Enclosed in its elegant original wooden case, it would be placed in this sturdy box. As for shipment, one of the ladies would personally carry the key onboard a flight to Paris. They asked when the French government would provide the air ticket and additional details on where the Mount Vernon lady would stay while in Paris.

This threw me for the proverbial loop. We never discussed anyone from Mount Vernon taking the key to Paris or being a part of the celebrations there. Fortunately, my USIA Paris colleagues came to the rescue. They negotiated an agreement with the French on providing a flight, hotel accommodation, and a role for the Mount Vernon lady as their honored guest. Problem solved, I thought.

Next, the ladies of Mount Vernon wanted to know what guarantee I could give them that the key would not be confiscated by French customs authorities as soon as one of their members arrived in the French capital.

No amount of my trying to calm them with reference to the provisions of the contract on such matters would appease the ladies. Finally, I said that someone from the embassy as well as a French Ministry of Culture official would be waiting at the airport and whisk the key and its bearer through customs. I must have been at my persuasive best because they were reassured by what I said. I then had to scamper to make sure all that I'd promised would actually happen.

The French media were beside themselves with amusement that one of the Mount Vernon ladies had traveled to Paris with the key to the Bastille. During the celebrations, she was treated like a celebrity. The fact that the event in France was the very first time the historic relic had ever been loaned provided great publicity for the association. When the bicentennial events ended, the association sent the same lady back to return with the key. It was then restored to its customary place of honor at Mount Vernon. I received a letter of thanks from the association with a facsimile key from its gift shop.

Beyond that amusing accomplishment, there were also a few times when I actually did things of importance to advance larger foreign policy goals. For example, after having agreed in 1986 to keep Spain in NATO, the country's Socialist government came under considerable pressure to reduce the U.S. military presence there. The U.S. lease of

Torrejón Air Base outside of Madrid, which dated back to the 1954 Pact of Madrid between Eisenhower and Franco, represented for many Spaniards a hated vestige of the dictatorship. The latest five-year base lease was set to expire in 1988, and the United States and Spain began often-contentious negotiations. They would eventually lead to the U.S. withdrawal from Torrejón, although not until 1992, following Iraq's defeat in the first Gulf War.

As part of its compensation to lease bases in Spain, the United States set up a U.S.-Spain Joint Committee for Cultural and Educational Cooperation and a U.S.-Spain Joint Committee on Science and Technology. When I served in Madrid, congressionally approved U.S. economic support funds (ESF) were drawn upon each year, with $5 million going to culture and education exchanges and another $7.5 million for science and technology grants between the two countries.

But in 1988, Spain said it would forgo future joint committees' ESF funds as part of a Torrejón base renewal. It used this tactic to put additional pressure on getting the United States to withdraw its F-16 jets from Torrejón as a condition of any new agreement. As negotiations dragged on and became more acrimonious, the State Department in its 1988 budget submission to Congress eliminated the $12.5 million request to fund the joint committees.

As I pointed out to colleagues at State, this was not legal. Our base agreement for Torrejón did not expire until the end of 1988, which meant the United States was obligated to provide JC funding through that year.

I wrote a memorandum to my bosses citing the ESF funding language in the 1983–1988 agreement. I prevailed, with lots of help from USIA's lawyers. The State Department was forced to restore $12.5 million to its budget request for a final year. Scholars in both countries benefited from my efforts.

After decades of being focused on Spain and serving in Spanish-speaking countries, my personal and professional life was about to change dramatically. As I was finishing my final year as a France, Spain, and Portugal desk officer, I was again passed over for promotion. This was significant. The 1980 Foreign Service Act established an up-or-out system of promotions similar to that of the U.S. military. In this system, you could only serve a maximum number of years at a foreign service grade (equivalent to a military rank). If you were not promoted during that time, you'd be "selected out," a bureaucratic euphemism for being forced into retirement.

By late 1989, I was approaching the limit of my grade for what the foreign service called time in class. Shortly after the 1989 promotions were announced, I received a letter from the USIA promotion panel chairman. He wrote that he and his colleagues were impressed by my achievements but noted I'd served only in Spanish-language overseas assignments. To advance to a higher rank, I needed a second foreign language. Reading between the lines, it was clear I was unlikely to be promoted unless I did so.

I began looking for assignments in Greece, Belgium, and Italy as I wanted to stay in Western Europe. But just about this time, Europe was changing in ways that would determine my future. From the fall of the Berlin Wall to Czechoslovakia's Velvet Revolution, 1989 was an exciting year to be in the USIA's Bureau of European Affairs. Almost all of the revolutions, including the eventual dissolution of the Soviet Union two years later, were peaceful. The one major exception was Romania, where Communist dictator Nicolae Ceausescu was overthrown after bloody street battles, followed by his and his wife Elena's execution.

I should have known that having served in a plum desk-officer assignment, I was unlikely to get my choice of assignments. My personnel officer thought it was time that I take a hardship assignment somewhere in Francophone Africa. Suffice it to say, I had absolutely no interest in doing so. I went to speak with my supervisor, the head of the West European division of our bureau. I said there must be some way I could stay in Europe for my next assignment. She listened silently and then said she'd see what she could do. A few days later, she appeared at my office door with a pleasing smile on her face. She said she'd come up with the ideal solution: Bucharest, Romania!

I grimaced but ignoring my reaction, she continued by saying it was a hardship post in Europe. Romanian was a Romance language I would find easy to learn as a fluent Spanish speaker. There were two good jobs there: cultural affairs officer and information officer, and the PAO was a top-flight officer. Finally, she said it would be an exciting time to be in this formerly Communist nation in Eastern Europe. My chances for promotion would be excellent.

My supervisor was right on every count, but I said, "Absolutely not!

All that I could think of was that during the brutal Ceausescu dictatorship, Romania was a bleak Communist backwater. Spanish speakers were often enticed to bid by being told Romanian was far easier to learn than Hungarian, Czecho-Slovak, or other similarly hard languages. In early 1990, my images of Bucharest were filled with violence and anarchy. There was the graphic footage of the Ceauşescus being convicted by a kangaroo court, lined up against a wall, and shot to death by a firing squad. In spite of this, after a couple of weeks of stalling, I finally came around to the idea that I should bid on Bucharest. It sounded a lot better to me than going to some isolated post in Africa.

In late spring 1990, I was assigned the cultural affairs officer job in Bucharest. By sheer chance, one of my JOT friends, Richard Lundberg, and his wife, Ann, were also headed for Bucharest, where he would be the information officer. Dick Virden, with whom I'd enjoyed working when he was PAO in Lisbon, was now in the same job in Romania. Things were looking up.

Of course, I had to learn Romanian first. Most foreign service officers study languages at the Department of State's Foreign Service Institute (FSI). However, one of the advantages of working for the USIA was that, unlike State, we had the option of going to a private language school for one-on-one lessons. Students there had a lead teacher and an alternate instructor to provide a different accent and teaching method. I hadn't particularly enjoyed FSI during my brief Spanish brush-up there, so I opted for a private school to learn Romanian.

A USIA colleague recommended I ask that the school arrange for an expat Romanian actor named Victor Strengaru to be my lead teacher. She'd studied with Victor and said he was phenomenal. He was available, and everything seemed set. Nothing, however, was simple when it came to Romania.

My first day of class in mid-November 1989 was at a language school on Dupont Circle in DC, just two metro stops from my apartment. There I met Victor and a middle-aged Romanian woman who would be the alternate instructor. Sad to say, my first impressions of them were not good.

On the first morning of classes, the school's director said, "Those are your Romanian teachers," pointing to Victor and the woman, whose name I don't recall. They were slumped in chairs toward the back of the school's reception area and wore sullen expressions. Looking for all the world like they wished they were anywhere else but at the school, they were shabbily dressed in rumpled clothing. I introduced myself to Victor and his companion, after which she motioned for me to sit down next to her.

In heavily-accented English, she whispered in my ear, "We hate this school! This man has a nice apartment where we'll teach you Romanian. Just go up and tell the director you're leaving with us. Let him know you won't be coming back."

Victor looked at me with hooded eyes. An overweight fellow with a maudlin wide face dominated by a drooping mustache, he nodded gravely, to which I replied, "Well, no. I'm sorry, but I can't do that. My agency has paid for me to study at this school. I have to study Romanian here."

The woman scowled, and Victor grumbled something to her in Romanian. She abruptly got up and marched to the front desk, where she began a violent argument with the director, insisting she would not teach at the school. Victor looked on as if enjoying the drama of it all. Suddenly, the woman turned around angrily and without saying anything to either Victor or me, left the office. Victor didn't move. I went to talk to the director, who told me not to worry as they would find another alternate teacher for me.

Victor and I then went into a windowless classroom with a small whiteboard. We sat in uncomfortable chairs at a square table on which he wordlessly plunked down a large, badly photocopied textbook. It had a pale-green cover with the title *Romanian for Foreign Students, Volume 1.*

In halting English, Victor made clear to me that we would spend the following weeks doing nothing except practicing Romanian phonetics. He said it was impossible to speak the language properly without getting the pronunciation and inflections down perfectly. I would have to master every sound of the language perfectly before he would allow me to proceed to grammar and vocabulary.

Our schedule was five hours a day from 8:00 a.m. to 1:00 p.m. with a couple of breaks. I had never studied a foreign language as the sole student before. I found the first classes intense, with the unsmiling Victor often frowning when I made an error, which was often.

Despite this, I found that Romanian was an intriguing language. It evolved from Latin after the Romans conquered the native Dacians during the AD first century. The Romanians liked to call themselves Latins in a sea of Slavs. Of all the Romance languages, Romanian is the closest in grammatical structure to Latin, with nouns that must be declined by number and case.

Beyond complex grammar, Romanian is exceptionally difficult to pronounce correctly. That's because, over the centuries, the language has been heavily influenced by Turkish, Greek, and Russian, with vocabulary and pronunciations drawn from all. This results in sounds that are totally unfamiliar to speakers of other Romance languages. Adding to my difficulty was the fact that unbeknown to me, I was coming down during the first days of class with a bad case of the flu. Victor would pronounce each syllable with great dramatic exaggeration and flourish. As my ears were gradually blocked up with an infection, I couldn't hear much of anything despite his booming actor's voice.

The more I struggled and failed, the more Victor became exasperated with me. Finally, after the second day of mutual torture, I told him I was too sick to continue. He gave me what I would come to know as the Balkan shrug, a combination of annoyance and resignation. It was often accompanied in Romanian with the phrase, "Ce pot sa fac [What can I do]?" I took a few days off. When I returned, the classes became considerably better for both of us.

I spent twenty-four weeks of intensive study with Victor. He was the best language teacher I've ever had. His forcing me to master Romanian

MARK L. ASQUINO

phonetics before doing anything else resulted in my speaking the language with an excellent accent. As time passed, Victor would suggest we occasionally have a class at his tidy small apartment on Capitol Hill. He would invite over Romanian friends. We'd eat typical food and drink homemade plum brandy known in Romania as tuica. It was there that I learned to speak colloquial Romanian, the sort of language filled with graphic swear words that I would never have learned at FSI!

Victor and I became friends and sometimes saw each other socially outside the classroom. But Victor remained a strict taskmaster. When I would get things wrong in the language, he would look at me fiercely and shake his fist. "Domnul Mark, te dau pumnul [Mr. Mark, I'm going to punch you]!"

Happily, I got a break once a week from Victor's linguistic version of "tough love". My new alternate teacher was the beautiful blonde Olga, a shapely, elegant young woman. One could not have wished for a more delightful teacher than Olga. Unlike Victor, she would look at me sympathetically when I made egregious errors. Gently correcting me in her soft voice, she had a beguiling look that conveyed, "Now, now, it's all right!"

Once every other week, I spent an afternoon at FSI, where I attended a three-hour seminar on the history and culture of Romania and the Balkans. This was both an informative and enjoyable break from language study.

I learned that Romania's history was both complex and tragic. Despite its ancient history, it became an internationally recognized nation only in 1878. Because of the squabbling among local aristocrats known as boyars, who couldn't agree on a local monarch or much of anything else, the German prince Karl of Hohenzollern-Sigmaringen was invited to come to Romania in 1866 as the ruling prince (Domnitor) of the Romanian United Principalities. He became king in 1881 and as Carol I of Romania, would reign until his death in 1914. During these years, the new monarchy looked to the West, both politically and socially. France exercised a strong influence on the country, with French becoming the preferred language of the educated class.

After his death, King Carol I was succeeded by Ferdinand, a distant relative, who attempted to keep Romania neutral during World War I. He would eventually yield to French pressure and enter the war on the side of the Allies. Despite disastrous campaigns against the Central Powers, Romania emerged on the right side of history. The Treaty of Versailles led to the country's expansion. It acquired Transylvania, which had been part of the Austro-Hungarian empire, as well as other territories.

The interwar period was a time of great economic prosperity and cultural achievement for Romania. Playwright Eugene Ionesco and sculptor Constantin Brancusi would get their start in Bucharest before immigrating to France. There was a thriving modernist movement in painting, and art deco became a defining style in Bucharest's striking architecture. The opulent Athenee Palace Hotel opened in 1914 and became a meeting place for intellectuals as well as foreign spies. Nearby, the elite class dined in the elegant Casa Capşa restaurant. Concerts at the Romanian Athenaeum often featured the music of famous Romanian composers, including George Enescu. Because of its wealth and cosmopolitan ambiance, Bucharest became known as the Little Paris of Europe, with Romania being called the breadbasket of Europe.

But storm clouds were on the horizon. They would darken the country's history for decades to come. Ferdinand's son, Carol II, ascended to the throne in 1930. Self-centered, dissolute, and corrupt, the Playboy King, as he was known, gradually usurped parliament's rights and acted like an absolutist ruler. He allied himself with the virulently anti-Semitic, nationalist Iron Guard movement. By 1938, he abolished parliament and became a dictator.

In 1940, with the winds of war sweeping through Europe, Carol II, having looted the country, abdicated and fled into exile, leaving his nineteen-year-old son Michael (Mihai) as king. But real power was exercised by the fascist dictator, Marshal Ion Antonescu, who was initially supported by the Christian nationalist, antisemitic Iron Guard. Under the marshal, Romania entered World War II and allied with Nazi Germany and the Axis Powers. Antonescu assisted Hitler with the arrest and extermination of the country's Jews and Gypsies.

By 1944, with the Allies turning the tide of the war, young King Michael staged a coup against Antonescu, who was subsequently tried and executed. Michael switched sides, and Romania joined the Allies. But it was too late. The Soviet Army had already entered and occupied the country. After the war ended, the Soviet Union awarded the young king the Lenin Peace Prize, but that didn't stop the Romanian Communists from seizing political power from him. By 1947, King Michael was forced to abdicate, stripped of his Romanian citizenship, and forced into exile. For the next four decades plus, Communist Romania would be a Soviet satellite state until the overthrow of Nicholas Ceausescu in December 1989.

During the history classes, I was joined by a dozen or so students studying Romanian at FSI who were also headed to Bucharest. They started language classes several months later than me and would not arrive in Romania until the summer. They included my entry-level classmate Richard Lundberg and Julianne Johnson, who had recently entered USIA. While at FSI, I also met the two Romanian teachers Cora and Ligia. Although Victor and Olga were my instructors, Cora or Ligia tested my progress in Romanian.

FSI, where I would have to take my test, has a language proficiency scale of 0–5 in speaking and reading. The top level of 5 approximates the fluency of an educated native. At the end of twenty-four weeks, I needed to achieve a passing grade of 3 in both speaking and reading, which was regarded as professional proficiency.

Cora, the younger of the two FSI teachers, was regarded as the tougher examiner. In my first midway progress test with her, I received a 2 in speaking and a 2+ in reading. Cora also administered my final test, in which I achieved a 3 in speaking and a 3+ in reading. Victor, of course, thought I should have scored far higher, saying FSI discriminated against his students. He may have been right, but I was just happy to have passed the final exam!

At this point, I'd been in Washington for almost five years. I visited my parents in Rhode Island every other month as it was just an hour's flight away. They were both in relatively good health with my mom, having made more or less a complete recovery. But all was not well in my relationship with her.

In 1986, when I returned from Spain and found my mom wasting away and refusing to eat, I considered, as previously noted, the last resort option of committing her to a private mental health facility to save her life. Thankfully, this was not necessary.

Unfortunately, sometime before my final visit to see my parents in the spring of 1991, my dad told my mother about our previous discussions of the mental health option. My mom took me aside at some point and said angrily she would "never forgive me" for having considered putting her in a mental hospital. In her view, I was a "bad son," even though my father and I saved her life during a harrowing time. No amount of telling her I loved her and had been trying desperately not to lose her made one whit of difference.

Sadly, that was the end of the very close relationship I'd had with my mother. It was hard to accept, and I was downhearted as I prepared to go to Romania. Despite this, my mom was now better, having recovered from her brush with death. While I would always regret the emotional chasm between us that lasted until her passing a decade later, I knew I'd done what was right for both of us.

II

When you are about to serve in places where shopping for everyday necessities is next to impossible, the Foreign Service allows you to ship several hundred pounds of "consumables," which you purchase at a local U.S. supermarket. These were canned and other non-perishable goods and personal care items most likely unavailable during your tour in a hardship country. I never needed to plan such a shipment in my past assignments.

When I arrived in Bucharest, there were no Western-style supermarkets or modern convenience stores. Two years after the 1989 revolution, Communist-era "state stores" were still poorly stocked. Going to one entailed waiting in long lines, especially after new shipments arrived. There were some farmers' markets that sold fresh vegetables, local cheeses, and sometimes meat of dubious quality. The U.S. embassy had a small "liquor locker" offering for sale, liquid "essentials," although I would find Romanian wine quite drinkable. There was also a government-run store for diplomats, but it had mostly overpriced Western goods.

Before I left for a two-year tour in Romania, I sat down and began assembling my consumables list. I was completely clueless when it came to doing so. Exactly how many rolls of toilet paper would I need for that amount of time? Not being much of a cook, I pondered the number of cans of beans, sauces, and vegetables I wanted and what varieties. Ordering lots of pasta sounded like a good idea, but how much? And then there were things like soap, shampoo, deodorant, toothpaste, and cleaning supplies. The list went on and on.

Then there was the matter of shipping a car. It was time to let go of my venerable Mustang. The chances of finding a mechanic, let alone parts, for a U.S. car in Bucharest were nil, so I sold it. I bought a new Volkswagen Jetta, thinking that perhaps having a German car (albeit one assembled in Mexico!) was my best bet. As with the consumable shipment, the U.S. government shipped the car by sea to Bucharest.

Unlike in my previous postings, embassies in hardship countries provide furnished housing. I only had to pack up books, a few of my favorite pictures, and other keepsakes. The rest went into government-paid commercial storage. As it turned out, I wouldn't see some of the things I put into the warehouse again until I retired some twenty-five years later.

In mid-April, a dear woman I'd dated in Washington took me to the airport. I was finally headed to Bucharest! I was happy to see PAO Dick Virden, who greeted me at the city's dilapidated Otopeni Airport. Driving into the center of Bucharest, we passed buildings still pockmarked with bullets and scorched by flames from the fierce fighting two years earlier. There were few streetlights, and Bucharest had a dark, forbidding quality. Dick and his charming wife, Linda, invited me to dinner that night in their grand 1920s Beaux Artes villa.

The U.S. embassy in Bucharest occupied two nineteenth-century mansions. The building where the USIA offices were housed was just down the street from Dick and Linda's house. My huge second-floor office, with its graceful double windows, had classical scenes painted on the ceiling. It had once been part of the mansion's grand ballroom. Without a doubt, it was the most opulent office I would ever have, but its enormous open space was also extremely cold in winter.

The ambassador and deputy chief of mission's offices, plus the political/economic sections, were in the chancery, an equally grand mansion just behind our building. There was yet a third, smaller mansion around the corner from the chancery, which housed the USIA Cultural Center and Library.

During the days after my arrival, I made courtesy calls with the ambassador, DCM, and others while meeting with the USIA local staff and the director of the cultural center and library. The new information officer, my friend Richard Lundberg, and junior officer trainee Julianne Johnson were still studying Romanian and would not arrive for another several months.

Several weeks before I traveled to Bucharest, I had a terrible nightmare. I dreamed I was in a rustic multistoried timbered building with a thatch roof. When I asked those in the room with me where we were, they refused to answer and ignored me.

Finally, I decided to leave, not knowing exactly where I was but feeling threatened in the building. I walked aimlessly through muddy streets until I arrived at a field. It was filled with skulls and bones protruding from the wet earth. Frightened by what I saw, I returned to the building where I'd been. Once there, I told someone what I'd just seen. The person answered with a harsh, menacing voice in Romanian, "You should not have gone there! You were not meant to see that!"

I woke up with a start, enormously relieved that what I'd experienced had just been a bad dream. But seeing the skulls and bones troubled me. I somehow couldn't get them out of my mind. I thought of the horrendous images in *The Killing Fields*, a film I'd seen years before. But what, I thought, did Cambodia have to do with Romania? Starting with my initial days in Bucharest and throughout the rest of my tour, the dream's meaning would gradually be revealed to me.

On my first Saturday in Bucharest, I took out the detailed city map the embassy had provided me. I headed off on a walk. As it was overcast, I carried an umbrella. I wanted to visit some of the old parts of the city, which included the Lipscani District, full of antique shops, and the Old Princely Court (Curtea Veche). This area contained the ruins of former royal palaces dating all the way back to the fifteenth century.

Most of all, I wanted to visit the nearby Hanu'l lui Manuc (Manuc's Inn). Built in 1808 as an inn and trading center by Hanul Bei, a wealthy Armenian merchant, it was one of the city's landmarks. As a huge two-story building with a pitched roof and more than one hundred rooms, it has a spacious interior courtyard surrounded by graceful columns supporting wooden balconies reached by winding staircases. Hanu'l lui Manuc was reputed to be Romania's oldest public inn, and I'd seen dozens of pictures of it in history books.

As I walked that day toward the old part of the city, I noticed something odd. The Romanians whom I passed on the streets all looked down to avoid eye contact with me. It was as if I didn't exist. I would later learn that during the Ceausescu years, the country's citizens were strictly forbidden from engaging with foreigners. Their reactions to me seemed a holdover from those days.

Seeing the Hanu' from a distance, I was impressed by its sheer size as it stretched for almost a full block. But as I got nearer, I saw the building's whitewash was smudged and dirty. The plaster was broken in places along its outer walls. Some of the windows were broken and boarded up. The inn had a derelict quality, and it was hard to imagine why anyone would ever wish to stay there.

Although it was a Saturday, the Hanu' courtyard was deserted. However, I saw a stand near the center with a wooden cask that said *bere* (beer). I went up to the unshaven middle-aged man standing behind the counter and in my best Romanian asked for a glass of beer. He said nothing. He poured it into a dirty-looking mug and then pointed to a sign with its price, which I paid. When I thanked him, the man grunted, turning his head and looking down at a newspaper. The beer was warm, watery, and sour tasting. After a few sips, I decided I'd had enough. Putting the mug back down on the counter, I walked to one of the staircases and climbed to the inn's main hall on the second floor.

Entering, I saw faded leafy green folk patterns painted on its walls and dim lighting. There were a few dilapidated chairs and a wobbly wooden table in the middle of the room. A bored-looking young woman was sitting behind a large desk with a sign behind her that said Receptie (Reception). Of course, pretending to read a book, she too ignored me.

What happened next was strange. At first, I thought, "This is all somehow familiar, and it feels as if I've been here before." I'd seen so many photos of the building. I thought that must be the reason, but it wasn't at all. I felt extremely uncomfortable and closed in. I wanted to leave but why? Then it suddenly occurred to me that this was the place I'd been in my nightmare. As in that terrible dream, I got out of the Hanu' as quickly as I could.

The temporary apartment where I was staying was about a half hour's walk away. Normally, this would have been a pleasant stroll, but it was now raining hard. Although I'd brought the umbrella, I was wearing flimsy old shoes, and water began drenching my feet. As I approached Bucharest's Great Synagogue, which survived the Communist era, I saw across the street an abandoned, Ceausescu-era construction site with overturned, rusting equipment. Something drew me to the place, making me approach it despite the intense downpour. For a few fleeting seconds what I thought I saw were skulls and bones protruding from the mud just as I'd seen in the dream. What did it all mean?

The experiences of that day would be the first of many I'd have, many in what remained of the old Jewish quarter. Inexplicably, I would find myself somehow linked to the 1930s Bucharest and the beginning of the Holocaust there.

I arrived at a time full of political and economic uncertainty. Following Ceausescu's overthrow in December 1989, Ion Illiescu, a former member of his Communist government who had been sidelined, gained prominence as a member of the new National Salvation Front (NSF) party. Despite his past ties to Ceausescu, Illiescu claimed that he and other members of the diverse NSF supported multi-party democracy and free-market principles for Romania.

But in a matter of weeks after the NSF established a provisional government with Illiescu at its head, protest demonstrations began once again in Bucharest. Mostly young people charged the party was led by former regime insiders like Illiescu, who had no commitment to democracy. They also said that Ceausescu's Securitate, the much-feared national security force, continued to operate as a force of repression. Nevertheless, Illiescu won the majority of the vote in the spring 1990 elections with a reported 85 percent of the vote. The NSF also won two-thirds of the seats in parliament.

Not surprisingly, the protesters rejected the election results as fraudulent. Their demonstrations soon became violent, with attacks on the Foreign Ministry and other government buildings. In June 1990, Illiescu invited coal miners from Romania's Jiu Valley, whom he referred to as "men of goodwill," to defend his government. Thousands of these miners arrived by train in Bucharest. They clubbed and beat demonstrators in the city's streets and ransacked the headquarters of opposition parties in addition to robbing the homes of opposition leaders.

Illiescu's calling in the miners and his increasing use of security forces temporarily allowed him by that summer to get the upper hand with the demonstrators. But when I arrived in Bucharest ten months later, there were still daily protests against the government by students and others on Piața Universității (University Square).

During my first few months in Bucharest, it was also clear to me that the economic situation in the country was deteriorating. The Illiescu government withdrew Ceausescu-era government price supports on bread, cooking oil, and other long-subsidized commodities. People complained about the high cost of living and the decreasing value of the leu, Romania's national currency. The black market dollar rate was ten times higher than that of the official exchange. Although it was summer, it was hard to find vegetables and fruits in street markets. Potatoes, a basic part of the Romanian diet, had to be imported from Poland because of Romania's poor harvest. Prices were high for what little was available. As the fall of 1991 approached, the economic and political situation gradually worsened.

If scarcity was the watchword on Bucharest's streets, it was just the opposite when it came to the programming resources I had as the embassy's new cultural affairs officer. President George H. W. Bush's administration saw a window of opportunity in the fall of Communism in East and Central Europe. Accordingly, there were a number of new programs and an expansion of old ones to promote democracy and a free-market economy.

For example, the 1989 Support for East European Democracy (SEED) Act provided millions of dollars in funding for grants to U.S. educational institutions to provide assistance in everything from improving agriculture to strengthening political institutions and university curricula. The Fulbright and international visitor programs were substantially increased, including in Romania. Teaching fellows were deployed throughout Eastern and Central Europe to increase English language skills among the younger generation.

The USAID had a wide range of assistance programs to help struggling economies in these countries, and they also received, for the first time, large groups of Peace Corps volunteers. The American Bar Association created the Central and East European Legal Initiative (CEELI), which sent U.S. judges and prosecutors to work on judicial reform with their counterparts with the goal of establishing the rule of law in the former Communist nations.

I was delighted to have such an abundance of resources but also overwhelmed. During my first year in Bucharest, I had no American assistant cultural affairs officer to help me manage my workload. There were just two Romanian foreign national employees (FSNs), Rodica and Ruxandra, to assist me. Both were smart and highly capable. Unfortunately, as my predecessors had warned me, they had been bitter rivals for years. The two women did whatever they could to undermine each other and spent endless amounts of time trying to establish themselves as my favored employee. Within my first weeks on the job, each would come to my office, close the door, and complain about the other in low, conspiratorial tones.

MARK L. ASQUINO

Sadly, this was a legacy of Ceausescu's long brutal dictatorship when ordinary citizens were co-opted by the Securitate, much as what happened with the Stasi in East Germany, to spy and report on each other. I will never forget the conversation I had one day with the rector of a provincial university. He was someone the embassy viewed as pro-Western and a modernizer, despite his former ties with the dictatorship. During a long walk after lunch at his home, he said to me, "Mr. Asquino, sometimes you Americans judge us harshly. You don't understand our situation under Ceausescu. Imagine if you had a sick child who desperately needed scarce medicine to survive. You were frantic because you had no way to obtain it. And then, one day, someone from the government approached you. He had the medicine your child needed and said he would be happy to give it to you. But then he added you had to do something for him in return. What would you do? Would you refuse and let your child die?"

I replied that although I didn't have children, I certainly understood what a horrible moral dilemma he'd presented. And I thought to myself that in such circumstances, I'd certainly save my child and agree to be an informer or worse.

He then smiled sardonically and said, "Well, Mr. Asquino, that's the sort of situation we found ourselves in all the time."

It was tantamount to an admission that he had been co-opted in the past and forced to report to the Securitate on his dealings with Americans. I respected him tremendously for his courage and honesty. It was possible he was still being forced to report. In this sense, I took it as a warning to be careful what I said to him and others.

Most of the time, though, it was just the opposite. Most Romanians I met would be anxious to prove their bona fides to me. They would tell me in the first few minutes of the conversation how much they had suffered under the dictatorship and how strongly they had opposed Communism. Sometimes these statements would be made in their homes, which had luxuries only available to ranking party members under Ceausescu.

What this taught me was that when it came to judging people's sincerity and past allegiances, there was little black and white in

Romania. Instead, most people had been tarnished for a variety of reasons, some quite understandable, as in the case of the rector, while others not at all honorable. I learned to navigate my way through the pervasive shades of gray that dominated almost every aspect of my personal and professional life, avoiding those who protested too much about past sufferings under the regime.

After several weeks in my temporary lodgings, I moved to my permanent house on Plantelor Street. It was a late-nineteenth-century one-story house surrounded by an ornamental black iron fence mounted on a long granite base. Coming up the front stairs, you entered a large vestibule. From there, you climbed a marble stairway to a landing with a spacious cloakroom on the left. This set the stage for your entry into an elegant, high-ceilinged dark wood-paneled reception room with two large crystal chandeliers.

To the right was the master bedroom suite with a full bath. On the left, there were two rooms. Presumably, one had been a library and the other a private office. Walking through the reception room, you came to two French doors with beveled glass and entered an inviting formal dining room with yet another chandelier and pale-yellow walls with white wainscoting. To the left of the dining room was a small corridor with a guest bathroom leading to the kitchen and a back bedroom where a maid once must have lived in. There was a heavy-iron work stairway that led to the attic, and another going down to the basement. Finally, a back garden was reached down a wide-sloping white marble stairway with stately granite balustrades.

The story I first heard about this magnificent house was that it was built by a Jewish businessman for his mistress. Certainly, the layout suggested this. It seemed more a place for masked balls and intimate dinners with a paramour than a residence to raise a family. Initially, the house had a dreamy quality for me. But that would soon change.

I learned there was a chilling history connected with this exquisite Beaux Artes manse. During World War II, the Nazi Gestapo requisitioned the house for its offices and interrogation center. It was not clear what had happened to its occupants. But the dismal, windowless basement was used to hold political prisoners, who were tortured, interrogated, and executed there. Those colleagues who had lived in the house before me told tales of the basement being haunted.

During what turned out to be the three years I lived at Plantelor 37, I avoided as much as I could going down to the basement. It had a heavy atmosphere everyone felt upon entering, whether or not they'd been told the Gestapo story. Sometimes at night, I would hear what seemed like creaks on the highly polished hardwood floors as if someone was walking in the reception area. Other times, I would discern the faint sounds of a piano being played.

There was also what seemed like the occasional cry of a child from the back bedroom. One of my successors in the house confirmed he and his wife had also heard the cries. He said he'd been told that a woman dressed in white had had a toddler who died in the room. The rumor was that there was a "lady in white" spirit who prowled the house and sometimes she would appear to those who lived there. For all of its foreboding qualities, my new home was a beautiful place to live and perfect for the frequent formal entertaining I did with the help of my housekeeper.

The summer seemed to go by quickly. My USIA colleague Richard Lundberg and his wife, Ann, and JOT Julianne Johnson arrived in July. The State Department officers I'd met at FSI, including Geeta Pasi and Stuart Hatcher, who would become close friends, also took up their new jobs.

In September, a group of U.S. Fulbright university professors, some with spouses, arrived in Bucharest. My predecessor had taken advantage of USIA's expansion of the program, accepting over a dozen academics, more than twice the number of previous groups. The professors were assigned to the University of Bucharest and the Institute for Economic Studies (ASE), a prestigious state-run economics school. They were to teach courses in English on business, social studies, journalism, religious studies, and American literature. As a former Fulbright lecturer, I looked forward to the arrival of the academics, thinking I would have much in common with them. Alas, I had absolutely no idea of what was in store for me.

First of all, the university and institute where the Fulbrighters would teach were required to provide them with housing. I asked Rodica, the older and more experienced of my two FSNs, to inspect their lodgings. She reported that everything was fine and that I had nothing to worry about. To my great regret, I didn't follow up by myself, a mistake I would not repeat again. After meeting the professors at the airport, I boarded a bus with them. We headed to where they would be living. Some were faculty lodgings in dormitories, and others were nearby rented apartments.

The dreary accommodations not only fell far short of Western standards but also in some cases were unlivable. For example, the unit assigned to the Fulbright journalism professor, his wife, and their young child lacked a kitchen sink and stove. We immediately moved the family to a hotel. A few of the single professors who'd previously lived in developing countries moved into their apartments without so much as a word of complaint. Bless them! But there were others who complained bitterly that I'd done a terrible job of preparing for their arrival.

Furious, I returned to the embassy and demanded to know from Rodica how she could possibly have assured me the housing was fine when it clearly wasn't. She was not one to be intimidated easily. She said in a dismissive voice that the Fulbrighters were obviously a spoiled lot. Giving me the Balkan shrug I knew all too well from Victor, she added it was not her fault if they were complaining. I replied that spoiled or not, the grantees deserved decent housing, and I expected her to address their issues. After looking at me crossly, Rodica swung into action.

We decided to move all of the Fulbrighters into hotels, not exactly luxurious places either, and then contacted the two schools. Rodica read the administrators the riot act and got results. The problems were fixed, and the grantees returned to their somewhat improved dwellings. Our efforts did little to assuage the grumblers among them. Despite my unhappiness with her on this occasion, I came to value Rodica as someone who could accomplish virtually anything in Romania.

By then, first-tour officer Julianne Johnson had arrived, and she divided her time between working for me and my friend Richard in the press section. She greatly helped me run the burgeoning international visitors and other programs I managed.

And there were others outside the embassy, who would also help me through that difficult first year. Linda Miller, a corporate attorney, took a year off and came to Romania on her own to teach business law at ASE, the economics institute. She was amazingly resourceful and had exceptional contacts and insights about the country. Another was a young actress named Victoria. She had been my teacher Victor's colleague at Bucharest's renowned Bulandra Theatre and one of the first Romanians I met. Tall and blonde, with high Slavic cheekbones and mischievous large brown eyes, Victoria was not only beautiful, but also a gifted actress. She introduced me to Bucharest's theater community, and as a non-English speaker, she patiently helped me improve my Romanian.

One cold winter evening, Victoria and I were walking back from the theater where we'd just seen a play. The sidewalk was icy, and. I put my arm around her trim waist, drawing her close to me. I asked if she ever thought of emigrating from Romania, perhaps to France. Given her fluent French, I added, she might find work there as an actress. She looked at me and said in a sad voice, "I would never do that because of what happened to Victor."

She was referring to my Romanian teacher. From the tone of her voice, I suspected she and Victor had once been more than colleagues. She said he was extremely unhappy in the United States because his heavily accented English prevented him from finding work as an actor. Instead, he eked out a meager existence teaching Romanian. Victoria added that although her French was good, it was not native, and she too would have to abandon acting if she were ever to leave Romania.

During most of my time in Bucharest, there was a "non-fraternization" policy that, among other things, forbade those of us serving at the embassy from having romantic relationships with Romanians. Such Communist-era U.S. restrictions were dropped in all of the other former East Bloc countries. Unfortunately, the U.S. government kept Romania under a dark cloud, viewing with deep suspicion both the Illiescu government and the country's people. I thought this was discriminatory and wrong. I protested the policy but got nowhere. And so Victoria and I remained just friends. As it turned out, that was all for the good as I soon met, fell in love with, and married the woman who would become my life partner.

By my second year in Bucharest, I could not have been happier as the cultural affairs officer. I truly believed it was the best job in the embassy. With the fall of Communism, Romania's rich cultural traditions in art, music, and learning sprang back to life after decades of censorship. But in my job, I also had contacts that went far beyond the arts and letters. The French have a saying, "Culture is politics, and politics is culture." Nothing could have been truer in Romania. Illiescu's first prime minister, Petre Roman, was a former university professor, and Emil Constantinescu, whom I first met and worked with when he was the University of Bucharest's vice rector, would one day be elected the country's president. Many of the writers I knew were also leading political activists.

My job was also not without its amusing moments. For instance, I sometimes would take visiting USIA colleagues to meet with Foreign Ministry officials. Romanians, as noted above, took culture very seriously and always were happy to see such visitors. There was an officious protocol assistant at the ministry who would always greet us upon arrival. He loved to practice his limited English, often with hilarious results. The Romanian polite command you use to ask someone to take off a coat is "Dezbracati-va, va rog." But he would translate the phrase into literal English, demanding, "Please undress!" This always elicited a startled look, especially from the women I was accompanying. And with a sly smile, I would reassure them, "Just your overcoat."

During my second year, the USIA sent me a superb assistant cultural officer named Jeff Jamison to help with my workload. He took over the international visitor program and a range of other projects, leaving me free to travel to universities throughout the country. In addition, most of the more disgruntled Fulbright grantees left after a year. Rodica and I carefully chose new grantees who seemed better prepared for the challenges Romania offered. We also began work on establishing an independent Fulbright Commission, which would have its own staff and take over the bulk of the program's administration.

Bucharest was a two-year hardship assignment, and by 1993, I was nearing the end of my tour. The USIA was pleased with my work and asked if I would be willing to extend for an additional year. It was a hard decision. PAO Dick Virden, whom I admired and for whom I'd enjoyed working, would soon be leaving. So would my classmate, Information Officer Richard Lundberg, and other embassy friends. I was not promoted during my two years there, which was a disappointment, making me think perhaps it was time to move on. But something told me I should stay on.

One day, for example, I had been walking in the old Jewish quarter near the Great Synagogue and historic State Jewish Theater. An older woman looked at me quizzically and then motioned for me to approach her. She said to me in Romanian, "I know you!" and then told me the story of her life. She grew up as a child in the neighborhood and immigrated to Israel with her parents in the late 1940s. She spent the rest of her life there, marrying and having children. During that time, she never had the opportunity to return to her homeland. Now, she was ill, and before she died, she wanted to see her old neighborhood.

She then made a sweeping hand gesture toward the mostly barren surroundings and continued, "It's all gone! The houses, the stores, even the streets I knew as a young girl. Only the theater and the synagogue are still here. But then I saw you. We knew each other in this neighborhood a long time ago. Your face is familiar to me. That's why I called you. I know you, don't I?" She looked at me expectantly.

"No, I'm sorry, but you're mistaken. I'm an American. But I come here often, as I feel a special bond with this place. It's hard to say why."

"But you speak Romanian without a foreign accent. Your parents, they're Romanians, yes? Surely, they once lived here."

I again told her this was not the case. She nodded, and slowly began to walk away. But then she turned, and looking back, she said, "I know you!"

And so I wound up staying an extra year in Bucharest. Yes, I loved my job, and everything about living in the country appealed to me.

But there was more to it than that. It was not time to leave. I needed to know more about what seemed to be my past life in this place. My grand house with its tragic history and uneasy spirits were perhaps the key to the mystery. I seemed to have been meant to live there too.

It was during my second year in Bucharest that the Peace Corps began sending volunteers to Romania. The actress Jessica Lange publicized the terrible plight of orphans who had been warehoused in orphanages during the Ceausescu years. The Communist dictator's mad, pronatalist policies forced poor families to have more children than they could support. For this reason, desperate parents put their children up for adoption.

Conditions were horrible in these orphanages. In a bizarre Romanian practice of giving infants transfusions to strengthen them, scores of babies had been infected with AIDS-tainted blood. Older children suffered from sexual abuse. There had also been a *20/20* television documentary showing the devastating impact of unloved orphans. Americans were flocking to Romania to adopt children, often through shady deals, which I would learn about from an American anthropologist friend.

The Peace Corps decided that volunteers were needed in the orphanages to "interact" with the children, picking them up and showing them affection. It was a well-intentioned but naive initiative. The young volunteers generally knew nothing about children or had any idea of how to care for them. New to Romania, they had only a smattering of the language. They couldn't communicate with either those running the orphanages or some of the older children.

The orphanages didn't need "babysitters" but carpenters, plumbers, electricians, and roofers to repair their dilapidated buildings. They also would have benefited from pediatric nurses and other health care professionals to help the orphans. But the volunteers had none of these skills. Soon, the orphanage directors, suspicious of these odd young foreigners, decided the Peace Corps had sent them as spies. Within a matter of weeks, all of the volunteers were ordered by the Romanian government to leave the orphanages. The Peace Corps country director frantically sought to have the volunteers teach English at any schools willing to take them as she tried to salvage the program. But the volunteers had no training for such work. Few of them had ever taught before, let alone in a foreign country. It was largely a wasted year, and the country director was replaced.

The new group of volunteers arrived in July of 1992 as I began my final year in Romania. Unlike their predecessors, no one was assigned to work in an orphanage. Instead, they were chosen for projects in three areas: assisting small startup businesses, promoting youth employment, and teaching English at selected schools. I heard that Art Flanagan, the new country director, was capable and experienced. The volunteers had their customary ten-week in-country language and orientation program during which they lived with host families. With new direction and leadership, the program seemed to be off to a good restart.

Every Friday evening, the embassy annex where I worked had a happy hour in its basement. The building's small cafeteria, which served lunches during the week, was open on Friday night and offered pizza, hamburgers, French fries, and other light fares. The get-togethers were popular. Back then, there were not many such places in the city where you could eat, drink, and relax at the start of a weekend. Bucharest remained grim, especially after the sun went down.

I was in my second-floor office late one Friday evening that summer and decided to take a break. I went down to the basement bar. Both the cafeteria and bar got little light through the basement's dirty half-windows. As I entered the bar, it took a few minutes for my eyes to adjust to its dim illumination. On this occasion, I noticed the place was full of unfamiliar people, mostly young American women. Pat Moore—the embassy's security officer, a former marine with thinning blond hair and a world-weary look—was at his usual perch. Sitting on a high stool at the end of the long bar with a beer in front of him, he was surveying the scene. After ordering myself a bottle of my favorite beer, Pilsner Urquell, I went over and asked him about these new folks, especially the women.

Pat told me they were the new Peace Corps volunteers. He added that the former country director did not allow her charges to attend such events because volunteers were told to steer clear of the embassy.

Romanians tended to view all of us as spies, and it was better not to go near the embassy. It was also standard Peace Corps policy for volunteers to avoid politics and in no way advocate for U.S. foreign policy. Pat told me this group of volunteers was at the embassy earlier that day for his security briefing. He persuaded the new country director to let them stay for the happy hour.

After telling me all this, Pat pointed to a pretty redhead standing in a corner off to the side of the room. "Now, that woman over there is really interesting."

When I asked him why, he continued, "Well, she's older than most of the others, has lived overseas before, and previously ran her own business in San Francisco. She's poised, mature, and outspoken."

I found that intriguing as Pat rarely mentioned those qualities when speaking about members of the opposite sex. So I decided I would go over and introduce myself.

The red-haired woman was thin and of medium height. She was also wearing an attractive summer dress. As I approached, she greeted me with a bewitching smile. "Jane Harader," she said after I told her who I was. We chatted for the next half hour. I learned that she would be working on an assignment in a small town in the foothills of the Carpathian Mountains, about two hours from Bucharest. She said there was a halfway house there for disabled teenage boys who had grown up in orphanages. Her job would be to persuade local business owners to hire the boys, with the goal of allowing them to begin normal lives.

I told her I had my doubts. Disabled for Romanian children could mean anything from being crippled to having a slightly crossed eye. It almost didn't matter, as such youngsters were all viewed as "damaged."

I then asked Jane how good her Romanian was, adding that although I spoke the language fluently and knew the country well, it would still be extremely challenging for me to persuade business owners to hire even mildly disabled boys. Jane answered that she'd tried hard to learn as much Romanian as she could during the ten-week course but lacked a gift for foreign languages. She also said that she was divorced, had no children, and didn't bring any other experience to working with youngsters.

Given all of this, I wondered why she hadn't been assigned to the small business program. She'd already told me that before joining the Peace Corps, she'd successfully run her own industrial signage company in San Francisco. But apparently only those with business degrees, which Jane didn't have, were chosen to work with small Romanian startups. That made little sense to me as it was clear that just having an MBA would be of little value if you lacked relevant business experience. Jane agreed but said that was not how the Peace Corps made assignments.

We might have talked for much longer, but the volunteers were told it was time to get on the bus and return to their host families. I enjoyed my chat with Jane and wanted to get to know her better. I suggested perhaps we could see each other again, to which she seemed amenable. So I gave her my business card, and she wrote her local telephone number on a piece of paper.

I called Jane after this, but she always seemed too busy to meet. We finally set a time one Sunday for her to come to my place for lunch. But when I went to pick her up, Jane said she was feeling ill and would have to take a rain check. I decided this was one of those relationships that wasn't going anywhere despite my finding Jane smart, attractive, and fascinating.

A few weeks later, the Peace Corps volunteers were gathered to take the oath of office and be sworn in by the ambassador at his residence. It was a sunny September day, and the ceremony was scheduled in the ample yard where the ambassador often held warm-weather receptions. I'd been invited to attend along with other embassy staff, but I also had an appointment later that afternoon to discuss a cultural grant with the director of a nearby museum.

For this reason, I planned to leave early. I'd seen Jane with the other volunteers when I arrived but decided not to greet her. Instead, I sat in a chair at the back and quietly left shortly after the ceremony began.

Jane called me the next day and said she wanted to talk with me after the ceremony. I explained why I left early and wished her luck with her Peace Corps assignment. I was going to end the conversation there, but Jane said she really hoped we could see each other. She proposed we do something during the afternoon of the following Saturday. So we finally agreed to have our much-delayed "date" then. Without having any great expectations, I thought it would be pleasant to see Jane again.

I just read *The Last Romantic*, a fascinating book by Hannah Pakula about Queen Marie of Romania. It tells the story of a British member of the royal family, Marie of Edinburgh, daughter of the Duke of Edinburgh and the Grand Duchess Maria Alexandrovna of Russia. Maria's grandmother was Queen Victoria. A high-spirited, intelligent, and beautiful young woman, Marie married Crown Prince Ferdinand of Romania in 1893. She would reign as queen of Romania from 1914 to 1927. It would be her son, who overthrew World War II Fascist dictator Marshal Antonescu and became King Michael, Romania's last monarch.

Because of her impetuous nature, Marie had many male admirers and a number of lovers. The most enduring was with a Romanian nobleman named Prince Barbu Ştirbey, who played a pivotal role in Romanian politics. Prince Ştirbey owned a large estate in the town of Buftea, some twenty kilometers from Bucharest. It was there that the young queen and her lover spent long periods of time together. Set on twenty hectares, the Ştirbei Palace had extensive riding trails, an artificial lake, and dense woods.

I had never been to the Ştirbei Palace, but I learned it had a restaurant, and its grounds were open to the public. So this is where I suggested that Jane and I go, telling her we could take a pleasant late-afternoon walk and then have dinner at the palace. Jane liked the idea. It was a late-September day, and there was just a hint of winter chill with a partly cloudy sky. As we drove up the tree-lined road leading to the estate, we saw a small parking area with several old, battered-looking Dacias, Communist Romania's version of the boxy little Fiat. After I parked, we began to walk to the main house. Despite Pakula's description of the well-kept palace and its manicured grounds in the 1920s, what we saw was quite different. What had been the formal gardens were now overgrown with weeds, some of the magnificent trees had been cut down, and the walls of the palace were stained with rust.

There was a sign for the restaurant, but when we entered to reserve dinner, it was deserted. I finally found a disheveled-looking older man in a dirty chef's uniform. He suspiciously looked me up and down as if wondering what this foreigner could possibly want. When I asked him about dinner, he said no, absolutely not, it was out of the question. Advance reservations were required! With that, he stomped off. This was not a particularly auspicious way to start our date, I thought. For all of its shabbiness, the palace and estate had a wildly romantic quality. The story of Marie and the prince's passionate affair, which I'd shared with Jane, made it all the more alluring. It was also apparent we had the whole place to ourselves as the Dacias evidently belonged to employees.

Jane and I began a long walk through barely trod-upon trails, seeing the ruins of wooden outbuildings that once had been part of a working farm. We talked about our lives. Jane had been married to an artist and lived in San Francisco for a number of years. Early in their marriage, they spent a memorable year in Florence, where he had a Fulbright grant to study sculpture. Her former husband's attempts to establish a successful art career failed. He decided to teach art at a junior college instead, and after Jane learned of his many infidelities with students, she obtained a divorce.

Now single once again, Jane ran a successful industrial signage business. After several years, she decided it was time for a major change in her life, so she joined the Peace Corps and sold her apartment, business, and car. Jane told me she had originally been assigned as a volunteer to Tunisia to provide instruction and activities for young girls.

But the religiously conservative elders of the village had been hostile to this unaccompanied middle-aged Western woman, whom they viewed as a bad influence on such girls. Finally, one day, when she was shopping at the market, an older man violently struck Jane from behind. The Peace Corps withdrew her from Tunisia for her safety but promised Jane another assignment. And that was how she came to Romania.

As she spoke about her life, I was drawn to Jane's openness and honesty. She seemed grounded, a quality that had often been missing in my tumultuous romantic relationships, especially with Spanish women. She also had a sense of adventure and she was not afraid to try new things in foreign countries. In turn, I told her about my own failed marriage, past affairs, and why I decided to spend an additional year in Romania. As darkness began to fall, I found myself enormously attracted to this thoughtful, mature woman.

We decided to have dinner somewhere in Bucharest. As we were getting ready to leave the estate, a waiter in a formal dinner jacket, white shirt, and black bowtie suddenly appeared. "Your dinner is ready," he announced, motioning toward the restaurant.

If I'd learned anything in Romania, it was to be prepared for the unexpected. To reach the restaurant, Jane and I ascended a handsome mahogany stairway to what had once been part of the palace's ornate ballroom. There were crystal chandeliers casting a soft light. Thick red velvet curtains hung from the floor-to-ceiling windows. We were led to the middle of the otherwise-empty room where there was a single small table with a linen tablecloth, a tall white candle, and a full dinner setting for two. There were to be no other guests.

Dining out in Romania was always an adventure. In restaurants like Bucharest's Casa Capşa, with its faded interwar French ambiance, you'd be given a large menu with page after page of entrées, main courses, and desserts. I soon learned this was just for show.

It was rare at Capşa and elsewhere that there was anything beyond some sort of pickled salad or soup for a starter, followed by overcooked carp fish or beef/pork with greasy potatoes. The carp came either from the Danube River or the Black Sea, both of which were heavily polluted, thus making fish a very bad choice. So this left what the Romanians called muşi de pork and muşi de beef, tough or grainy meat cutlets. Romanian wine could be excellent, but it lacked quality control. Even when you ordered what you thought was one of the better brands, you might get spoiled or gritty wine you had to send back.

Given the impossibly romantic atmosphere and how we were looking into each other's eyes that evening, the quality of the meal and wine was of little importance. Queen Marie had woven her spell. Jane and I became inseparable after that magical visit to the Ştirbei Palace.

A few weeks later, I helped Jane pack up her belongings in Bucharest and move to her lodgings in Ramnicu Valcea, the small town near her project site. Her apartment was on the first floor of a typically dirty-gray cement Soviet-style apartment block. After several tries with the key, we opened the door, and we turned on the light switch, which did not surprisingly provide any illumination. There was an odd warmth coming from the apartment's pitch-black interior, and the small flashlight I always carried soon revealed the cause. A pipe had burst and the floors were flooded with several inches of steaming water, making the place uninhabitable. Jane would later learn there was hot water for only a few hours each week in the block, and the pipe had broken at one of those times. So we found a not-so-warm hotel room for the night and woke the next morning to the season's first beautiful snowfall.

It took a while for Jane's apartment to be mopped up by the landlord, and when she returned to start her project, there were problems of a different sort. The teenage boys for whom she had been asked to find employment had not been socialized during their years in orphanages. They also had virtually no verbal skills, and they would often respond to Jane's attempts to communicate by trying to grope her breasts. She had no luck with the town's small businesses, which lacked interest in employing young men.

Finally, the Peace Corps concluded what seemed to me evident from the first time I'd met Jane. The project was simply not feasible. Before the Christmas holidays, she was reassigned to a project in Bucharest, writing grants and doing other administrative work. She quietly moved in with me. The Peace Corps country director, Art Flanagan, was aware of our increasingly serious relationship and much to our relief, looked the other way.

Late that fall, I learned that my long-delayed promotion had come through. It was an enormous relief, as it meant I would not be "selected out" (i.e., fired) for "time-in-class" without advancement. The PAO who replaced Dick Virden spent most of his career in Francophone Africa. His Romanian was spotty, and he seemed to have little interest in understanding the country, preferring to see everything through the prism of his past postings.

The flip side of his limited interest in our work was that I had free rein to focus on important projects I wanted to finish before I left. These included working with U.S. legal experts to revise Romania's Communist-era court system. I also worked closely with the country's first Fulbright Commission. When I'd arrived in Bucharest almost three years earlier, Fulbright grants had been almost exclusively for Americans coming to the country. But with the new Fulbright Commission director Maria Berza, a highly respected Romanian educator, we expanded grants to include promising Romanian scholars who went to the United States.

Jane and I were happy together. I told her all of the stories about the house, and she too sometimes heard the odd sounds in the middle of the night. We both loved Romanian culture and went to classical concerts at the Athenaeum and art exhibits. On weekends, we would often go to Sinaia, where the embassy had a villa available to staff. We'd take long hikes in the mountains and sometimes visit Peleş Castle, the former summer palace of the Romanian monarchy.

Commission director Maria Berza and her husband invited us one snowy night to come to their nearby apartment for drinks. The inclement weather precluded driving, so we walked. We were feeling cold when we entered the Berzas' gracious apartment with its antique furniture and paintings. Maria served us a teapot full of piping-hot tuica, the same Romanian plum brandy I'd first had at Victor's place. The warm, fragrant beverage had a delightful, warming effect. We spent an enjoyable evening with the Berzas, full of laughter and cup after cup of the sweet-tasting brandy. When Jane and I stood to leave, we discovered we were quite pleasantly drunk. We staggered back home in the now-deep snow, holding on to each other but still occasionally falling together into huge drifts, which seemed hilarious to us. We finally made it home, completely drenched from the snow but deliriously happy. It was one of many nights to remember.

But of course, my assignment was coming to an end, and it was time to bid again. After three years in Romania and traveling throughout Eastern and Central Europe, I wanted to stay in the region. I decided I would learn a Slavic language, which would allow me to serve as a PAO in a nearby country such as Bulgaria, the recently separated Czech and Slovak Republics, or one of the new nations of the former Yugoslavia. However, I failed to get any of these assignments. In the USIA, you had to bid on more than one region, so I added the information officer (IO) in Santiago, Chile, to the list. But I didn't particularly want to return to Latin America, and as the job in Chile was sought after, I figured I'd never get it. In the parlance of the foreign service, it seemed like a safe bid.

Yet another adage came into play: never bid on anything you really don't want! For whatever reason, my personnel officer thought Santiago would be ideal for me. "After all," he said, "you're coming from a three-year hardship tour, you now have a second language, and just got promoted." "So," he argued, "it's your turn to have something nice." The fact that it was not what I wanted didn't carry much weight.

I consulted with Dick Virden, who was now PAO in Warsaw. He immediately advised me to "go for it!" He heard that Barbara Moore, the PAO in Santiago, was excellent. He added that if I wanted to advance in the USIA, I needed to do a tour as a press attaché. This was the fast track to becoming a PAO as information work was regarded as more demanding than culture and education. Dick's advice made sense, and I accepted the position, which would start in the summer of 1994.

There was just one problem. Chile was literally on the other side of the world from Romania. Maintaining a long distance with Jane as she started her second Peace Corps year didn't appeal to either of us. But having had unhappy marriages, we were not eager to roll the matrimonial dice again. Finally, we decided to throw caution to the winds, and I proposed to Jane. We made our engagement public on Valentine's Day at an embassy dinner/dance. Now, we just had to figure out how to get married in Romania!

Jane had grown up as a Congregationalist but was not particularly religious, and I was a non-practicing Catholic. Accordingly, we both wanted a simple nondenominational church wedding. As it turned out, one of the Fulbright grantees, Earl Pope, was an ordained Presbyterian minister. He said he'd be honored to officiate. He and his wife Mim were also only too happy to help us find a venue for the ceremony. We settled on Bucharest's intimate Anglican chapel and set May 21 for the wedding.

The USIA needed a fair amount of time to process the paperwork for Jane to travel with me to Chile as my new wife. For this reason, we decided to first wed in a Romanian civil ceremony to get things rolling, but this proved not at all easy to arrange.

For starters, all foreigners wishing to be married in Romania were required to provide authorities with medical records showing they were in good health. Jane and I both had been cleared by the United States to work overseas, but this was not acceptable to the Romanian government. Fortunately for us, there was an American nurse working in Bucharest who helped us by providing everything needed. Then the forms sat at the Ministry of Health, which had to approve them.

My assistant Rodica did everything she could to push the ministry but to no avail. She said what we needed to do was meet with the health minister and ask for his intervention. Rodica was able to set up an early-morning meeting for us, and we went to the ministry to see him. But when we arrived, no one seemed aware of our appointment, and we were shuffled from one surly official to the next. Finally, we spoke with someone who said the minister was having breakfast with his staff but would soon receive us.

What followed was something out of a Fellini film. We were ushered into the minister's plush huge office, lined with bookcases full of medical tomes, many quite old and dusty. The minister was dressed in an immaculate white lab coat and flanked by similarly attired men at a long table in the room. They were all eating a sumptuous multicourse breakfast served by waiters in crisp green uniforms.

The minister, a heavy-set man with a florid face who had once been Ceausescu's personal physician, looked up at Rodica and me as we entered the room. He was clearly not happy to have his breakfast interrupted. An assistant scurried over and whispered something in his ear. The minister then said to me, "So I understand you wish to marry this woman." He glanced at Rodica.

Rodica and I were horrified! She was a lifelong spinster and many years my senior. Under other circumstances, the idea of our marrying each other would have evoked howls of laughter, followed by screams of protest.

To her credit, Rodica ignored the minister's remark. She evenly explained that no, I was engaged to an American Peace Corps volunteer, we had submitted all of the necessary forms and were there in the hope that he would be so kind as to sign them.

The minister then motioned to the underling who had whispered in his ear, instructing him to do the necessary. Rodica had a copy of the forms, and as soon as we got out the door, she cornered the official and got him to stamp the minister's signature on them.

A couple of weeks later, with a small group of friends, Jane and I went to the city hall, where an assistant mayor, after making us wait for almost an hour, emerged in a large unadorned hall and announced he was ready to begin the ceremony. Realizing as if for the first time, we were foreigners, he announced in an officious voice, "Where is the translator? I will not conduct this solemn act unless a certified translator is present!"

Rodica explained that Jane and I both understood Romanian. But no, he insisted we could not be married without a state translator. At this point, to my great surprise and relief, Rodica pulled out an official-looking card from her purse that said in Romanian *certified state translator*.

The deputy mayor took a good look at it on both sides, apparently suspicious it might be a forgery. Satisfied it was not, he began reading from what was obviously a Communist-era text. Invoking Ceausescu's brutal pronatalist policies, he said we were immediately to start having children in support of the state. Rodica translated this part in an arch voice as Jane and I tried not to laugh. In our mid-forties, we were not planning to have children; but if we had, it would certainly not be for the glory of the Romanian state! After another few minutes of similarly exhortatory rhetoric, he said we were man and wife. That was it. No congratulations or invitation to kiss the bride, which I did anyway.

We were then brusquely directed to a small table where he signed some papers. The deputy mayor put his signature on them, sealing everything up in an envelope. Rodica asked if we could have a copy of the forms as she knew Washington would need them, plus translations, to certify we were married. He refused, stating the documents had to go to the registry where they would be logged. We could then apply for an official copy. In her most solicitous and servile voice, Rodica offered, as the ceremony's official translator, to hand-carry the envelope to the registry. I was sure the deputy would shake his head, but he said this was fine and handed the envelope to her.

We took photos on the steps, and I think some people even threw some rice or confetti. But I was concerned about how we could get a copy of the document to send to the USIA. Rodica looked at me and smiled coyly. "Don't worry, I'll steam the envelope open, make a copy, and then reseal it. No one will be the wiser at the registry."

I was tempted to ask Rodica where she had acquired such impressive skills. Assuming it was in the service of an organization to which she probably still reported, I kept quiet. The next day, she gave me a copy of our civil marriage certificate with a translation, and off it went to Washington.

Both Jane's and my parents were advanced in age, and they decided against attending the religious ceremony in May. In any event, we planned to see them that summer. We were wed in the charming red-brick Anglican chapel on a bright, sunny day. It was quite an ecumenical service! Our minister Earl was a Presbyterian. My best man and dear friend Jacques was a Fulbright grantee and Orthodox Jew. Sarah, Jane's maid of honor, was a fellow Peace Corps volunteer and observant Roman Catholic from Boston. A married couple from the embassy belonged to the Greek Orthodox Church. They were professional singers and lent their beautiful voices to the ceremony. Talk about an ecumenical event!

Art Flanagan, the understanding Peace Corps country director, accompanied Jane, who wore a lovely long blue dress, down the aisle. Those who witnessed our taking wedding vows included a large number of embassy friends, Fulbright and other grantees, Peace Corps volunteers, and Romanians we'd come to know. Few things in life are perfect, but our wedding was one of them.

After the ceremony, Jane and I hosted a festive reception at the Plantelor manse. We engaged a local restaurant to cater the meal and found a keyboard player to provide music. The house, as noted earlier, was ideal for such a happy event, and "the others" who haunted the place were on their best behavior. I would like to think they too were happy for us. We set up tables in the garden where there were peonies in full bloom. The guests helped themselves to an ample buffet with wine in the dining room. The wife of someone at the embassy made a large multitiered wedding cake with green and white frosting. There was only one small "local" touch.

During the course of the reception, Jane and I noticed that the chef overseeing catering seemed increasingly tipsy. At one point, when he brought out a large knife to help us cut the cake, he was unsteady on his feet, and his large hat fell off his head. As the afternoon wore on, his waitstaff also appeared to be in an increasingly jolly mood.

We would later learn that they raided my well-stocked liquor cabinet. What they didn't drink at the reception, they carried off with them. It really didn't matter; I would have given away most of the bottles anyway. However, a couple of days later, I went by the restaurant and told the Romanian owner the reception food was excellent but that I was unhappy with the larcenous behavior of his staff. He listened with a rather amused look on his face. Then without addressing the substance of my complaint, he said he wanted to invite Jane and me for a sumptuous, post-wedding meal at his restaurant. We were to order anything from the menu we wanted, including a bottle of expensive imported wine, and enjoy a wonderful evening at his expense. It was a kind and delightfully Romanian way to compensate us for what had happened.

A few days later, Jane and I packed up our belongings in what would become for her the first of our many moves together in the foreign service. We said our goodbyes and flew off to the United States via Warsaw.

Dick Virden and his wife, Linda, had invited us to spend our honeymoon in Poland, where they were now posted. They put us up in a grand Warsaw hotel and hosted a festive dinner in our honor. We spent the next week exploring Warsaw and Krakow before leaving for Washington, where I had consultations. And then we were off to Chile.

CHAPTER 7

Chile: Preparing for Bigger Things

A S I WAS going on a direct transfer to be the information officer at the U.S. embassy in Santiago, there was no time for Latin American area studies at FSI in Washington. I had a couple of days of consultations and stopped by to see the USIA desk officer who handled Chile, as well as had meetings with those in charge of press work at the agency. I already possessed high scores on the Spanish test I'd taken after my tour in Madrid, so this meant that I didn't have to do a language brush-up or test again.

After a week in DC, we flew to Rhode Island. Jane had never been to New England, and she was excited to be going there. We were both somewhat apprehensive because my parents had not met her. That would be the same for me when we met her folks in Wyoming. I'd warned Jane that my mom could be difficult.

Despite the lukewarm welcome from my mom, Jane and I had a nice visit. We went to Newport with my parents, where Jane thoroughly enjoyed exploring this historic oceanside city. I gave Jane a tour of Brown University and downtown Providence and introduced her to members of my small family.

Next, we flew to Denver and took the colorfully named Armadillo Express, a local van service, to Cheyenne, Wyoming, where Jane's parents would meet us. She had told me in advance that her father Frank had a hair-trigger temper and suffered from a lifelong stutter that affected how he interacted with others. But Jane's parents could not have been more cordial or welcoming.

We drove from Cheyenne to Wheatland, a small town of thirty-five hundred residents. Jane's parents, Frank and Mary-Alice, lived on an eight-hundred-acre high-plains ranch that had once belonged to his aunt. Frank was employed as an aeronautical engineer by contractors working for NASA's space program. His work took him, Mary-Alice, and their three daughters to Washington State, Southern California, and Louisiana. When he retired early, Frank and Mary-Alice moved to Wheatland, where he indulged his great passion for collecting and restoring 1930s classic cars. I enjoyed my visit with Jane's parents and developed an affection for them both.

The six weeks of home leave went by quickly. We returned to DC for a few additional days and then boarded the eight-hour flight to Santiago via Miami. A new and exciting chapter in my professional and our married life was about to begin.

For more than a century, Chile enjoyed the reputation of being the most democratic and stable nation in Latin America and had often been called the Switzerland of the Southern Hemisphere. But in 1973, democratically elected president Salvador Allende, a Socialist, was overthrown in a military coup by General Augusto PinochetUgarte Although his regime claimed Allende committed suicide at La Moneda, the seat of government that had been a colonial-era mint, he most likely was executed by Pinochet's troops.

In the immediate aftermath of the bloody coup and the establishment of a military dictatorship that followed, thousands of Chileans were tortured, murdered, and "disappeared" by the military junta. Civil liberties were suspended, as was the Chilean Constitution. Opponents of the regime were hunted down, jailed, and often never seen again. During Pinochet's brutal seventeen-year dictatorship, an estimated two hundred thousand Chileans fled into exile. Pinochet admired Franco and modeled himself after the Spanish dictator.

The Nixon administration had opposed the Socialist Allende government from the start. Questions still remain about the exact role the United States played in supporting the military's 1973 coup. In the years that followed, Nixon provided major economic assistance to Pinochet.

In 1980, the Pinochet regime drafted a new constitution, stipulating he would continue to serve as president during an eight-year "transition period." In 1988, there would be a referendum on whether Pinochet would be granted yet another eight years in office. Much to his shock, Pinochet lost the referendum, with Chileans decisively rejecting granting him another term. Under the provisions of the constitution, he was allowed to remain in power for another year while preparations were made for democratic multiparty elections.

In December 1989, Christian Democratic Party candidate Patricio Aylwin was elected president. His Center-Left political coalition was called La Concertation. Following his four-year term, there was a peaceful, democratic transition. Leading the same coalition, Eduardo Frei, another Christian Democrat, was elected president in 1993. He assumed the presidency in March 1994, just months before Jane and I arrived in Santiago, and it was an exciting time to be going to Chile.

However, not all was sunshine because Pinochet had not retired from political life. Under the terms of the constitution drafted during his dictatorship, he was allowed to remain in the powerful role of commander and chief of the army until March 1998. After this, he would become an appointed senator for life and loom over Chile's reestablished young democracy.

When Jane and I arrived, Chile had lively media. The newspaper of record was Santiago's conservative *El Mercurio,* but there were numerous other dailies, including sensationalist afternoon tabloids. There was also an array of television and radio stations spanning the political spectrum and first-rate schools of journalism. The United States recently opened a state-of-the-art, architecturally striking new embassy in the northeast part of the city, several miles from the historic city center. I had a large office on the second-floor public affairs section, and a staff consisting of seven Chilean national employees and an American assistant.

Barbara Moore, the PAO, was an experienced USIA officer who had spent her entire career in Latin America. Several years younger than me, she entered the foreign service straight out of college in 1974. We both grew up in New England as ambitious Italian American kids.

Barbara would become not only my friend but also another important career mentor.

I had done a limited amount of press work in both Venezuela and Panama, but running a large press section and being immersed in Chile's free-wheeling press environment was something altogether different. Being a successful information officer requires an ability to move quickly in responding to breaking-news stories about the United States. In Santiago, I needed in-depth knowledge of bilateral policy issues and a familiarity with Washington media guidance to be prepared for questions from journalists. My job also entailed setting up media interviews and press conferences for the ambassador and visiting U.S. government officials who came to the country.

Interestingly enough, the first career officer ambassador I worked for in Santiago could not have cared less about the media, especially local outlets. During my introductory meeting with him, he recited a litany of complaints he had about local reporters. He claimed they consistently misquoted him and ran articles that distorted U.S. foreign policy. He warned, "I've stopped having anything to do with the media here. If you get requests for interviews with me, just tell them I'm not interested. And I also strongly recommend that you avoid contact with this country's journalists."

I responded that certainly I understood and would respect his wishes regarding interviews. I noted though that as press attaché, my job was to interact with local media and provide them with information. The ambassador said nothing in response, and it was clear the meeting was over.

Completely deflated, I went back to the public affairs section and stopped by Barbara's office to relate what I'd just been told.

"Oh, don't worry about that!" Barbara said. She reassured me she was well aware of the ambassador's views. Despite them, we had to do our job and work with journalists. If there were problems with the front office, she would handle them.

As it turned out, I would indeed not need to worry. Within a matter of months, the ambassador finished his tour and moved on. His successor was a Clinton administration political appointee who'd briefly been a foreign service officer. He left the government, received a law degree, and eventually became a Democratic Party fundraiser. As Barbara and I would soon find out, our new ambassador would present us with just the opposite problem when it came to journalists.

This is because he loved media attention and especially wanted to be included in *El Mercurio*'s society pages. These ran prominently in the front section of the newspaper. In his view, it was my job as press attaché to make sure he appeared there. If he didn't see photos of himself in *El Mercurio*, he became annoyed with me.

Despite this unpleasant aspect of my work, the rest of my job was substantive. The fact that Chilean journalists could be aggressive and persistent was something that I came to admire. During my four years in Santiago, I developed good relations with most of them. I learned from Barbara that the one thing you never did was mislead or lie to the press. If you didn't know an answer or were unsure of the policy line, it was always better to say, "Let me get back to you." You were then obliged to do so in a timely manner. Once you lost the respect of journalists, your credibility was gone.

After seventeen years of repression, Chile's media thoroughly enjoyed their ability to criticize their government and go after foreign countries, especially the United States. I took that as a given and felt privileged to work in a place with a free press. Although I am not naturally a "morning person," I learned that in my job I needed to be among the first to arrive at the embassy each day. That gave me a chance to go through the daily newspapers and meet with Juan Pablo, the senior foreign national employee in the press section, and his colleague Cacho, who focused on radio and television. They were both former veteran journalists who would brief me on news programs from the previous evening, which Cacho had recorded, as well as print coverage that morning.

I would also have a short "vespers" meeting with my senior press assistants to discuss what was in the afternoon tabloids, which often broke sensational, wildly inaccurate stories. As hard as we worked to anticipate breaking stories, it was often the ambassador who\caused some of our biggest problems. A native Spanish speaker, he couldn't resist going off policy guidance to express frequently abrasive views. Given that Spanish was his native language, it was impossible for me to tell the media afterward that he'd "chosen the wrong words."

Equally odd, the ambassador thought journalists were fond of him, which was not at all the case. He regularly asked me to set up press conferences so he could "chat" with them. I would always ask what it was he wished to announce at such events, and he would say he simply enjoyed speaking with the local media and the few international journalists in town. My response was that unless there was "something in it for us" in terms of advancing U.S. policy, press conferences were a bad idea and could be dangerous. Both Barbara and the DCM supported me on this issue, and with their help, we were able to discourage the ambassador from convening the media whenever he felt like it. But on one occasion, that didn't happen, and it turned out to be one of my worst days as a press attaché.

It occurred when neither Barbara nor the DCM was in town. The ambassador called and asked me to set up a press conference for him, and before I could reply, he said, "Listen, Mark, I know what you're going to say. Just do it."

With that, he hung up and I had no choice but to work with my staff to arrange a press conference for the following day. Of course, the journalists all wanted to know what the purpose of the meeting would be, and we simply had to say the ambassador wished to see them. In advance, I updated the talking points on U.S. policy issues I regularly shared with the ambassador and visiting U.S. officials. We had various trade disputes with Chile, and I sent the talking points on these and other issues to the ambassador, asking that he follow them.

The next day, we gathered in the embassy's large multipurpose room on the embassy's first floor. As usual, my staff set up a large round table, and we also arranged space with a riser off to one side for television cameramen. It had been some time since the ambassador had last given a press conference, although he frequently gave press interviews. Those were easier because when he strayed from policy, I would often tell the journalist afterward that the ambassador had misspoken and then cleaned up his remarks. This usually worked. But it was impossible to do so in a large press conference. As usual, we took the precaution of recording the event just in case he was misquoted.

All went well enough, with the ambassador more or less staying on the policy line as time was about to run out on the hour-long session. I could tell the journalists were not happy, as there was nothing he said that was newsworthy. That was fine with me and I signaled the press conference was over, thanking them for coming. But just then, a reporter for the British Reuters news agency raised his hand. I knew and liked the journalist, but I had already closed the conference, and other journalists were packing up to leave, so I ignored his raised hand. But then the ambassador said, "Yes, I'll take your question."

The press conference alternated between English and Spanish, and the American journalist chose to use his fluent Spanish to ask the ambassador the following, "There has been much recent discussion about the power of the military in Chile, especially because General Pinochet remains chief of the army. So do you believe, Mr. Ambassador, that there is full civilian control of the military in Chile?"

It was a dangerous question. Chile had returned to democracy just six years earlier, and many argued that President Frei was weak vis-à-vis the military. U.S. policy was clear: Chile's civilian leaders had control of the military, which was crucial to democracy. I had this in the talking points I'd given the ambassador, and I hoped he would simply say *sí*, and that would be it. I was shocked, as were other embassy officers in the room when he began in Spanish, "Claro que no [Clearly no]."

"No!" I thought to myself, trying not to gasp. Did you just say Chile's civilian government is not in control of the military?

That was exactly what the ambassador seemed to be saying, and it was a complete departure from U.S. policy. Then he continued with a long convoluted answer that Chile's return to democracy required its civilian government to reassert full authority over the military. This was challenging after so many years of dictatorship. But the ambassador thought that was exactly what the government was doing, which the United States supported.

Nobody cared about the rest of his answer. The sound bite and headline would be that the U.S. ambassador had just said in no uncertain terms, "There is no civilian control of the military in Chile." Of course, that was not quite what he said. His answer had been nuanced, albeit awkward, in qualifying his "Claro que no" gaffe. Thankfully, we had the tape with exactly what he'd said. But of course, the media had their bombshell story and were out the door before the ambassador even got up from the table.

As he was leaving the room, the ambassador turned to me and my embassy colleagues and said, "Everything okay?" We were speechless. As acting public affairs officer, the task fell to me to go to his office and tell him he'd just made an enormous blunder. And that is exactly what I did, explaining to him why.

He listened and then snapped, "Well, go fix it!"

And here was where I made one of the greatest mistakes of my foreign service career. I focused on having my staff provide local reporters with the ambassador's full response to the question. But the "U.S. Ambassador Says No Civilian Control of the Military in Chile" story was already on the Reuters international wire. It would soon be picked up by news outlets around the world and garner front-page headlines in the United States.

We were only an hour ahead of Washington time, but that would have been enough for me to immediately call the State Department Press Office and alert them to the gaffe. Had I done that, we would have worked on guidance for the daily press brief that would soon be conducted in Washington by State Department spokesperson Nick Burns. Barbara certainly would have told me to reach out first to Washington and then to local journalists. But she wasn't there, and I got it wrong, missing the big picture, much to my regret.

The first question Burns got at the briefing was about Chile and the ambassador's answer. Although blindsided, he calmly replied that he knew the ambassador and was confident he must have been misquoted. He added that the United States strongly believed there was complete civilian control of the military in Chile. In any case, he would get back to the press once he had more information.

It was a smooth, polished recovery. Within minutes of Burns's reply, I had State's press office on the line with a furious staffer wanting to know, "What the hell is going on down there?" I didn't blame him for being angry because I knew I had screwed up. I immediately sent the staffer the original Spanish and English translations of the ambassador's full answer. The State put it out in a press release. I felt terrible, but things were about to get even worse for me.

I returned to the ambassador's office to brief him on how the story had quickly spread, including to the State Department's briefing room. I added that I worked with the Office of the Spokesperson to get out a correction to the misleading reports.

The ambassador's pink face slowly flushed to a deep red. He then said in a voice just short of a scream, "This is horrible! How could you have let such a thing happen? It's all your fault!"

As I stood there mutely, taking his tongue lashing, I could feel my temper rising. I had the enormous desire to reply, "Mr. Ambassador, you demanded holding a press conference after I warned you against doing so. I'd ended the session, but you insisted on taking that last question. You provided a confusing answer that has set off this media firestorm. So, it's all your fault!"

I thought back to my younger self as a new junior officer, and I was sorely tempted to say exactly that. It was what the pompous ass deserved to hear. Of course, I was now a seasoned midlevel officer who'd learned over the years when to bite my tongue and how to control my temper. So, I merely said evenly that my staff and I were doing everything we could to correct the story. I would keep him informed. With that, I quietly turned and walked out of his office.

Working with my staff, I drafted a statement for local media, pointing out that stories already running in the afternoon tabloid press had taken the ambassador's initial remark on civilian control out of context. The next day, numerous Chilean journalists telephoned Juan Pablo, my senior press assistant, charging that I was claiming they had misquoted the ambassador. Their sense of professional pride had obviously been wounded.

I asked Juan Pablo to read word by word exactly what the embassy statement said as there was nothing in it about "misquoting." Despite this, they demanded to meet with me. When I had my staff provide them with the recording of the ambassador's words in Spanish as contrasted with their misleading headlines and stories, they backed down. That was the end of them wanting to string me up. The story gradually faded away.

When Barbara returned, I explained what had happened, how I responded, and the outcome. I took the blame for my error. She said she understood and, as always, backed me with the ambassador, who was still angry. The State Department got over my delayed input, as the flash fire had been squelched.

Of course, the ambassador never thanked me for cleaning up the mess he'd created or apologized after he yelled at me. But that's often what happens in the foreign service. When things go wrong, whether it's your fault or not, you usually wind up taking the hit for your superior, especially if he or she is the ambassador.

Other than such occasional unpleasantness at work, life was good for Jane and me in Santiago. We lived in a stately three-story 1930s French colonial-style house. It had a large wooden ramada in the front that was covered in the summer with bright-orange trumpet vine flowers. There were apricot trees on the manicured lawn that led to high hedges. It was absolutely delightful to live in this gracious home.

However, two years into our tour, real estate speculators began knocking down nearby similarly graceful old residences and putting up in their place silo-like apartment buildings surrounded by concrete. A twenty-floor edifice went up right next to us, creating construction noise and dirt for almost a year. Once it was built, the huge tower shut out the light from our lovely home and robbed us of our privacy. As the song goes, "They paved paradise."

During our time in Chile, Jane and I fostered and then found homes for the many stray cats that made their way into our yard and hearts. That itself was quite a surprise. When Jane had first come to my home in Bucharest, she'd noticed a large feral cat prowling around the perimeters of the yard. "Oh, you have a cat!" she exclaimed. I said this was definitely not the case, as I was horribly allergic to felines. They triggered severe asthmatic attacks that could last for days. For that reason, I avoided getting anywhere near them. But as to the cat she'd seen, I fed it from a distance. The ferocious animal stayed in the yard, chasing away and often killing the rats found everywhere in the city. Jane was clearly disappointed, telling me she loved cats.

When we arrived in Santiago, she cared for the many strays in our neighborhood. Gradually, Jane introduced them to our home, keeping the cats outside. Little by little, I became less allergic to them until we began allowing the more friendly ones in the house. We took two of them with us when we left Chile, and when they passed away we had a succession of other felines. That, too, is a happy memory of our time in Santiago.

In the summer of 1997, Barbara's four-year tour was coming to an end, although I still had one more year in Chile. By then, it was clear that bowing to pressure from Republican Senator Jesse Helms, the Clinton administration would soon agree to merge the USIA with the State Department. The reason was that as the chairman of the Senate Foreign Relations Committee, Helms told Clinton that he must come up with a way to "revamp the U.S. foreign affairs apparatus." Helms warned the administration that if this didn't happen, he would block a vote on the Chemical Weapons Treaty, which Clinton wanted to become law.

Senator Helms claimed USIA, USAID, and the Arms Control and Disarmament Agency (ACDA) were outmoded relics of the Cold War and needed to be abolished. He presented the administration with an ultimatum: choose two of these three independent agencies and then merge them into the Department of State. This was the price of dropping his opposition to a vote on the chemical weapons accord.

Barbara and I, along with the majority of other USIA officers, were vehemently opposed to the merger. In our view, it would deprive the United States of a vital means to promote U.S. foreign policy through the use of soft power. Nevertheless, by the summer of 1997, it was obvious the USIA's days were numbered. Clinton eventually chose our agency and ACDA to be merged with State, allowing USAID to remain independent.

Under the terms of the Foreign Affairs Reform and Restructuring Act of 1998, the deadline for the merger would be no later than the end of 1999. Although the USIA's demise was two years into the future, I told Barbara that the merger would put us both at a great professional disadvantage. Neither of us had ever worked for the State Department, and suddenly, after more than two decades at the USIA, we would be thrust into a completely new bureaucracy. She strongly disagreed with me. After naming a number of our State Department officer colleagues at Embassy Santiago, she said, "Look, Mark, you and I are not only as good but also far better officers than most of those people. This merger with the State Department opens up enormous career opportunities for us. I intend to become deputy chief of mission for my next overseas tour. After that, I'm setting my sights on an ambassadorship. You should do exactly the same thing!"

Being a DCM, let alone an ambassador, was not something I'd ever thought about. I knew that only a handful of senior USIA officers ever got State Department assignments as DCMs. An even smaller number, perhaps one or two each year, became ambassadors. But Barbara was right. Once we became State Department officers, we would be able to compete for these positions on a more or less equal basis with our new colleagues.

Indeed, within a few years after the 1999 merger of the USIA with the State Department, Barbara returned to Latin America as the deputy chief of mission at the U.S. embassy in Bogota, Colombia. Not long afterward, she became our ambassador to Nicaragua. Tragically, cancer ended Barbara's life at age fifty-eight, preventing her from continuing to rise even higher within the senior ranks of the foreign service.

Barbara's successor as PAO in Chile was Kathy Brion, also a highly capable and accomplished officer. We worked extremely well together, and I benefited from having her as my boss during that final busy year in Chile. The Second Summit of the Americas was scheduled to take place in Santiago in April 1998. Both President Clinton and the First Lady would attend, and the press section and I were fully engaged in providing support for what was a successful summit followed by Clinton's bilateral meetings with the Frei government. In preparation for the summit, I volunteered the previous October to assist our embassy in Buenos Aires, Argentina, with press support for President Bill Clinton's official visit there. Working on high-pressure presidential visits in both countries, plus what I learned during my four years as a press attaché in Chile would prove invaluable to me in my upcoming assignment.

By early 1998, it was time to bid once again. Jane and I wanted to stay overseas so that I could become a PAO. I wondered if there might be a PAO position in Equatorial Guinea, as I was still fascinated with the country. I learned, though, that due to deteriorating relations with the Obiang regime, U.S. embassy Malabo had been closed three years earlier. So I focused on staying in Latin America. Unfortunately, none of the major PAO jobs was open.

At about that same time, people I knew in the USIA's European area contacted me. They were trying to find good candidates for hard-to-fill PAO slots in the newly independent Central Asian republics, which had been part of the former Soviet Union until it collapsed in 1991. Derided by many as the Stans and ridiculed by others as the Icky Stans, these new nations included Kazakhstan, Uzbekistan, Kyrgyzstan, Tajikistan, and Turkmenistan. Jane had followed a family tradition of becoming a serious quilter while in Chile and was fascinated by fabric art. For her, Central Asia was an intriguing place.

As it turned out, I was offered and accepted the PAO job in Tashkent, Uzbekistan, which included the fabled Silk Road cities of Samarkand and Bukhara in its territory. After Romania, I'd been interested in learning a Slavic language so that I could remain in East and Central Europe. Now, I had the opportunity to learn Russian, the lingua franca throughout Central Asia, which might open opportunities for me to serve in other Russian-speaking countries.

One of our last vacations in Chile was a trip to Iguazu Falls in Brazil to see one of the world's most spectacular waterfalls. While there, we struck up a conversation one day with a young American couple. I told them that I would soon be studying Russian for a year, and Jane and I would then be heading off to Central Asia. The woman frowned and said, "I'm sure you know that Russian is a hard language." I was unfazed, replying that, of course, I knew it would be hard, but I was a good language learner.

"No, you don't understand. What I'm trying to tell you is that Russian is really hard. I was a Russian major in college and struggled with the language. You've just said you don't have another Slavic language, and that means Russian will be extremely difficult to learn."

It was one of those odd admonitions, and I was puzzled by the emphatic tone of the woman's warning. I would begin Russian classes at FSI in September 1998, just four months shy of my fiftieth birthday. Jane and I were enormously excited about this new direction in our lives. Little did we know what a harrowing year was in front of us.

CHAPTER 8

The Russian Bear

ONE OF MY Russian language classmates at FSI was Larry Memmott, who was also going to Uzbekistan and had been the economic affairs officer in Santiago. When international journalists would ask me about Chile's economy, Larry was the person to whom I always turned. He had an encyclopedic knowledge of the subject and was skilled at providing reporters with detailed background briefings. Having been a Mormon missionary in Latin America, Larry had superb Spanish. Over the course of the next forty-four weeks of language study, we would become good friends and bunker mates in confronting the "Russian bear," as I came not so affectionately to call the language.

Few of FSI's Russian instructors were trained teachers. As emigrants from the former Soviet Union, they had a variety of backgrounds and found work teaching their mother language. While some of them had subsequently taken education courses and developed excellent teaching skills, most had not. They taught Russian with a harsh "Why can't you learn my language!" attitude.

There were forty of us about to embark on learning Russian, and during the first two weeks of instruction, we were divided into orientation groups of ten. The stated goal was to provide us with a quick overview of Russian. But it soon became apparent that the true intention was to gauge our learning skills. Some in the groups had previously studied Russian or other Slavic languages, which put them far ahead of the rest of us. And it was during those two weeks that I came to appreciate just how difficult it was going to be to learn the language.

I had always done well in other language classes, but during the first few days of this introduction, I found myself struggling and falling behind most of my classmates. I have a slow, methodical approach to language learning. But because this class was meant to provide a quick overview, the instructors had neither the time nor patience with those of us who couldn't immediately pick up on complex linguistic concepts. By the end of two weeks, I was completely demoralized, wondering if I would ever be able to learn Russian.

Evaluating how we'd all done during the overview introduction, the instructors then assigned us to classes of four, and to my pleasant surprise, Larry and I were in the same group. Our instructor for the first sixteen weeks was someone who'd taught Russian at FSI for many years but was not one of the better teachers.

At the end of eight weeks, all of the Russian students were given a progress test. After a slow start, I found that with hard work, I was doing well and received an excellent grade. The program administrator was pleased with my progress and told me I was on track to achieve the 3/3 score in Russian speaking and reading needed by the end of the course. That was great but short-lived news. Within days, a family-related health crisis would occur in my life that not only threw my studies into disarray but also jeopardized my career.

After our return to the United States in the summer of 1998, Jane and I visited my parents. Unfortunately, my mom had descended into another deep depression, refusing to see doctors and rarely leaving the house. We sensed that a time would soon come when my father, then in his late eighties, would no longer be able to care for her. I gently suggested that my folks might consider moving into an assisted-living facility. Jane and I would be there to help them make the transition.

My mother's reaction was as quick as it was categorical. "Absolutely not, Mark! This is my home, and I'm not leaving it!"

Jane and I looked at each other and knew that further urging would be useless. My father, for all of his many fine traits, rarely stood up to my mother and certainly would not do so on this delicate issue. So, we did not push the matter any further, but we left Rhode Island concerned about my parents' long-term well-being.

After my Russian exam in early November, I decided to make a quick trip back to Rhode Island over a three-day weekend to check in on my folks. I told Jane it would be better if I made the visit alone as I wanted to stay with them and assess the situation. When I arrived, it was apparent, just as I'd feared that things had become significantly worse for my mother. I was alarmed that she had become a complete shut-in once again. Even worse, she was now in a state of constant fear and anxiety, often muttering unintelligibly to herself. When I tried to suggest she needed medications to help reduce her state of agitation, my mom told me to mind my own business. I knew I was in for a tough visit.

The second day that I was there, my father said he had been having some chest pains and asked if I would take him to a nearby hospital's emergency room for a quick diagnosis. It was a Saturday, and not surprisingly, we waited for more than two hours before a doctor on duty saw my dad. He checked his vital signs, and noting my dad's advanced age, he said he wanted to admit him to the hospital for further testing.

My father hesitated and called his personal doctor, who was on the hospital's staff. My dad's doctor said he agreed that checking in for a thorough exam was a prudent idea. A kind man whom my father trusted and who had cared for him over many years, this personal physician promised us both that even though the next day was a Sunday, he would stop by to see how my dad was doing. And so, Louie was admitted to the hospital.

When I returned home, my mom was sitting in the partial darkness of the house's narrow hallway. After I told her Louie would be in the hospital at least overnight, she immediately said, "Who will take care of me?" I assured her I would and did my best to prepare something simple for us both to eat.

My dad would remain in the hospital for most of the coming week. His personal doctor told me Louie's lungs were congested, and it was possible he had pneumonia. I canceled my flight back to Washington and called Jane to let her know what was happening. I also contacted my Russian-language classmate Larry, asking him to let our instructor know I would have to miss some classes.

Staying with my mom and trying to take care of her were even more difficult than I had imagined. She was accustomed to my father doing virtually everything for her. Without him, she became highly agitated and was prone to expressing all sorts of irrational fears. I'd brought some Russian work with me, but it was impossible to study as my mom demanded my constant attention. Most of all, she needed assurances that I would not leave her, but oddly, she rarely asked about Louie. I explained to her that I needed to go to the hospital briefly each day to make sure he was getting proper care.

Whenever I saw him, Louie was anxious to go home, expressing concern about my mother. Finally, after he'd been in the hospital for four days, his personal doctor said he didn't have pneumonia but rather a bronchial infection. He was given medications and set to be discharged from the hospital the next day. I rebooked my flight and picked up my dad from the hospital, planning to return to Washington later that afternoon.

When we arrived back from the hospital, my mom barely looked at my father. Instead, she turned to me, saying: "You can leave now. You're no longer needed here."

With that, she gave me a peremptory goodbye wave. I told her I needed to gather my things and would soon be on my way. As I left the house, my father thanked me, and we hugged each other as we'd become accustomed to doing. My mother watched silently as I went out the door.

Of course, I realized Eleanor was seriously disturbed, both mentally and emotionally. This caused her to do and say hurtful things to my father and me. Still, her harsh words were impossible to forget. No matter how tough, capable, and resilient I'd become as a diplomat, there was still the small child within me who wanted and needed my mother's love and approbation. Preparing to board the plane to DC, I reflected on how I was leaving my parents in a difficult situation. My feelings of guilt and unease would not go away either then or anytime in the near future.

When I resumed classes the following week, I struggled to catch up. Although I'd missed only five days, it seemed like I was far behind. Worried I could not keep up with my classmates, I began to suffer from insomnia. The less I slept, the harder it was for me to concentrate, first on Russian and then on other things as well. It was a downward spiral. Soon, I was having trouble making decisions about simple matters. I started to suffer from anxiety attacks, worrying about everything from how my parents were doing, to getting through to the next day's Russian class with little or no sleep.

Jane saw that there was something seriously wrong with me. I lost my self-confidence and expected more and more from her in our everyday life. I became defensive when she brought up the changes she was seeing in my behavior. Deep down, I recognized I was sinking into a clinical depression, having observed my mother's lifelong struggle with the disease. So, when Jane firmly insisted that I needed medical help, I agreed.

What followed during the next eight months were regular sessions with a wonderful psychiatrist. At first, I was reluctant to share much of anything with him. Like many strong, independent people, I felt that I could pull myself out of it. After all, I told myself, there'd been so many times in my life when I'd felt down or rejected and then been able to "snap back." Surely, I reasoned, I could do so again. The first step toward recovery from depression, as I soon learned, was accepting that I was seriously ill and needed medical help. As long as I refused to acknowledge this, things would only get worse.

I was fortunate in my choice of a therapist. Born in India, he was a middle-aged man with a soft voice and a nonthreatening manner. As a foreign service officer, I think I was more comfortable exploring my feelings with someone from another culture than I might have been with a fellow American. We started discussing my family history and my mom's depression and then worked our way forward. I told him that despite my lifelong driving ambition, there were now times when I wanted not only to give up on Russian but also to leave behind my career.

For years before I became ill, I'd had a recurring nightmare. I would dream that I was a scuba diver deep underwater when I spotted an intriguing-looking cave. I began exploring its winding tunnels full of beautiful brightly colored tropical fish. All of a sudden, I found myself in a pitch-dark cavern with no idea of its dimensions or how I could get out. I became disoriented and felt trapped. I knew I would soon run out of air and thought, "How could I have let this happen?" For me, that became the perfect metaphor for clinical depression. Without Jane and my doctor to guide me, I would never find my way out of the deep abyss.

After a short time, my psychiatrist prescribed a fairly high dosage of a psychotropic drug that initially made me jittery. At a lower dose, though, the medicine made me feel less anxious, and I started to sleep again. I called my father regularly to see how he and my mom were doing. I told him that perhaps it would be better if Jane and I did not go to Uzbekistan. It was far away, and I worried about them. My father could not have been more adamant in saying he wanted me to continue my career. He added he was now feeling much better and completely able to take care of Eleanor. It was vintage Louie and —exactly what I needed to hear.

Weeks passed, and I still found myself barely keeping up in Russian. Before the Christmas holidays, I took the next progress test. This time, I did not do well. Rather than encouraging me, the program administrator told me how disappointed she was. It was impossible, she said, for me to get the 3/3 final score I needed to go to Uzbekistan. I listened calmly and knew I was on the road to recovery when I replied, "I'm sorry, but I don't agree at all." The administrator gave me an annoyed look. She had thrown down the gauntlet, and I now was determined to prove her wrong.

During the next months, I gradually started the long climb back to normalcy. I couldn't have done so without Jane's steadfast love and support, for which I can never adequately repay her. For anyone who has suffered from depression or other mental issues, I cannot recommend more strongly regarding getting medical care. It is sadly true that there remains an unfair stigma attached to such diseases.

When I informed the Department of State that I was undergoing therapy for depression, the Office of Medical Services was neither empathetic nor helpful. Fortunately, my doctor provided that office with information on my recovery and positive prognosis, and I was able to continue my career. In doing so, I emerged a much stronger person, and I believe far more capable and more compassionate toward others.

After Christmas, Larry and I moved to a different group with a much better teacher. Just as with economics, he had a remarkable analytical ability to break down challenging linguistic concepts and make them easier to understand. He created flashcards that provided grammatical patterns and kindly shared the cards with me, which helped a great deal.

I worked tremendously hard in the last month of Russian to prepare for the final three-hour test in June. I felt I did well on the oral presentations and conversation in the speaking part of the test Reading though is harder in Russian as you need to be very careful not to misconstrue grammatical constructions, which can lead to missing the meaning. From previous tests, I knew the examiner would start with the easiest-level reading text. If I did well on that, she'd move to the next. Assuming I got through this level, she'd see how I would handle a tougher passage. I only needed to do well on those first two levels to score a three, which was the professional proficiency I needed.

When the test ended, it was customary for the examiner and a linguist, who sat in on the exam, to ask the student to leave the room. I knew from having taken final exams in both Spanish and Romanian that they would then decide on a score. As I sat outside, I was quite confident I'd gotten a 3 in both speaking and reading.

After being called back into the room after what seemed like a long time, I was asked to take a seat by the examiner. She then complimented me on my speaking, saying that I'd scored a strong 3. That was good, I thought, but then she and the linguist looked at each other frowning. Unfortunately, they said I'd fallen just short in reading. They were giving me a 2+ rather than a 3. I told them this surprised me, noting my translations for the first two levels had gone smoothly, and I'd held my own on the most difficult, final passage. Of course, this was not an argument I was going to win, and I left feeling I'd done the best that I could.

In succeeding days, I heard that other classmates, including Larry, had had the same experience in receiving scores they felt were unfair. I knew from my previous testing that the sessions were recorded and that as students, we had the right to ask for a review of test results. That would allow another FSI Russian teacher and linguist to evaluate my performance. Of course, these were not outside evaluators but rather in-house teachers who all knew each other. It was extremely rare for one teacher to overturn a colleague's grade. I'd never challenged test scores in the past, but thought it was worth appealing on this occasion. I decided I had nothing to lose.

With great reluctance, the administrator of the Russian program agreed to allow another teacher and linguist to assess my recorded performance. She told me I was wasting her and FSI's time. Weeks passed, and I heard nothing back. Finally, after many calls, I tracked the administrator down in her office. She told me the cassette recording of the test in which I translated the readings was too faint to hear, so no assessment could be made. She gave me a look that conveyed, "So tough luck for you, kiddo!" Not so fast, I thought. In that case, I told her, I was entitled to retake the reading portion of the test. The administrator said that no, in her opinion, I had no right to be tested again.

By now, I was getting back to my old argumentative self and said this seemed extremely unfair. In fact, I was prepared to appeal her decision all the way up to FSI's dean of the school of languages. The last thing the administrator needed was for me to make a big ruckus about my Russian test. So, she backed down and said sourly that I'd be allowed to redo the reading test in two weeks.

I worked intensively to improve my skill in reading Russian, When the day finally arrived for my test, I breezed through the readings. After a brief wait, I was welcomed back to the room by the examiner and linguist who congratulated me for having scored a solid 3. Having been told in no uncertain terms I would not achieve a 3/3 in Russian, I'd done just that. Even more importantly, I'd overcome clinical depression, and my doctor had persuaded the State Department to allow me to go to Tashkent. It had been a long brutal year for Jane and me, but we were about to head off to the wilds of Central Asia.

CHAPTER 9

9/11 in Uzbekistan

C ENTRAL ASIA IS a part of the world that is still largely unknown and often misunderstood. Until the 1991 dissolution of the Soviet Union, the five Central Asian states of Uzbekistan, Kazakhstan, Kyrgyzstan, Turkmenistan, and Tajikistan were separate Soviet Socialist republics ruled by local leaders obedient to Moscow. The Central Asian region is bordered by Russia to the north, China to the east, Afghanistan and Iran to the south, and the Caspian Sea on its western border. Shortly after their independence in the summer of 1991, these new states were often lumped together as the Stans. However, each has its own distinctive history, indigenous languages, and cultural traditions. Arguably of the five, Uzbekistan is the Central Asian republic with the strongest identity and the most self-confidence.

In ancient times, it had been part of the Persian empire and was known as Transoxiana and Turan. In the seventh century, a majority in these two provinces converted to Islam. Caravans along the Silk Road, which connected China with Europe, passed through what would become Uzbekistan. The great cities of Samarkand, Bukhara, and Kiva were along this route and soon became rich resting and trading places for huge caravans.

The Mongol invasion and conquest in the thirteenth century led to an influx of Turkic peoples and their languages to these lands. Eventually, the Mongol ruler Amir Timur, known in the West as Tamerlane, would make Samarkand his dazzling capital, greatly expanding and embellishing the city with plunder from his brutal conquests stretching as far away as northern India and modern-day Pakistan. During the rule of one of his successors, Ulugh Beg, the empire would become renowned for accomplishments in science, mathematics, astronomy, and medicine.

During what historians call the nineteenth-century Great Game, czarist Russia and Great Britain vied for imperial domination of territory stretching from the Indian subcontinent to Afghanistan and Central Asia. Eventually, Russia successfully expanded its borders to incorporate Central Asia, with Tashkent serving as the capital of Russian Turkestan.

Following the 1917 Bolshevik Revolution, Central Asia became a part of the new Soviet Union. In 1924, the Soviets created the Uzbek Soviet Socialist Republic (SSR) and the Turkmen SSR. The Tajik SSR was created from territory previously allotted to Uzbekistan. The Kyrgyz and Kazakh SSRs were later created by Stalin with arbitrary and artificial borders.

When Jane and I arrived in Tashkent in the summer of 1999, Uzbekistan was being led by Islam Karimov, who had served as president of the Uzbek SSR at the time of Uzbekistan's 1991 independence. As with other Soviet-era leaders in Central Asia, he used his position to consolidate power in the new nation. In December 1991, relying on the levers of control at his command, he was chosen as Uzbekistan's first president in elections that were deemed neither free nor fair by international observers. In subsequent years, he kept himself in power through repression and by holding periodic undemocratic elections, winning with close to 100 percent each time. A ruthless, brutal leader, Karimov ruled Uzbekistan until his death in 2016, allowing no opposition.

The offices of USIA, the Foreign Commercial Service (FCS), and the USAID were located in the drab 1950s-era Sharq (*east* in Uzbek) office building, which was next to the National Theater on a pleasant tree-lined boulevard. The embassy itself was several miles away on one of the city's noisy main thoroughfares. It occupied a building that had once served as the headquarters for Uzbekistan's Communist youth Komsomol organization. Unlike the Sharq building, where my staff and I had ample office space, my State Department colleagues, including the ambassador and DCM, were crammed into tight little offices. The embassy's large ground-floor hall, which everyone called the bullpen, was where the local Uzbek employees sat in open cubicles.

I was pleased to be out of the hive-like embassy building. I got along well with my FCS and USAID colleagues. One of them named us the Sharq Troops, which I rather liked. In the summer of 1999, we were all heads of independent foreign affairs agencies with a high degree of autonomy from the State Department. This included separate budgets and our own carpools and drivers. Alas, this was all to change for me in just a few months with the USIA's imminent incorporation into the State Department. I had ten local employees on my staff, divided almost equally between ethnic Uzbeks and Russians. And that, as I would learn, it was not only a source of tension in the embassy but also in the country at large.

From my reading, I knew that during the Soviet period, the Russian language and culture dominated all aspects of life in the country's many non-Russian majority, Socialist Republics. Those of Russian ethnicity in places like Central Asia were favored for employment and given other privileges. That dramatically changed with the independence of these republics in 1991.

Uzbekistan's population was 85 percent ethnic Uzbek and only 5 percent Russian. And Uzbek, a Turkic language that the Soviets had adapted to the Cyrillic alphabet, has a rich literature and an ancient history of which ethnic Uzbeks are rightly proud. Not surprisingly, it became the newly independent country's official language, with Russian designated to be used for "interethnic communication." In fact, I heard far more Uzbek both in my office and on the city's streets than I did Russian.

By 1999, speaking Uzbek became a matter of both ethnic pride and national identity. As citizens of the Soviet Union, all Uzbek citizens were required to study and become fluent in Russian, but the vast majority of Uzbek ethnicities learned and used their indigenous language at home. In contrast, Russian-ethnic Uzbeks usually spoke only Russian, once the dominant language, and this put them at a distinct disadvantage in their now-independent country.

In the office, everyone spoke fluent English, but the Uzbek speakers conversed among themselves in their native language and reluctantly mixed with their non-Uzbek-speaking, Russian-ethnic colleagues. The two groups clearly did not get along, and this often made it challenging for me to have them work together cooperatively. I would remind my staff that once inside our offices, I expected them to set their ethnic differences aside.

Another challenge was that although not the largest country geographically, Uzbekistan has half of Central Asia's population, which should have meant that as PAO, I would have several USIA officers assisting me. There was a reason why this was not so, and it accounted for my being a one-man band as I sometimes thought of myself. In contrast, my PAO colleague in neighboring Kazakhstan had a staff of three American officers, and this was directly related to Central Asia's fascinating post-Soviet history.

At the time of its independence, Kazakhstan possessed a large arsenal consisting of over 1,400 strategic nuclear missiles and an undetermined number of tactical atomic weapons. It also had the Semipalatinsk nuclear test site, one of the largest in the former Soviet Union. That would have made it the fourth largest atomic power in the world had it kept its nuclear weapons, which none of its Central Asian neighbors possessed.

Through a series of agreements with the United States, Kazakhstan completely denuclearized. The test site was closed, and all of the nuclear weapons were transferred to the Russian Federation. Kazakhstan's president Nursultan Nazarbayev, who'd previously ruled the country as a Soviet boss, insisted his newly independent nation did not want to have nuclear arms. For this, he won worldwide acclaim. But as a tough, shrewd politician, Nazarbayev insisted that as a reward, he expected major financial and other benefits from the United States. And that was exactly what happened.

The largest U.S. embassy in Central Asia was established in Kazakhstan, even though it has a far smaller population than Uzbekistan. In recognition of voluntarily renouncing nuclear weapons, Kazakhstan also received the lion's share of U.S. government assistance to the region.

The USAID's Central Asia regional mission was established in the then-capital of Almaty, with Kazakhstan benefiting from a wide range of U.S. government economic development programs. The country was allotted twice as many international visitor grants as I received in Tashkent, as well as far more Fulbright and other exchange fellowships.

Admittedly, not all of this was solely in return for Kazakhstan's decision to dismantle its vast nuclear arsenal. The country has far greater geostrategic and economic importance to the United States than other Central Asia nations. It shares a 3,500-mile border with Russia and a 950-mile frontier with China and is one of the world's largest producers of oil and gas. U.S. petroleum companies are among Kazakhstan's major foreign investors.

Clearly, I was envious of the greater human and financial resources that went to my PAO colleague in Almaty, including two American assistants. Nevertheless, there was more than enough to do in Tashkent, and it was arguably more satisfying work. To begin with, most international media attention was focused on Kazakhstan. After spending four grueling years as the U.S. embassy information officer in Chile, I was only too happy to have little press work in Uzbekistan. This allowed me to return to working on cultural programs with local institutions, something that I'd missed doing in Santiago. I especially enjoyed supporting Tashkent's Ilkhom (*inspiration* in Uzbek) Theater. Mark Weil, its young director, founded Ilkhom in 1976. His troupe became not only the best theater in Central Asia but also developed an international reputation.

From a Jewish-Ukrainian family that had immigrated to Uzbekistan a generation earlier, Weil was a political dissident who used theater during the Soviet period to challenge and satirize state authority. As in other Communist nations, this often led to his being harassed by Soviet officials who tried to censor his work. But he and his actors were relentless and continued their productions in both Tashkent and Moscow. When independence came to Uzbekistan, Weil became even more daring. In often original avant-garde plays in Russian and sometimes Uzbek, Ilkhom explored controversial themes for Uzbek society, including homosexuality, ethnic conflict, and official corruption.

I worked closely with Mark, providing Ilkhom with grants and other assistance to the extent my limited budget allowed. This was in recognition not only of the artistic brilliance of their work but also to promote free expression in what was a highly repressive country. It was always easier to get funding for promoting democracy than it was for the arts, and I used political arguments in justifying grants to Ilkhom.

In addition, I pointed out to Washington that the theater's relationship with the U.S. and other Western embassies provided Ilkhom and its director with a degree of protection from retaliation by the government and others. However, as Mark Weil and his company knew, there was real danger in what they were doing. Sadly, this would eventually result in tragedy for him and also a great loss for Uzbekistan and the world of theater.

During my three years in Tashkent, I found Mark to be personable and surprisingly modest despite his growing international reputation. His talented company toured overseas, and Mark, who was fluent in English, was asked to direct off-Broadway productions. But in response to threats against him starting in the 1990s, he decided to move his wife and two children to Seattle, Washington, where he established a twin-city theater-exchange project.

In 2010, seven years after Jane and I left Uzbekistan and were living in Sudan, we were devastated to learn that Mark had been viciously stabbed by assailants outside his Tashkent residence. He died at age fifty-five several days later in a local hospital. At the time, there were no arrests or even a serious investigation of his brutal murder. For those of us who knew Mark and witnessed the government's open hostility toward him, it's impossible not to believe the Karimov regime was behind his murder.

In the summer of 2000, I began working on a project that was even less popular with Uzbekistan's government than the Ilkhom Theater. Even before I'd arrived in Tashkent, I had been fascinated by how the five Central Asian states were using language, ethnicity, and culture to help define separate identities as independent nations no longer part of the Soviet Union. With my senior assistant Elnora, we planned to invite civil-society participants and academics from each country to make presentations and participate in a symposium with the provocative title "Language, Ethnicity, Cultural Diversity, and Democracy in Central Asia."

Not surprisingly, none of the state-run universities in Uzbekistan was willing to host the symposium. Similarly, when we contacted hotels, also owned by the government, they politely declined to rent us conference space.

The reason was apparent. With the exception of Kyrgyzstan, whose president Askar Akayev had been a physicist before his country's independence, all the other then Central Asian heads of state had served as loyal Soviet apparatchiks. Although evaluating post-independence "governance" was not an explicit topic of the symposium, the symposium title made it clear we would discuss the creation of national identity as a process leading to democracy. This, of course, implied consideration of why former Soviet-era strongmen remained in power through undemocratic means. Just when it looked as if we would be unable to find a venue, Elnora told me that Yusuf Abdullaev, the rector of the Samarkand Institute of Foreign Languages (SIFL), was willing to cosponsor the symposium in September.

The institute was founded in 1996, with Dr. Abdullaez as its first rector. A larger-than-life character, he built SIFL into one of Uzbekistan's leading postsecondary educational institutions. Abdullaez viewed himself as an internationalist and saw the symposium as a way to enhance its prestige and profile, as well as his own. With that said, he took a considerable risk in hosting us, but at the time had enough political power to do so. Nevertheless, he would fall out of favor with the government just three years later, going into a long self-imposed exile as an educator in South Korea.

The other indispensable person in making the symposium a reality was Professor William Fierman, a leading expert on Central Asia who directed Indiana University's Inner Asian & Uralic National Resource Center. A fluent speaker of both Russian and Uzbek, he had done part of his Harvard PhD research in Tashkent.

Bill agreed to come to Uzbekistan as a speaker and played a leading role in organizing the symposium program. He delivered the opening-day keynote lecture entitled "Language Policy and Political

Development." Participants came from all of the other Central Asian countries except Turkmenistan, whose fanatical government refused at the last moment to provide exit visas for those whom we'd invited.

The symposium program was a lively and productive one that included formal presentations and panels. Students from the institute packed the hall for the two-day sessions. They were delighted to hear experts from throughout Central Asia speak on political topics seldom discussed in Uzbekistan. They took advantage of breaks to ask the experts questions they dared not raise in public.

There was another successful Samarkand project that became one of the most meaningful of my foreign service career. While we were in Samarkand, my assistant Elnora introduced me to a remarkable woman named Dr. Bibisora Oripova, who had been trained in the 1970s as a surgeon specializing in the treatment of burns and reconstructive surgery. This was a time when specialists were in high demand to care for Soviet soldiers who had suffered disfiguring burns while fighting in Afghanistan. After the war ended, Oripova began treating young women who had tried to commit suicide through self-immolation.

Almost all had been victims of domestic violence who had been forced to wed at an early age and go to live in the home of their in-laws. It was here that these women had been physically and psychologically abused not only by their husbands but also by their mothers-in-law and other relatives. Although Uzbekistan is an Islamic nation, prior to the seventh century, Zoroastrianism, a religion based in ancient Persia that includes worship of a fire god, dominated the region.

Vestiges of this religion were incorporated into Islamic practices, especially in cities like Samarkand and Bukhara, where Tajik—a variant of Farsi, the language of modern-day Iran—is widely spoken. As one researcher has noted, Zoroastrian rituals can still be found in Uzbekistan, especially in rural areas, where the bride and groom hold hands and circle a bonfire before their wedding ceremony.[6] There are differences of

---

[6] See Campbell, Elizabeth Ann, "Perspectives on Self-Immolation Experiences Among Uzbek Women." PhD diss., University of Tennessee, 2005 (https://trace. tennessee.edu/utk_gradiss/1893) Accessed on 07/31/20.

opinion on whether Zoroastrian beliefs, including purification by fire, play a role in self-immolation in Uzbekistan. But deliberate self-burning by desperate women trapped in abusive marriages is frequent.

Women who survived immolation were rejected, along with their children, by their husbands, in-laws, and their own family. Consequently, they had nowhere to live or the means to support themselves. In 1998, Dr. Oripova created the Umid Center in a two-story house with a large central courtyard and outlying buildings. *Umid* means "hope" in Uzbek. The center provided survivors of self-immolation and their children with a safe temporary shelter from domestic abuse. There, they learned vocational skills, including sewing, carpet weaving, and how to use a computer to help them make a living. They also received psychological counseling and legal assistance at this residential facility.

The Karimov regime denied that domestic abuse existed in Uzbekistan, which meant that Dr. Oripova and Umid were forced to keep a low profile so police would not shut down the shelter. The house appeared to be just another private residence but had a secure entryway to prevent angry husbands from entering. Umid functioned with small grants that came mostly from international organizations. At any given time, a dozen or more women and their children lived at the center, where they studied as well as did housekeeping tasks, including cleaning and cooking.

Elnora suggested we meet and discuss with Dr. Oripova how the U.S. embassy might help her work. A staff member allowed us to enter Umid through its thick heavy wooden gate, secured by sturdy iron bolts on the inside. As we went in, I saw a number of small children playing happily in the courtyard. From there, Elnora and I went up a short stairway and into the downstairs office where we were met by Dr. Oripova, or Bibisora, as everyone called her. She was a small plump woman in her early fifties with intense brown eyes.

That first visit was the hardest of the many I would make to Umid. The women I saw who had arrived recently still had raw, sometimes oozing, wounds and many had suffered terrible disfigurement. I soon learned to avoid looking directly at their injuries to minimize making the women feel uncomfortable in the presence of a foreign male stranger.

MARK L. ASQUINO

Others who had been there for a longer time and whom the doctor had helped with reconstructive surgery seemed more comfortable with my presence. All were engaged in productive activities.

One of the problems Bibisora shared with us was that she would often have to go to rural areas after a woman had survived self-immolation and bring her back to Samarkand for medical care. The challenge, she said, was not having an ambulance for such urgent transportation needs. Months later, Bibisora told me she found an old Russian van that could be converted into a makeshift ambulance. Elnora helped her prepare a grant application, which stressed the vehicle would be used to provide treatment and transport burn victims. Umid received a grant of around $10,000 to buy the vehicle and refit it as an ambulance. But that was not the end of the story. I was about to have my first deeply unhappy experience as a new Department of State officer.

The USIA had been "consolidated" into the State Department a year earlier. The biggest impact I felt was no longer controlling how I used my allotted public affairs budget for projects like Umid. Everything now had to be analyzed and approved by State Department administrative officers in Washington, many of whom knew nothing about public diplomacy work. When these officials reviewed my grant for the ambulance, they apparently concluded that I'd used taxpayers' money to buy a car for some Russian woman doctor! They accused me of malfeasance and God knows what else.

In response, I provided them with all of the previously approved grant information on the sort of vehicle Umid had bought and the purpose for which it would be used. Democracy funds, I pointed out, could be used to help victims of domestic abuse. But this was to little avail.

Finally, in exasperation, I sent my new fiscal minders color photos of a badly burned woman, obscuring her face, being gently placed on a stretcher by Bibisora and an assistant, and then lifted into the back of the reconverted Russian van. It was only then that they stopped questioning why giving Umid a grant for the vehicle had been so important to its life-saving work.

Jane and I were very much enjoying being in Uzbekistan, with its fascinating historical cities and gracious, hospitable people. Jane loves fabric art, and Uzbekistan opened incredible horizons for her to learn about and collect a wide variety of beautiful traditional works of all sorts. These included suzanis, highly decorative embroidered textiles made throughout Central Asia but developed into a high art form in Uzbekistan.

She also collected Central Asian chapans, traditional silk robes, often with elaborate ikat designs in silk and lined in cotton. Jane found a wide array of small embroidered women's caps, which we now display at our home in Santa Fe, New Mexico. Finally, we both were captivated by Central Asian tribal rugs, especially those from Turkmenistan.

In March of 2000, I flew back to Washington to attend a worldwide public affairs officer conference at the Department of State. Jane had left Tashkent a week earlier and flown to Wyoming to spend time with her parents. Our plan was to meet in Rhode Island and visit my mom and dad after the four-day-long DC conference. In those pre-cell-phone days, I always provided my father with the telephone number of the place where I would be staying. When I arrived at the conference hotel early in the afternoon, I had a message to call my dad immediately.

As soon as he picked up the phone, I knew there was something terribly wrong. He tried to speak but then started to sob. Uncle Paul, my mother's only sibling, came on the line and said she had passed away in her sleep the night before. Although I knew from my last visit that her health was declining, Eleanor's death was still a shock. So many images of her from my childhood, adolescence, and adulthood came to mind. Now she was gone, literally days before I'd planned to see her. I knew I needed to get to Rhode Island as quickly as possible.

I told my uncle that I would try to get a flight that evening. I called my PAO colleague from Kazakhstan and asked her to inform the conference organizers that I would not be able to attend the sessions. Then I called Jane in Wyoming, who consoled me and said she'd rearrange her flight to arrive in Providence as soon as possible.

I got a flight that same evening. My dad was still up, and when he came to the door, I could see he was exhausted. Sitting at the kitchen table, he slowly began telling me there had been no warning signs of my mother's imminent death. For years, they slept in separate rooms, and as usual, she went to bed very early while he stayed up until around 9:00 p.m. My dad checked on my mother before turning in and said she was sound asleep. He heard nothing during the night, but when he awoke and went to see her in the morning, she was gone. With my uncle's help, he contacted a local funeral home to make the necessary arrangements.

The next day, Jane arrived from Wyoming and she was an enormous help. The wake, funeral, and burial were dignified. Afterward, we spoke to my father about being alone in the house. To our relief, he agreed to let us put his name on the waiting list for an independent-living unit at the nearby Methodist Retirement Center. Six months later, we returned to Rhode Island to help him move in. Gregarious by nature, he made many friends at the center. He would spend eleven happy years there, moving from independent to assisted living and finally nursing care.

We all grieve the loss of a parent in different ways. In the case of my mom, I was thankful that she passed away peacefully in her sleep at home. I knew this was exactly what she would have wanted. The close bond we shared sustained my relationship with Eleanor into my early twenties.

But this closeness eventually proved to be suffocating, leading to my rebelling against what I felt to be her domineering influence and overprotectiveness. I deeply loved my mother. I know she also loved and wanted the best for me. I will always be grateful to her for instilling in me a fascination with exotic places and romantic adventures. When it came to action, Eleanor was a sedentary dreamer, whereas I chose to be a traveler on a journey through life.

Perhaps it was inevitable that we would disappoint one another, drifting apart and finally becoming permanently estranged. I will always be sorry that happened, but I have come to accept it was due to the choices we both made.

Following the funeral, Jane and I returned to Uzbekistan. Shortly afterward, in October 2000, John Herbst arrived in Tashkent as the embassy's new career-officer ambassador. I welcomed his arrival because I had not gotten along with his predecessor. The latter did not value public diplomacy, often disparaged my work, and ridiculed my Russian. In contrast, Ambassador Herbst greatly appreciated my experience and public affairs advice.

This was true from the very beginning of his tour when he arrived around midnight at the Tashkent airport with his family. New ambassadors are not allowed to take questions from the media or do substantive work until they present a copy of their "credentials" (i.e., a signed letter from the U.S. president confirming the envoy's appointment to the country) to the foreign head of state. My excellent Uzbek ethnic press assistant Odil told me no local journalists would show up for the ambassador's arrival at such a late hour. I countered that the journalists, all employed by state-monopoly media, should be there because the ambassador was going to make a brief arrival statement that would be of interest.

Ambassador Herbst, like his predecessor, was a fluent Russian speaker. I had previously contacted him in Washington, and he agreed to make an airport arrival statement. When I suggested he deliver his brief remarks in Uzbek, he asked me why, noting he hadn't studied the language. I explained that no previous U.S. ambassador had ever spoken a word of Uzbek to the press, and if he could say just a few words in the country's much-loved native tongue, this would be warmly received. He immediately saw the value in my suggestion, found an Uzbek teacher at FSI, and worked with her on the short Uzbek text my staff had written.

Odil dutifully informed the media that the new ambassador would say a few words without tipping them off that Herbst would speak in Uzbek. The DCM and I greeted Ambassador Herbst and his family as they came off the plane. I was not completely sure just how my gamble would turn out. What if he butchered the Uzbek words, mispronouncing them in a way that offended the journalists?

Tall and thin, the fifty-year-old ambassador strode confidently to the podium we'd set up. Surveying the dozen print and other media journalists who were there, he slowly and smoothly delivered his two minutes of remarks in what Odil would later tell me was flawlessly pronounced Uzbek. To say the journalists were astounded would be an understatement.

Before they could barrage the ambassador with questions in Uzbek, the DCM and I whisked him out the door and into his official vehicle. Sure enough, the accounts of Herbst's arrival in the media the following day were glowing. They wrote he was the first U.S. ambassador to show respect for the country's history and culture by delivering remarks in its ancient language. No one cared much about what he'd said. Thus, Ambassador Herbst and I were off to a strong relationship that we would both come to rely on. A few months later, an event would occur that would never allow any of us to forget exactly where we were when we received the horrendous news.

Late in the afternoon of September 11, 2001, Jane and I were at the Tashkent Intercontinental Hotel with a group of high-school-aged Uzbek students. They had recently returned from a year in the United States as grantees in the highly competitive Department of State Future Leaders Exchange, or FLEX program as it was known. Established in Russia and countries of the former Soviet Union, FLEX allowed students to learn firsthand about the United States by attending public high schools, living with American host families, and volunteering for community service in states across the country.

FLEX was one of my favorite programs and this was to be an enjoyable afternoon for Jane and me as the youngsters shared their experiences with us. It was exactly what was happening when a half hour into the program, someone from the hotel front desk came into the room and whispered in my ear that I should come to the lobby immediately. There a large-screen television was showing CNN footage of the first plane, American Airlines Flight 11, crashing into the North Tower of the World Trad Center. And then, CNN went back live as United Airlines 175 hit the South Tower.

I watched the footage of people running as fast as they could from the crumbling towers while fire engines, police cars, and emergency vehicles convened on the site. Earlier coverage had shown desperate men and women jumping from the upper stories of the buildings. Commentators provided details on the World Trade Center attack carried out by hijackers who'd commandeered U.S. airlines.

Shortly afterward, another American Airlines plane, Flight 77, would deliberately plunge into the Pentagon. I would later learn that a fourth plane United Airlines Flight 93, had crashed into the Pennsylvania countryside after brave passengers tried to seize control of it, preventing the hijackers from another attack in Washington. In reports that followed, the terrorist group Al-Qaeda led by Osama bin Laden took responsibility for the atrocities.

After the first plane crashed into the World Trade Center, I immediately called Ambassador Herbst at the office. He asked that I contact the members of the Emergency Action Committee (EAC) for a meeting at the embassy within the next half hour.

U.S. embassies have groups that meet for different situations. What is called the country team, consisting of all senior officers who head sections as well as those in charge of independent agencies, meets once a week with the ambassador and the DCM. But the EAC is different. It is a smaller group that convenes only when there is an emergency or threat that potentially jeopardizes not only the embassy and its staff but also the larger American community. In addition to the ambassador and DCM, other EAC members included the regional security officer and other security professionals at the embassy, plus the head of the political/economic section, the consular chief, the defense attaché, the USAID director, and me as the public affairs officer.

Led by the DCM and occasionally by the ambassador, this group considers the emergency in the context of the embassy's emergency action plan (EAP). The latter has a set of what are called trip wires, which have been approved in advance on possible threats against the embassy and other resident Americans. The EAP includes a range of actions the embassy can take in response to emergencies, including man-made disasters and terrorist attacks.

For American embassy staff, these actions may include a voluntary or ordered departure from the country of those deemed by the embassy as "nonessential" to responding to the emergency. Embassies are required to share information about a credible threat to official Americans with other American citizens in the country via telephone and/or text messages. Public bulletins are also issued on the Internet by the consular section with Washington's approval.

After I'd alerted the EAC to the embassy meeting, I returned to speak to the FLEX students to inform them of the attack on the World Trade Towers in New York. Some of the young Uzbeks began to cry; others looked shocked. Of the close to three thousand people who died in New York on that day, it would turn out three hundred and seventy-two were non-Americans, of which two were Uzbek nationals.

After I arranged for Jane to return home, I went directly to the embassy. Entering the secure conference room, I was met with the grim and, in some cases, angry faces of my colleagues. The ambassador chaired the EAC and began by summarizing the information we had at that time. This included the developing news that Al-Qaeda had planned the attacks from the sanctuary provided by the Taliban government in Afghanistan. He noted that, as we all knew, Uzbekistan shared an eighty-nine-mile border with the latter. The Amu Darya River in the south formed a natural border between the two countries. Most of us were already aware that in 1999, the Uzbeks had closed the "Moct Druzbie" (Friendship Bridge in Russian) over the river after terrorists from the Islamic Movement of Uzbekistan (IMU) were accused of a series of bombings in Tashkent. Uzbek officials charged that the Taliban had trained and equipped the IMU terrorists in Afghanistan. This made an already tense relationship between the countries even worse.

The committee discussed the threat against the embassy and the larger American community posed by Al-Qaeda from Afghanistan. We decided against having an immediate ordered departure of American staff and their families from Tashkent. This would have left only a small number of us at the embassy. We realized that Uzbekistan had gone from being a relative backwater to a "front-line state" in what the George W. Bush administration would soon call the global war on terrorism (GWOT). Under these circumstances, it made no sense to drastically downsize our staff. We agreed that any American staff members or their family members who wished to leave the country should be able to do so through a voluntary departure.

In this case, there was no "credible" evidence of a "specific" threat against either official Americans or other U.S. citizens living in Uzbekistan. However, as we were allowing some members of our staff the option of leaving the country voluntarily, we decided we should issue a general statement warning that following the attacks in the U.S., it was possible Al-Qaeda members in neighboring Afghanistan could strike Americans living in Tashkent or elsewhere in the country. As a precaution, some nonessential embassy staff would be departing, and we advised nonofficial Americans to consider this option as well.

It was dark when I left the embassy, which faced out directly onto a major street. The building was surrounded by a high iron fence. Uzbek citizens had already begun placing bouquets of flowers with condolence messages against the embassy's outer wall. By the following day, the floral tributes would be stacked high. When Jane and I saw our Uzbek neighbors, they would look at us solemnly, putting a hand over their hearts in sadness and respect for our loss. These were unforgettable gestures and continue to endear us to the people of Uzbekistan.

On the foreign policy front, there was also solidarity between our two countries. The Karimov government immediately saw an advantage in forming a post-9/11 strategic alliance with the United States. As noted, it viewed Afghanistan as a dangerous adversary following the 1999 IMU bombings in Tashkent. The Bush administration had begun planning its incursion into Afghanistan after the Taliban refused to turn over Osama bin Laden. Uzbekistan offered invaluable geographic resources for the October 7, 2001, launch of the United States' Operation Enduring Freedom campaign to destroy Al-Qaeda's camps in Afghanistan and overthrow its Taliban allies.

Uzbekistan had a Soviet-era air force base in the southern city of Khanabad, just ninety miles north of its border with Afghanistan. The Soviets had used the base for air support of its 1979–1989 invasion and occupation of the latter. Shortly after 9/11, Karimov offered the use of this key facility to the United States. In early October, the Bush administration signed a status of forces agreement (SOFA) with Uzbekistan. This allowed for the immediate deployment of 1,500 U.S. Air Force, Army, and Special Forces personnel, in addition to fighter and transport aircraft to the base, which became known as K-2 because of its proximity to the Uzbek cities of Kharshi and Khanabad.

None of this was lost on the U.S. and international media, which sent hundreds of journalists to Uzbekistan following 9/11 to cover the military buildup and the imminent war in Afghanistan. All saw the bridge from southern Uzbekistan into Afghanistan as a route for them to enter the country once the ground war began.

Within a week after 9/11, most major U.S. news outlets including the *New York Times*, CNN, the *Washington Post*, and others had reporters on the ground in Tashkent. Having had only sporadic press work during my first two years in Uzbekistan, I was now deluged with requests for briefing and other support from these journalists. Once the Karimov regime realized international media were requesting visas, it immediately demanded that all foreign journalists register to be "accredited" in Uzbekistan.

The day after the journalists arrived, they were required to report to the Foreign Ministry's Press Office to fill out forms and wait for an accreditation document. Media organizations that didn't comply risked having their reporters expelled. The purpose of this was to keep track of the reporters by getting personal data and restricting their movements. I soon found myself spending time with the ministry's press officer on behalf of U.S. journalists who were being harassed despite having registered. The official proved to be quite helpful, and over time, we came to work well together.

In response to the journalists' wanting information about American-Uzbek cooperation, Ambassador Herbst asked that my friend, political-economic section chief Larry Memmott, and I do briefings "on background." This meant that the reporters could attribute to a "U.S. government official" what we told them but not specifically refer to us or the U.S. embassy by name. Rather than speak with reporters individually, Larry and I began weekly briefings for groups of U.S. journalists, answering questions about the U.S.-Uzbekistan relationship. Gradually, I built rapport with the media representatives.

The skills I used in press work after 9/11 were the ones I'd learned in Chile. It's hard to imagine my being able to navigate through often-choppy media waters without those four years as press attaché there. As in Chile, having Larry with me during the group briefings helped enormously when reporters wanted a deep dive into economic and political issues.

During the briefings, our official line was always telling the media how much the United States appreciated the cooperation of Uzbekistan. What we didn't say was that Islam Karimov was intent on exacting a high price from the United States for its support. Having long been viewed by successive administrations as an especially cruel Central Asian despot guilty of egregious human rights abuses, Uzbekistan's president now demanded U.S. political recognition as well as large amounts of development assistance in return.

On December 7, just two months after the launch of the strikes by United States. and coalition forces on Afghanistan, Secretary of State Colin Powell visited Uzbekistan as part of a multi-country tour of coalition partners. He arrived in Tashkent with a large State Department press pool. Powell was there to get the Uzbek government's agreement to reopen the Friendship Bridge on its southern border with Afghanistan. With support from the United States, Afghanistan's Northern Alliance had pushed the Taliban from its northern strongholds, including the strategic city of Mazar-i-Sharif. There was a railroad line that crossed the Friendship Bridge from the Uzbek city of Termez to Hairatan, a small Afghan town on the other side. The United States wanted to use the bridge to funnel personnel across the border as well as bring desperately needed humanitarian relief to Afghans in the north.

Powell started his visit by meeting with the ministers of foreign affairs and defense. But as in all authoritarian states, the most important meeting was on the following day with Karimov at the presidential palace. By December, the State Department provided me with a series of Russian-speaking civil service employees on one- or two-month assignments. All were bright, energetic young women who took over running all of Tashkent's cultural and education programs. This allowed me to devote myself full-time to working with the U.S. press and high-level visits, such as that of Secretary Powell's.

Along with the State Department press pool, roughly fifty other U.S. and international journalists and a similar number of Uzbek reporters filled the presidential palace's main hall for the December 8 press conference that would follow the Powell-Karimov meeting. It was my job with help from the Uzbek presidential press office, to get the U.S. press pool journalists through tight security and into the briefing area.

The meeting continued beyond its scheduled hour, and I would later hear that inside the conference room, Secretary Powell placed on the table a letter from President George W. Bush to Karimov. In the letter, Bush had written of "developing a long-term partnership" and "qualitatively new level" of cooperation. U.S. assistance to Uzbekistan would be tripled. Most importantly for Karimov, Bush extended an invitation for an official visit to Washington, something the Uzbek president had never done and dearly wanted.

In their meeting, after thanking Karimov for signing the October agreement allowing the U.S. access to K-2, Powell raised the question of opening the Friendship Bridge. According to what I was told, Karimov hedged, noting that it had been closed for several years. He required an engineering assessment, especially if it were to be used again for the transport of heavy materials. For that reason, it was premature to speak of reopening it.

The secretary jumped in, saying that the United States had a team of technical experts standing by who were ready to inspect the bridge and do all necessary repairs in a matter of days. Karimov again dodged, asking about financial assistance. Powell informed him that President Bush was prepared to triple the amount of U.S. aid to support political and economic reform in the country. He also would be pleased to welcome Karimov to Washington.

While he said all of this, the letter, with its U.S. presidential seal and addressed to the Uzbek president, remained face-up in front of Powell. Karimov could see the missive, but it became clear that Powell had no intention of giving it to the Uzbek president unless he agreed to open the bridge. Karimov eyed the letter as Powell calmly looked at him. Who would be the first to blink? After several moments of silence, Karimov said Uzbekistan would allow the U.S. access to the bridge.

Only then did Secretary Powell hand the letter over, which Karimov read in translation.

After Powell and Karimov entered the press conference room, the Uzbek president began by speaking in rather broad generalities about how pleased he was with Secretary Powell's visit. He noted that in their meeting they'd discussed ways of strengthening relations between the two countries. He pointed to Uzbekistan's support for the Bush administration's Operation Enduring Freedom against the Taliban as a demonstration of such cooperation. Karimov then announced that the secretary had just given him a letter from President Bush inviting him to make an official visit to Washington. He said nothing about the Friendship Bridge.

It was now Powell's turn to speak, and he said in a booming voice how happy he was to announce President Karimov had agreed to reopen the Friendship Bridge. A team of U.S. engineers would arrive in the coming days to work with Uzbek specialists to prepare it for use as soon as possible. Powell spoke at length about the importance of providing food and other supplies to Afghans now living in liberated parts of the north. He turned to the subject of Karimov's Washington visit, saying the two sides would be working beforehand on a series of agreements to be signed then.

Of course, it was very unusual for Secretary Powell rather than President Karimov to announce the reopening of the Friendship Bridge. After all, it was a decision that Karimov alone could make and share with the public. But it was clear that having obtained Karimov's agreement during the meeting and then watching him remain silent on the matter, the secretary was taking no chances. Whether the Uzbek president liked it or not, Powell was making it official at the press conference. In response, Karimov kept a straight face.

By December, many of the United States and international journalists who had come to Tashkent were anxious to cover the fighting in Afghanistan. A large number of them were what I came to call "danger junkies." They were professional wartime correspondents who had covered armed conflicts from Africa to the Balkans. Some like C. J. Cheevers, of the *New York Times*, had served in the U.S.

military. Even before the Friendship Bridge reopened, a number of the reporters had somehow managed to cross its one-kilometer span into Afghanistan. There were also barges laden with United Nations' World Food Program relief supplies that regularly crossed the river. Many journalists found a way to use this transport to get to the war zone.

There was just one problem with this. The journalists left Uzbekistan illegally without getting an exit stamp on their passports. This meant it would be extremely hard for them to reenter the country, especially after Uzbek officials beefed up security along this maritime border with Afghanistan. When U.S. journalists became burned out after covering the war, they often contacted me for help in returning from Afghanistan the same way they'd entered. In such cases, I would talk with the head of the Foreign Ministry's Press Office. And for what I am sure was a hefty "fine" that the news organizations were only too happy to pay, the Uzbek authorities allowed the journalists back into the country either via the bridge or on a barge across the river.

I'd helped any number of such U.S. journalists return, but two stand out for me. One was a lanky former U.S. military veteran who worked for the Knight Ridder organization. He partnered with a female journalist who was fluent in Russian and worked as the Moscow bureau chief for the *Los Angeles Times*. For several weeks, they filed reports from any number of dangerous places in northern Afghanistan. After this, they were eager to return to Uzbekistan, which I helped arrange. Once they were back in Tashkent, I received a call from the Knight Ridder journalist saying he and his partner were deeply grateful for my help and wanted to take me out to lunch.

Socializing with journalists is always tricky business for an embassy press attaché. While I came to like and respect most of the American journalists I worked with in Uzbekistan after 9/11, my ironclad rule was never to consider them friends or engage with them on anything other than official business. It was far too easy over drinks to say something you would later regret. But I made an exception for these two journalists because we agreed no business would be discussed. I was eager to hear about what they'd done in Afghanistan.

The three of us met at a Tashkent restaurant, and I was glad to see them again. They spoke of having had to rely on Afghan guides and interpreters who often served as middlemen in arranging interviews. The journalists never knew when they walked down an alley for a meeting with some shady figure if they would be kidnapped or killed. They told me that finding safe places to sleep at night was particularly hazardous, as there was always the chance foreign reporters could be attacked in "safe houses." They added that criminals had entered one such house at night in northeast Afghanistan, where Swedish journalists were staying, killing one of them in the course of robbing the group. The two Americans said this episode was one of the reasons they'd decided to return to Uzbekistan.

I asked them how they'd felt when they arrived back again in the Uzbek border town of Termez and away from the dangers they'd faced on a daily basis in Afghanistan. Both replied that at first, they experienced an enormous sense of relief. After a few hours, this feeling passed, and they began to miss the adrenaline high of reporting from a war zone. They said that while doing so you might be frightened and constantly alert to threats, but these highs also made life intensely exciting. This gave me insight into the appeal of being a danger junkie. Although we would never see each other again, I knew it wouldn't be long before they found another armed conflict to cover. As fate would have it, I too would soon be crossing the Friendship Bridge myself into Afghanistan under less-dangerous circumstances.

In February 2002, a congressional delegation (codel) led by Senator Tom Daschle, a Democrat from South Dakota who was the Senate majority leader, arrived in Tashkent. It had become fashionable for such codels to visit Central Asia and Afghanistan after the fighting had wound down. As public affairs officer, I was responsible for arranging press support for these groups. What was different about Codel Daschle was that his delegation, which included other senators and their spouses, was scheduled to make a visit to the town of Termez. There, they would see the famous Friendship Bridge and meet with the city's mayor, who had been highly supportive of U.S. military operations after the span reopened. It was meant to be a short photo-op and a way to build goodwill with local officials.

Ambassador Herbst was with the group. I'd sent two members of my Uzbek staff, including Dima, the talented young man who was my office's computer specialist and photographer, to assist the delegation. A half hour after the codel was set to arrive, Dima called from the airport to say their small U.S. Air Force jet hadn't arrived. He asked if the group had been delayed or the visit postponed. I told him no and said I'd get back to him as soon as possible.

I alerted the embassy security officer and the DCM. They too had no information about the delegation. We all began to fear the plane had crashed with the U.S. Senate majority leader, other prominent senators, spouses, and our ambassador onboard. But just then, I got a call from Ambassador Herbst saying they were in Bukhara, the great Silk Road city. He said he'd explain what had happened when he returned. All of us felt great relief. But it fell to the DCM to inform the mayor, who was still waiting with his delegation in Termez, that, unfortunately, the visit had been "canceled."

Once back in Tashkent, the ambassador explained that as the plane was approaching Termez, someone in the delegation suggested it would be far more interesting to return to Bukhara, which the group had visited on the previous day. Ambassador Herbst had objected, noting that the mayor and other city dignitaries were awaiting their arrival and had arranged a brief program for the codel. But Senator Daschle said he agreed that the delegation would go to Bukhara, and so that's what happened. The ambassador concluded, using his characteristic irony, "What could I do? It was their plane!"

Of course, the mayor of Termez was irate, as was the Uzbek government at what they took to be a deliberate snub. I met the ambassador in his office a few days later, and he asked me what I thought we should do to address the situation. I suggested that the two of us make an official visit to Termez as soon as possible. Once there, we would spend time with the mayor and then walk with him and other Uzbek officials across the Friendship Bridge to Hairatan. This was the Afghan city recently liberated from the Taliban. As with my proposal that he speak Uzbek upon arrival two years earlier, Ambassador Herbst listened carefully and then asked why this would be a good idea.

I explained that a visit would get excellent coverage in the Uzbek press. He would be the first U.S. ambassador to cross the same bridge that the Soviet Union had used for its 1979 invasion of Afghanistan. Doing so would go a long way toward repairing hard feelings with the city's mayor. Ambassador Herbst then said, "And you think you can pull this off and get the Uzbek military and Afghans guarding the other side of the bridge to agree?" The answer was yes, as I'd developed excellent relations through my assistance to the journalists with the Uzbek general in Termez. I also had a good working relationship with the Foreign Ministry's Press Office. The ambassador mulled over what I'd proposed and then said, "Fine, arrange for security, and let's go for it."

When I spoke to the embassy security officer, he thought my Friendship Bridge idea was both crazy and dangerous. Gradually, he came around. He worked on a safe bridge crossing for us using his security contacts, and I touched base with the Foreign Ministry and others. The greatest concern was making sure there weren't Taliban sympathizers ready to shoot us in Hairatan once we crossed the bridge!

I've often told this story to non–foreign service friends, and they've asked me how the ambassador and I could take such a "risk." I understand this reaction, but when you're a diplomat, there is danger every time you step outside the embassy. It's impossible to do your job if you are constantly worried about security. You always take as many precautions as possible after you've decided to do a public event. That is what the ambassador and I did in deciding to cross the bridge. In weighing the pros and cons of going to Termez and crossing the bridge into Afghanistan, Ambassador Herbst and I considered the risks. We concluded that we would have adequate security. As it turned out, the event on that cold, sunny day in February was an enormous success that got excellent local press coverage.

As my tour was drawing to a close, I was happy to receive a State Department Superior Honor Award for my work in Uzbekistan. And after having been passed over by a succession of evaluation boards, I was promoted to the senior foreign service with the rank of a counselor.

MARK L. ASQUINO

Until 9/11 occurred, it seemed like I was in a rewarding job but not likely to get promoted from this out-of-the-way place. Had this happened, I would have been forced to retire for time in class. But it didn't happen largely because of 9/11. From a professional perspective, I was in the right place at the right time.

Of course, during this time I could have fallen flat on my face and failed to perform well. Had I not been able to rise to the challenges that 9/11 presented, this too would have led to the end of my career. To a lesser degree, had USIA not ceased to exist, I would have had virtually no opportunity to become either a DCM or an ambassador. Instead, with this promotion, my next assignment would be as DCM in Kazakhstan, an enormous career leap. As the job didn't open until 2003, this meant that I would have a bridge year in Washington before returning to Central Asia.

So, rather than end my diplomatic journey in Tashkent, I was now on a path that would eventually take me to be an ambassador in Equatorial Guinea. Life is full of so many unexpected twists and turns. Ultimately, the principal thing I have learned is that nothing is ever a given or even all that predictable. The most you can do is adjust to unanticipated change and then try to make the best of it.

CHAPTER 10

A "Bridge" to Kazakhstan

OFTEN IN THE Foreign Service, assignments requiring language proficiency are advertised two years in advance. This allows those bidding either to acquire a new language or brush up on an old one needed for the assignment. By the end of my tour in Uzbekistan in 2002, I already had serviceable Russian for the job in Kazakhstan. The question arose as to what I would do during the gap year as a bridge to that assignment.

As it turned out, Dick Hoagland, director at the State Department for a regional bureau called EUR/CACEN, provided the answer. He was responsible for all of the former Soviet "Eurasian" countries in the Baltics, the Caucasus, and Central Asia. During one of his post-9/11 visits to Uzbekistan in 2002, after I'd been assigned to Almaty, I asked him what he recommended I do with my gap year. He immediately said that I should work for him as the desk officer for Georgia.

Now, that struck me as strange. I'd just been promoted to the senior foreign service, and the EUR/CACEN job he was proposing was two grades below my current rank. I pointed this out to him, asking why taking such a "down stretch" job made any sense. Being on the Georgia desk, I concluded, didn't seem like a good career move for me.

Dick and I were sitting in the noisy lobby of the Intercontinental Hotel, where I'd learned about the 9/11 attacks. Dick was in his fifties. He had short-clipped salt-and-pepper hair and wore heavy dark-frame glasses. A chain smoker, he silently listened to me, took a long drag on his cigarette, and finally said that as a former USIA officer, I had never worked at the Department of State. Now I was going to be the deputy chief of mission at the largest embassy in Central Asia.

In that job, he said I would need to know whom to turn to when I need help at the State Department. That would require an understanding of how the building works and what was reasonable to ask for from my desk officer. Beyond that, Dick added that I'd need to understand what Washington's interagency process was all about.

He continued that decisions at the Department of Defense, the National Security Council, and elsewhere in government all impacted Kazakhstan. Knowing which levers to pull in these places is essential. If I worked for a year on the Georgia desk, he said, I'd learn all of that because it was one of the most demanding and busy ones in CACEN. Doing so made sense because it would help me in Kazakhstan and beyond.

He told me this with a rather annoyed look on his face, and I had the sensation he was talking down to me, which I didn't like. In fact, Dick and I would frequently clash during the year I worked for him. However, what he said that afternoon made absolute sense. My taking the job would be invaluable.

As a USIA officer, I'd occasionally gone to meetings at the State Department and always found the building intimidating. The corridors are winding and confusing. The numbering sometimes doesn't seem to make sense, and the floors' color coding and maps offer only limited assistance. I sometimes used to say about the building to visitors, "If it seems confusing, it's meant to be that way!" So when Dick Hoagland said a year at EUR/CACEN would help me understand "how the building works," that was as true about State's physical layout as much as it was about how it functions.

I was excited about my new job at the Georgia desk. The country is located in the Caucasus region of Eurasia. Its western border is the Black Sea, with Russia in the north and Turkey and Armenia in the south. Its southeastern neighbor is the oil-rich nation of Azerbaijan. Georgia's capital is Tbilisi. The country's history includes hundreds of years when it was an independent Christian monarchy. In the nineteenth century, it gradually was incorporated into the Russian Czarist empire. After the 1917 Russian Revolution established the Soviet Union, Georgia briefly became independent again as a republic. The country was invaded by the Russians in 1921 and forcefully merged as a republic into the Soviet Union the following year. After the fall of the USSR, it returned to being an independent republic in April 1991.

As a newly independent country, Georgia pursued a pro-Western policy. It sought to become a member of NATO and join the European Union. Given its long and conflictive history with Russia, the years after independence were challenging ones. Interethnic violence led to the regions of Abkhazia and South Ossetia breaking away from Georgia, which they did with strong backing from the Russian Federation.

During the year I spent on the Georgia desk, much of my focus was on U.S. concerns about terrorist groups operating out of a lawless Georgian region called the Pankisi Gorge, which is close to the Russian border. Russia also saw the Pankisi Gorge as a dangerous area that provided refuge to separatists it was battling in Chechnya.

In early 2002, Washington established the Georgia Train and Equip Program (GTEP), an eighteen-month sixty-four-million-dollar military assistance initiative aimed at increasing the capability of Georgia's armed forces to fight terrorists and defend itself from Russian incursions into its territory. Not surprisingly, Moscow denounced GTEP as a brazen ploy to increase U.S. military influence in the Caucasus. There were occasional skirmishes between Georgian and Russian forces in the Pankisi Gorge during 2002–2003, but none that led to prolonged conflict.

The U.S. interest in Georgia during the early 2000s also had an economic dimension. Washington actively supported the construction of the Baku-Tbilisi-Ceyhan (BTC) oil and gas pipelines. These would bring Caspian Sea oil and gas from Azerbaijan's capital and major port city of Baku, through Georgia, to Turkey's Mediterranean depot of Ceyhan. From there, it could be shipped to energy-hungry Europe. BTC's geostrategic goal, as viewed by Washington, was to provide European countries which were dependent on Russian fuel shipments with an alternate Western source of oil and gas. In the process of mastering what BTC was about, including some of its technical details, I learned a great deal about the politics of energy that would assist me both as DCM in Kazakhstan and ambassador to Equatorial Guinea, both major oil-producing countries.

I was expected almost immediately to be one of the State Department's resident "experts" on Georgia. This made the learning curve a steep one as I immersed myself in the country's political and economic history. Fortunately, there was a woman in the Bureau of Intelligence and Research (INR) who was a genuine expert on Georgia and kindly helped me get up to speed. In the fall of 2002, I spent a week of consultations at our embassy in Tbilisi, visiting the Pankisi Gorge and getting a firsthand perspective on the challenges faced by the United States in Georgia.

I loved my work in Georgia, which required that I engage with virtually every part of the State Department. I also spent time at the Department of Defense, the USAID, and the Department of Energy on the range of U.S. interests affecting the two countries. I could not have had a better introduction to the Department of State or preparation for being DCM in Almaty than my year on the Georgia desk. But now it was time for Jane and me to go to Kazakhstan.

Kazakhstan

The Kazakhs are descended from nomadic tribes going back to the Scythians and followed by a succession of Turkic nomads in more modern times. There is nothing in Kazakhstan's history comparable to that of Uzbekistan, whose settled peoples founded and resided in the great cities of Samarkand, Bukhara, and Kiva. Kazakhstan was not on any of the major routes of the Silk Road, which brought its southern neighbor an infusion of new ideas in science, medicine, mathematics, and other fields, in addition to great riches from trade. With its over four-thousand-mile border with Russia, the vast territory that would become modern-day Kazakhstan has particularly close linguistic and cultural ties to that country.

Immediately after World War II, Stalin established a huge nuclear testing facility near the northern Kazakh town of Semipalatinsk, where the first Soviet atomic test took place in 1949. It would become a major testing ground for increasingly more powerful explosions until 1989. When the Soviets left that year, their legacy in Semipalatinsk was environmental destruction and high incidences of nuclear-related cancers and related ailments affecting its population.

In 1953, Soviet leader Nikita Khrushchev began what was called the Virgin Lands campaign to exploit Kazakhstan's vast northern plains for the production of winter wheat and develop its agricultural potential. This would remain Kazakhstan's main source of revenue until the late 1990s when the country became one of the world's largest producers of oil and gas.

The U.S. embassy in Almaty was near the historic center of the city. The political and security sections, plus the ambassador's and DCM's offices, were in a charming, nineteenth-century former dwelling on one of the city's major streets. The consulate, management, public affairs, and several other sections were about a mile away on several floors of a modern building complex called Samal Towers.

I would be working for Ambassador Larry Napper. Born to a family of modest means in San Antonio, Texas, Larry contracted polio as a child. Through sheer determination and unceasing efforts, he overcame this disability, attending Texas A&M University, where he was a member of its elite Corps of Cadets. After graduation, he entered the U.S. Army and rose to the rank of captain before joining the foreign service. Larry is a remarkable human being. He proved to be a superb boss from whom I would learn everything I needed to know about being an ambassador.

When Jane and I arrived in Kazakhstan in 2003, former Soviet Communist Party boss Nursultan Nazarbayev, the country's first and at that time only president, had been in power since 1990. In 1997, he announced that the capital of the country would be moved from Almaty, located at its geographic center, to Astana, not far from the Russian border. Many argued at the time that Nazarbayev feared Russia would encroach on its provinces in the far north, where Russian ethnicities dominated. It was also maintained that Almaty was in an earthquake zone while Astana was not. With that said, Nazarbayev, his family, and their cronies pocketed hundreds of millions of dollars in kickbacks and control of contracts for the construction of the new capital.

Moving the U.S. embassy from Almaty to a new compound in Astana would dominate my 2003–2006 tour and provide an excellent experience for me in Sudan and Equatorial Guinea, where I would also oversee the construction of new embassies. Astana had been a frontier settlement called Akmolinsk during the czarist and early Soviet periods. It became the administrative capital of the Virgin Lands campaign in the 1950s and was renamed Tselinograd in 1963. By then, it was a growing city that included high-rise housing blocks for agricultural administrators and workers.

After the fall of the Soviet Union, it returned to being Akmola, which means either white tomb or according to some, holy city in Kazak. Given the region's white-out blizzards, arctic-like winters, and isolation, White Tomb always seemed to me a more likely, if not more appealing, name for the place. Apparently, Nazarbayev thought the new capital required yet another name change. In 1998, it became Astana, which means "capital" in Kazak, certainly an improvement over White Tomb. This city of many names became Nur-Sultan in 2019 in honor of Nursultan Nazarbayev. It has now reverted back to Astana following Nazarbayev's fall from grace in retirement.

The embassy found a splendid house for Jane and me near the ambassador's residence. It was a modern two-story dwelling with a large enclosed porch at the rear, which was ideal for entertaining. It had a large well-equipped kitchen, a spacious living room, and an elegant dining room. We hosted many receptions and elegant dinners during our three years there.

As we were settling in, Jane and I decided we should find a feline companion for Chessie, our Maine Coon from Chile. One day she went to the pet section of Almaty's sprawling mostly open-air market. There she found a Russian ethnic woman who was selling a litter of white kittens with thick lustrous fur and huge amber eyes. Jane asked if they were Turkish Angoras, to which the seller answered, "Da [Yes]!" One of the kittens immediately attached himself to Jane, snuggling up and purring. It was love at first sight, and she bought the adorable little tyke for the equivalent of $9. We named him "Pasha" for his regal presence.

A voracious eater, Pasha soon began to grow, eventually becoming a huge cat—not at all the petite Turkish Angora Jane thought she was buying! With a bit of online research, I discovered that he was actually a Turkish Van. Originally from Turkey's Lake Van region, many of this breed are multicolored. Still, the all-white felines are rare and highly prized. It is said that just such a pure white Van was Turkish president Mustafa Kemal Atatürk's favorite feline companion. According to one story, Atatürk, the founder of modern Turkey, forbade the export of white Turkish Vans from the country. Highly intelligent and stunningly elegant, Pasha loved to strike cat-show poses. Fortunately for us, he and Chessie got along famously.

Our new home was situated on a spacious walled-in lot with lovely, manicured lawns and imaginative gardens. Although Pasha and Chessie were indoor cats, they were perfectly amenable to having us put them in harnesses for long walks outside. Yes, you can walk a cat! The house had a narrow decorative ledge a few feet from the ground, and we would often let Pasha off his leash so he could walk with grand agility around the dwelling's perimeter.

My office in the U.S. embassy, along with those of several others, faced the main street that ran parallel to the building. Its location might have provided a pleasant view of the nearby tree-lined sidewalk and beyond, except for the fact that being on that side of the building was dangerous from a security perspective. We were separated from the sidewalk by a few feet, bordered by a high iron fence. This meant that a suicide bomber or a car laden with explosives could easily be detonated and destroy that side of the building with us inside. Widespread global opposition to the U.S. invasion of Iraq earlier that year placed all American embassies on high-security alert, especially in the Middle East and Central Asia, where Islam was the majority religion.

The embassy's security officer erected two side-by-side eight-foot-high rows of sandbags in the gap between the building and the iron fence. He also installed sheets of Mylar plastic on the inside of our windows, which after a blast was meant to prevent the glass from

MARK L. ASQUINO

shattering into dangerous shards. Nevertheless, neither would have done much good to protect us in the event of a powerful explosion. Indeed, this was—and is—the sort of danger foreign service officers often face overseas.

The U.S. embassy in Almaty was one of the largest overseas missions in which I would serve. As the DCM, part of my job was to oversee the work of a regional medical officer; several Department of Defense offices, including a large military cooperation assistance program; plus representatives from the FBI and Drug Enforcement Agency. The U.S. Agency for International Development (USAID) had its own multistory building several blocks away from the embassy. It was a regional operation with a large staff that provided support to smaller USAID offices throughout Central Asia.

I'd learned from a DCM whom I met in Washington that in embassies with many different offices providing a range of assistance, there was frequent overlap, duplication, and a lack of coordination. From my year on the Georgia desk, I was well aware of how these sorts of problems could lead to interagency turf battles. After a few weeks on the job, my solution was to create a mission-wide assistance coordination committee that I chaired every week. During the meetings, I would have each representative describe his or her ongoing projects.

When I saw overlap or duplication, I asked what we could do to eliminate wasteful spending. Sometimes projects had no connection whatsoever to the annual country plan priorities that the entire mission had helped write. If so, why was that section or agency doing such projects rather than undertaking work that supported overall mission objectives? The questions were uncomfortable ones, and those attending sometimes became defensive. That was the point of the meetings. If government money was being spent on activities of marginal or no value to what the embassy was trying to accomplish in Kazakhstan, the ambassador and I needed to put an end to them, which we did.

On the positive side, there were also conversations among the section and agency heads that would often begin, "Well, if you're doing that, we'll focus on something different" or "Why don't we work together on that issue to reduce costs?" Sometimes one organization would be bringing in a specialist who had skills needed by another, and that too fostered cooperation. Just getting such folks out of their stove-piped offices and talking with each other once a week worked wonders. Within a matter of months, I had a far better command of our multiple assistance programs. There was enhanced cooperation on everything from military training to economic assistance to law enforcement programs. I was off to a good start.

One of my first in-country trips was by air to Astana, almost eight hundred miles away. It was a rocky flight in a small plane with lightning flashing all around us. I feared it might be my one and only trip to the new capital. Fortunately, we landed safely. There had already been a groundbreaking ceremony for the new embassy complex, which included a chief of mission residence and housing for the detachment of marines that would be assigned there. By late 2003, all of Kazakhstan's ministries and government workers relocated from Almaty to Astana.

My principal task was to work with the management officer to find a temporary office space in Astana. We needed the entire floor of a building for American and locally employed staff (LES). We would begin to transfer employees there starting in early 2004. New incoming political, security, and management officers, including a new branch office head, were assigned to Astana rather than Almaty, where we had to find suitable, secure housing for them. Having this branch facility allowed us to have them do most of the routine work with the government of Kazakhstan. When the ambassador and I were needed in Astana, we now had office space in the branch.

The construction of new embassies by private U.S. contractors is always supervised by an on-site officer from the State Department's Bureau of Overseas Building Operations (OBO). Jack Whitney had overseen dozens of major projects in his long career and was in charge of doing so for the Astana embassy. I was his chief contact. While Jack could sometimes be difficult, he was a thorough professional. He soon learned that because I'd grown up spending time with my dad at construction sites, I was comfortable wearing a hard hat and climbing ladders.

MARK L. ASQUINO

Astana presented some extraordinary challenges as the site of a new embassy. The only place in the world with a U.S. embassy that is colder than Astana is Ulaanbaatar, the capital of Mongolia. Winter temperatures in Astana can plunge to negative forty degrees Fahrenheit. To pour concrete in such extreme conditions, the embassy's U.S. contractor, B. L. Harbert, recruited skilled workers with building experience in Alaska. There were challenges of a different sort due to the fact that Astana is only several hundred miles from the Russian border.

As is customary, we had a State Department security officer assigned to the construction site. He explicitly warned American workers upon arrival that due to the risk of Russian espionage, they were forbidden from fraternizing with local women. Those working in what was secure, classified embassy space were told they were at the greatest risk. Women (and sometimes men) engaging in such espionage are known in spy craft as honey traps for an obvious reason. They readily offer sexual favors in return for sensitive information. Not surprisingly, a fair number of construction workers were caught breaking the fraternization rules, and I immediately sent them home.

Embassy Almaty's local employees were essential to staffing the new embassy. We realized moving from Almaty to distant Astana was asking a lot of our Kazakh staff. Still, we wanted to keep as many of these fine workers as possible in our employ. This was especially true of the technically skilled ones. Accordingly, the U.S. government offered local workers a generous moving and resettlement allowance. We were pleased and relieved that 80 percent of the local employees with their families said they were willing to relocate.

By the summer of 2006, when I finished my tour in Almaty, the new embassy complex (NEC) was almost ready for occupancy. By then, almost all of Embassy Almaty's employees, both American and Kazakh, had moved to Astana. Only the ambassador and I, plus a handful of support staff, remained in Almaty. The United States would maintain its main consulate in Almaty's Samal Towers, with a smaller consular section in Astana. Almaty is still the country's largest city where most visa applications are processed and American citizens' services are needed. The large USAID mission also opted to remain in Almaty, arguing that a. As a regional organization, there were advantages for it to be in what remains Kazakhstan's bustling commercial capital.

The role of a DCM is to be the embassy's chief operating officer. Accordingly, most of my responsibilities entailed supervising personnel operations, keeping an eye on the budget, and working closely with the management counselor to provide administrative support services not only to State but also to other agencies at the post. I served as the acting chief of mission or chargé, short for the French *chargé d'affaires* (CDA in diplomatic parlance) when the ambassador was out of the country. This required that I follow political issues close so that I could shift seamlessly into that role. For the most part though, I was not directly involved in the political side of the mission's work. Nevertheless, I developed a close acquaintanceship with a leading opposition figure, which would have far-reaching consequences for the United States and Kazakhstan.

Sometime in early 2004, I met Altynbek Sarsenbayev, a former mayor of Almaty and member of the country's security council. He had recently returned from Russia, where he'd been Kazakhstan's ambassador. In his early forties, he became a trusted confidant of President Nazarbayev and was seen as a rising political star. But when we met, Sarsenbayev just had a major falling out with the president and joined the opposition Naghy Ak Zhol (True Bright Path) party.

Sarsenbayev was bald and wore wire-rimmed glasses, which gave him a rather owlish, professorial look. Intelligent and quick-witted, he had a whimsical smile and open manner. We met at a diplomatic reception, and after a brief conversation, the two of us immediately hit it off. I asked Sarsenbayev why he had left the government, and he suggested we talk one-on-one somewhere else.

A couple of weeks later, he sent me a note proposing we meet at a restaurant/bar not far from the embassy. He asked that I have my embassy driver drop me off and wait about a block away so that my official car would not call attention to our meeting. I'd lived long enough in the former Soviet Union not to be surprised by his request. In the late afternoon of the appointed day, I walked to the restaurant and entered its dark dining room. It was easy enough to spot Sarsenbayev's clean-shaven head over the top of a wooden booth at the back of the room.

There was loud Euro-rock music playing, which made it difficult for someone to eavesdrop on our conversation. This meeting style was familiar to me after living in other countries ruled by authoritarian governments. What made it hard, though, is that Sarsenbayev didn't speak any English. As my Russian wasn't great, I had to concentrate on hearing everything he said. In a low voice, he relayed the story that shortly after returning from Moscow, he'd met with Nazarbayev. During their conversation, Sarsenbayev said he was blunt in expressing concern over the president's oldest daughter Dariga Nazarbayeva's corruption and the growing power she wielded along with her thuggish husband, Rakhat Aliev.

The president did not welcome the criticism of his then-heir apparent, daughter Dariga. Sarsenbayev subsequently decided he could no longer serve in Nazarbayev's government, which led to his joining the opposition and becoming a regime critic. But he realized in doing so, he had placed himself in danger.

As if on cue, Sarsenbayev discreetly motioned toward two heavy-set men who had just entered the restaurant and seated themselves in a booth not far from us. "Security police," he said in a whisper. "Someone must have tipped them off that we're here." Our conversation over, I thanked him for meeting me and got up to leave. The two security men avoided looking at me. Sarsenbayev came out of the restaurant a few minutes later, and we walked in different directions. I saw the government goons emerge and follow him. They made no attempt to hide from me who they were or what they'd been sent to do. When I returned to the embassy, I immediately sat down and wrote a reporting cable to Washington on my conversation. One never took notes in such situations, and I wanted to get down every detail.

My next meeting with Sarsenbayev occurred several months later in Astana under astonishingly different circumstances. By then, he'd decided to change his Russian last name to Sarsenbayuly, its equivalent in Kazak. Even more surprising, he'd returned to the government as Nazarbayev's minister of information. Accompanied by a political officer who had recently arrived at our branch office, I went to see Sarsenbayuly in his new role. He had a large well-appointed office in one of the new capital's modernistic buildings. He was wearing a well-tailored suit and tie and greeted me warmly.

After initial pleasantries about our families and my asking how he liked living in Astana, I told him the setting for this meeting could not have been more different from when we'd last seen each other in Almaty.

"So why, Mr. Minister, have you decided to return to the government? What's changed since our last chat?"

Sarsenbayuly was seated behind a massive desk. He gave me one of his signature whimsical smiles. He said he did not step down from being a member of the opposition. Despite this, President Nazarbayev offered him the key information minister's job in the run-up to parliamentary elections in September. Sarsenbayuly said he believed he could play an important role from inside the government in assuring that these elections would be the first step toward democracy. If polling was free and fair, he thought that the country's opposition parties would win a majority in the Mazhilis, as the parliament was called. I wished him well in his new job, saying I hoped he was right about the possibility of greater democracy in the country.

Unsurprisingly, in the fall elections, Nazarbayev's ruling Nur Otan Party (Radiant Fatherland) won forty-two of seventy-seven seats in the Mazhilis, easily retaining its majority. Sarsenbayuly stepped down from his ministerial position before the elections and charged government intimidation against the opposition. When I saw him afterward, he said he'd been mistaken in believing he could make a difference as a government minister. The only path to democracy was working as an opposition member against Nazarbayev.

Many months would pass before I saw Sarsenbayuly again. The occasion for our meeting occurred in the late summer of 2015 after the announcement that former president Bill Clinton would be coming to Kazakhstan in September. It was a private visit, and Clinton was scheduled to meet with President Nazarbayev to discuss ways Kazakhstan could support the Clinton Foundation's HIV/AIDS

Procurement Consortium of nations to reduce the cost of antiretroviral drugs to treat the disease.

Sarsenbayuly called me and asked if I could meet with him and other senior leaders of the Ak Zhol party to discuss the visit. When I arrived at the party's Almaty headquarters, he and his colleagues said they were upset that Clinton would arrive just weeks before the December 2005 presidential elections.

Ak Zhol and other opposition parties had candidates who would be running against Nazarbayev, and the Kazakh government would surely use Clinton's visit as an endorsement of Nazarbayev's candidacy. My boss and mentor Ambassador Napper had recently ended his assignment in Kazakhstan, leaving me in charge until his successor arrived. Sarsenbayuly asked me as acting ambassador if I could have Clinton postpone coming to Kazakhstan until after the election.

I explained that unfortunately I could not. Kazakhstan was just one brief stop on President Clinton's multicountry private tour on behalf of the Clinton Foundation. However, I could see if he would be willing to meet with Ak Zhol and any other opposition party after seeing President Nazarbayev in Almaty to discuss HIV/AIDS.

Sarsenbayuly was skeptical. He said such a meeting with the opposition would be little more than an afterthought. I countered by asking what the opposition had to lose by meeting with Clinton. If they didn't, Nazarbayev certainly would use the former president's visit to claim an endorsement. Gradually, I brought Sarsenbayuly around. Now, all I had to do was persuade the Clinton Foundation, where I knew no one, that the former president should meet the opposition! I informed the State Department of my plan and got the green light to approach the foundation to make my pitch on Clinton's spending time with Ak Zhol and other opposition parties.

If my friend Sarsenbayuly had questioned the value of a Clinton-opposition meeting, this was nothing compared to the reaction I initially got from the foundation staffer in charge of the Almaty stop. He told me this was a "private visit" by the president. It had nothing to do either with the embassy or foreign policy. Therefore, he saw no reason for adding such a "political" meeting. He became a bit more receptive when

I told him that I'd had the great honor of working as a press officer for Clinton's presidential visits to both Argentina and Chile several years earlier. It turned out we knew some people in common from those trips, which kept the conversation going.

I explained at length why it was so important, given the upcoming presidential election, for Clinton not to see only Nazarbayev. I noted how Kazakhstan's authoritarian government would use Clinton's presence to imply he'd come to endorse Nazarbayev's reelection. Finally, the staffer agreed that Clinton would see the opposition for "no more than thirty minutes" after his dinner with Nazarbayev. "And one more thing, absolutely no photos with the opposition!" I said, "Of course," and thanked him.

President Clinton was set to arrive in a private plane late in the afternoon of September 5. I would be at the airport to meet him along with Kazakh government officials. Clinton and those traveling with him would then be taken to a fancy restaurant on the picturesque road that led to the nearby Tian Shan mountains. Clinton was scheduled to meet President Nazarbayev and Kazakh health specialists at the restaurant to discuss the HIV/AIDS initiative. I was not included, nor was there any reason why I should be for a private visit.

It had been agreed in advance that Kazakhstan would sign a memorandum of understanding, adding it to the forty other member countries in the consortium working to lower the price of retroviral drugs. This would be followed by a lavish outdoor dinner and then a folkloric show. On the way back to the airport, President Clinton was scheduled to stop at a hotel along the way to meet briefly with the opposition party representatives. Political section chief Deborah Mennuti and I would attend this meeting. She and her staff had worked out all of the details with the Foreign Ministry. Of course, the Kazakhs weren't happy at all about this but reluctantly agreed.

I departed for the airport in the ambassador's armored black Cadillac sedan. The Kazakh government had stopped all traffic on the road to the airport, and people were positioned along the entire route to greet President Clinton. Although he was no longer a sitting president and this wasn't an official visit, the Kazakhs had pulled out all the stops for his arrival.

The driver and I were headed down the hill on our way to the airport, and the Cadillac had a small U.S. flag flying from a metal clasp attached to the passenger side of its hood. And here I was, a mere "acting ambassador" who had come close to being forced to retire a couple of years earlier, sitting ramrod straight in the backseat, watching scores of Kazakhs waving wildly and cheering as we passed. At each intersection, policemen in dress uniforms stood at attention and saluted me. What to do? I waved back and returned their salutes, thinking I would never again be given such a grand reception. I was right about that. While the experience was deeply humbling, it was also wildly surreal. But things were about to get even stranger.

We arrived well before the plane touched down, and I took my place in the front of the receiving line. Standing to my side was a statuesque young Kazakh woman in a brightly colored traditional Central Asian dress. She was holding a loaf of typical bread in one hand and a small dish of salt in the other, ceremonial offerings for honored visitors. Clinton came down the stairs of the corporate jet, looking tired and rumpled. I shook hands with him, as did the mayor of Almaty and other dignitaries.

It was then that the young woman, whose low-cut bodice was quite revealing, came forward. Unfortunately, the former president was looking directly at her bosom when she suddenly bowed, hitting him on the top of the head with her long pointed purple hat. It was just hilarious. It took all of my diplomatic reserve to keep a straight face and not burst out laughing. Both of them looked embarrassed but quickly regained their composure.

The Kazakh government took President Clinton and his assistants to the meeting and dinner at the restaurant. As agreed with the Ministry of Foreign Affairs, after this part of the visit, the embassy would provide transport to the hotel for the meeting with the opposition and then proceed to the airport. We'd heard that given how unhappy the government was with Clinton's seeing members of the opposition, President Nazarbayev would do everything he could to prolong the dinner. If it went on too late, the government hoped Clinton might go straight to the airport.

As originally planned, the former president was scheduled to arrive at the hotel for the 11:30 p.m. meeting. Deborah and I were there thirty minutes in advance, followed shortly by the arrivals of Alikhan Baimenov, the Ak Zhol party's candidate for president in the upcoming December elections, my friend Altynbek Sarsenbayuly, and several other members of their party. Although we'd invited all of the other opposition parties to send representatives to meet with President Clinton, only one chose to do so.

Deborah was waiting outside the hotel entrance to greet President Clinton and escort him to the meeting room directly off the lobby. By 12:30 a.m., we received word from the embassy security officer waiting outside the Kazakh government's meeting place that the events there were finally ending. I'd later learn that Kazakh officials tried to stop Clinton's official party from attending the opposition meeting. In a potentially dangerous diversionary tactic, Kazakh police on motorcycles "escorting" the motorcade down the hill tried to block Clinton's car from making the left turn to the hotel. The U.S. embassy security officer was in another car and took action to make sure the official motorcade was able to turn.

It was after 1:00 a.m. when Deborah escorted the former president, his four staff members, and the Secret Service detail to the room where the opposition members and I had been waiting for more than an hour and a half. Despite the late hour, Clinton was on. No longer looking tired, he heartily greeted the opposition members and me, apologizing for being late.

Just as I'd often heard, President Clinton was one of those people who drew energy from those around him. Once so animated, he could keep going for hours on end, supercharged by adrenaline. At such times, he had an uncanny ability to make you feel you were enormously important to him and had his undivided attention. I was far from being a Clinton fan after the Lewinsky scandal. Added to that, I held him personally responsible for the disastrous dismantlement of the USIA when he was president. But it was impossible not to be mesmerized by the man.

The president and I sat down at a small table with a Secret Service agent to his left and an embassy translator behind Clinton. On the other side of the room, the six opposition members were seated at a larger table. Deborah, the president's staffers, and several other Secret Service agents settled into folding chairs behind the Kazakhs. Baimenov, Sarsenbayuly, and the other party's leader thanked the president for finding time to see them. They emphasized how important U.S. support was to them and other members of the opposition. They then spoke at length about Nazarbayev's long repressive rule, appealing to Clinton to do everything he could to make the December presidential elections free and fair.

Clinton listened attentively and, following the consecutive translation, said he appreciated the difficulties faced by opposition parties in Kazakhstan. Then he shifted in a different direction, noting that following his presidency, former president Jimmy Carter had founded the Carter Center, which was dedicated to advancing democracy and promoting human rights throughout the world. Clinton said that after leaving office, he'd chosen instead to work on global health issues, especially HIV/AIDS. He then turned to me. Putting his hand on my back, he told them, "The chargé here is a good man, and I'm sure he'll convey your concerns to President Carter. You can certainly count on the United States to help you in any way that we can."

Now, I wondered how Clinton had concluded I was a good man based on the fact he'd just met me. Furthermore, the notion that I could pick up the phone and have a chat with Carter was quite a stretch. The Carter Center only observed a limited number of foreign elections each year. We'd asked months before if it might include Kazakhstan's upcoming presidential contest. The answer had been no, as the center believed it would have no constructive role in what was seen as an inevitable Nazarbayev victory. Still, the opposition members seemed genuinely pleased Clinton had given them a hearing, albeit then tossing the ball into my lap.

At this point, forty minutes had elapsed, and I could see that Clinton was just warming up. But one of his aides was chopping his right hand vertically into his left one as a signal to me that it was time to cut off the conversation. I leaned over and whispered to the president that I thought perhaps we should wrap things up. He replied in a loud voice, "Oh no! I'm enjoying this."

As I looked at the aide, my expression clearly conveyed, "Well, I tried."

Clinton was in office from 1992 to 2000, shortly after Kazakhstan's independence and Nazarbayev's decision to denuclearize. The opposition members wanted to know more about that process and the sorts of interactions he'd had with Nazarbayev in those years.

Clinton leaned back and launched into an animated discussion about that period, emphasizing it was only after prolonged negotiations that Kazakhstan, Belarus, and Ukraine signed a 1993 agreement in Budapest committing them to give up all the nuclear weapons on their territories. Obviously, he continued, Kazakhstan had had the lion's share of weapons, and Nazarbayev's participation and agreement to denuclearize had been crucial.

It was now almost 2:30 a.m. and I could see Clinton's aides were frantic to get him on the plane. Fortunately for everyone, the president was now ready to go. Before he did, the opposition members, who all had in front of them Russian translations of Clinton's recently released book, *My Life*, asked if he'd sign their copies. He said he'd be glad to do so and walked over to their table and started signing. And then someone in the group said in halting English, "Mr. President, photo, please!" Clinton's aides began mouthing to me in an exaggerated fashion. "NO PHOTO!" but he smiled broadly and said, "Of course!" They all stood up with Clinton in the center, and Deborah snapped several shots with a camera one of them had brought.

Before Clinton left, he looked intensely at me, and said with seeming sincerity in his deep, Arkansas drawl, "Thank you for your service, Mr. Chargé!"

Now, that's not something frequently said to diplomats, so it was a surprise, especially coming from a former president. Clinton made me feel at that moment as if I was the only person in the room. I'd just experienced firsthand one of his great talents as a politician.

Within an hour, the two opposition parties uploaded to their websites the photo with Clinton which did much to undercut the claims of Kazakhstan's state-controlled media the next day that the former U.S. president had come to endorse the country's authoritarian leader. It was no great surprise, though, in December that Nazarbayev won a "resounding victory" with 91 percent of the vote compared to Ak Zhol's mere 1.6 percent.

In late December, Jane and I held a large holiday party to ring in the new year. The house was elaborately decorated with two Christmas trees, holiday lights, and garlands. Jane used her gourmet cooking skills to prepare delicious appetizers and dozens of homemade cookies. We invited our many friends and my professional contacts to the festive late-afternoon open house. I was pleased to see Altynbek Sarsenbayuly among our guests. Despite the opposition's electoral loss just a few weeks earlier, he was in an upbeat mood. We talked about his plans to strengthen civil society organizations in the coming year. We joked about how cold it was outside and agreed the dark clouds promised heavy snow later that evening. It was the last time I would ever see him alive.

On February 13, 2006, Sarsenbayuly, his bodyguard, and driver were found dead, lying facedown on the ground near their vehicle in a deserted clearing outside of Almaty. All had been murdered execution-style with a bullet to the back of the head. The bodyguard's and driver's hands had been bound behind them. They had been forced to kneel before being summarily assassinated. I was in my office when I got the ghastly news. The details of the crime made me nauseous.

We immediately reported to the State Department what had happened. I then helped draft a press release sent out that same day in which the U.S. government deplored the brutal murders and called on Kazakhstan's government to conduct an immediate and thorough investigation. I'd written a number of similar statements in the past but never about the death of someone whom I knew, liked, and deeply respected. As a diplomat, you're supposed to keep your emotions in check and not personalize events. In this case, I found that hard to do.

Initially, the response by Kazakhstan's government came from its deputy interior minister. In his statement, he tried to downplay any political motivation for the killings, speculating unconvincingly that what happened had occurred over some sort of financial dispute involving Sarsenbayuly. The widely held view among those in the opposition and the international community was that he had been murdered on the orders of the government for his outspoken opposition views and activities.

As if to confirm this, on February 22, five members of Kazakhstan's elite paramilitary Arystan Tiger intelligence unit were arrested. They confessed that they had been paid $25,000 to assist in abducting Sarsenbayuly and those with him. A day later, the government's chief national security officer resigned, saying the group of men under his command had betrayed the interests of the people.

The jailed security operatives said that a former law enforcement officer named Rustam Ibragimov had organized the plot and been the triggerman. After his arrest, he confessed he'd been paid $60,000 to carry out the killings and claimed the person who had ordered the crime was Yerzhan Utembayev, head of administration in the country's Senate. Prosecutors would later claim that Utembayev had been enraged over Sarsenbayuly's criticism of him in a newspaper article. This led Utembayev to retaliate by having him killed. But there was never any corroborating evidence to link Utembayev to the crime, and the opposition believed he was merely a low-ranking bureaucrat who had been made the scapegoat.

The new ambassador, John Ordway, and I attended Sarsenbayuly's wake, which was held in a large hall near Almaty's city center. There were hundreds of mourners outside as we were led by security guards through the crowd to the door and allowed to enter. Once inside, we waited our turn with a small group of men to approach the casket. We bowed our heads as the imam said a prayer. Each of us then touched the casket, and I paused to say a personal goodbye to my friend.

The ambassador and I offered our condolences to Sarsenbayuly's wife and small children. To this day, what I remember most was the expression of inconsolable grief on the face of his youngest daughter.

What a horrible way to lose your beloved father, I thought. There was nothing I could say that would provide any meaningful solace or comfort to her. I will always believe her father's murder extinguished a spark of hope for the future of Kazakhstan.

Few of us who were there at the time believe justice was done in this case. All signs point to high-level government involvement in the killings, perhaps including members of the Nazarbayev family. Sarsenbayuly was viewed as someone who knew a great deal and presented a direct threat to their power. This included his investigation of corruption in the media empire owned by the president's daughter Dariga Nazarbayeva and her husband, Rakhat Aliev.

By the spring of 2006, I had only a few months left in Kazakhstan. I continued to make monthly trips to Astana to supervise the final preparations for moving the staff into the new embassy compound. It would be formally inaugurated several months after Jane and I left Kazakhstan. Seeing the completed facility just before I left was enormously rewarding.

Another project in which I'd become involved would lead to my next assignment. Early in my tour, I met senior diplomat Carlos Pascual during a visit he made to Almaty as the State Department's coordinator for U.S. Assistance to Europe and Eurasia. I accompanied him to a number of ongoing projects funded by his office, and we got to know each other quite well.

Several months after his visit, the embassy was informed that because of Kazakhstan's increasing oil and gas wealth, the country would be zeroed out in the following year from this program. The USAID director George Deikun and I felt that the assistance being provided to Kazakhstan to build its financial infrastructure and train those in its economic ministries was crucial. We opposed shortsighted cutting off such aid.

Although he was now in a State Department position, earlier in his career, Carlos had spent more than a decade as a USAID officer. He was unpersuaded when George and I argued that the U.S. economic assistance was so valued by Kazakhstan's government that it was willing to pay for at least part of it in the future. Carlos proposed that if we felt so strongly about this, we should come to Washington and make our case to him and his assistant office colleagues. This was not something that embassies normally did. However, the ambassador agreed with us and approved the trip.

George thoroughly knew the financial assistance programs, as USAID oversaw most of them. There were also other embassy officers who worked with the institutions being aided and contributed to our preparations. The plan we came up with was to have the Kazakhs begin during the coming year to contribute 10 percent of the cost of the programs, which included having U.S. financial experts come to Kazakhstan to work on strengthening financial infrastructure and train officials. Over the next five years, the Kazakh government's contributions would gradually increase to 25 percent, 50 percent, and 75 percent until the final year, when they would pay for the entire cost of the programs if they wished them to continue.

We spent two long days in Washington with Carlos and members of the Office for U.S. Assistance to Europe and Eurasia. What we proposed had never been done before with other former Soviet republics. It was a tough sell, with George doing the heavy lifting on the financial side while I made the political justification arguments. At the end of our stay, Carlos agreed to give our approach a try. It turned out to be a great success, and the plan we devised for Kazakhstan would become a model for other countries.

Before I left Washington, Carlos mentioned that he would soon be taking a job as the first coordinator of a new State office for worldwide reconstruction and stabilization. He said that I should contact him if I were looking for a Washington assignment at the end of my tour. I thanked him but thought this was highly unlikely. Having spent six years in Central Asia, I hoped to return to Washington and become director of EUR/CACEN, the regional office that covered Central Asia and the Caucasus. Being a CACEN director would provide me with a good launching pad to become an ambassador in one of the smaller Central Asian republics.

As I've said throughout this book, things in the foreign service never turn out quite the way you think they should. In 2005, there was a major reorganization in the Department of State that resulted in the countries of Central Asia being moved from the European Regional Bureau to the South Asia Regional Bureau (SA). EUR/CACEN was transferred to SA which was renamed the South and Central Asia Regional Bureau (SCA). I'd never served in South Asia, knew no one in the new SCA, and accordingly had absolutely no chance of heading the Central Asia office there.

CHAPTER 11

A Turn toward Africa

THE STATE DEPARTMENT'S Office of the Coordinator for Reconstruction and Stabilization (S/CRS) was created in 2004 during the Bush administration when Colin Powell was secretary of state. In a post-9/11 world, the United States viewed some of its greatest national security threats as coming from failing and failed states. S/CRS's role was to address these threats worldwide, and its mission statement could not have been more ambitious:

> The office will lead, coordinate and institutionalize a U.S. government civilian capacity to prevent or prepare for post-conflict situations, to help stabilize and reconstruct societies in transition from conflict and civil strife so they can reach a sustainable path toward peace, democracy and a market economy.

When I joined S/CRS as its deputy coordinator in the summer of 2006, it had a staff of eighty. In addition to the Department of State, we had employees on interagency details from USAID, the Department of Defense (DOD), the Army Corps of Engineers, and the Department of Labor. S/CRS had an experienced foreign or civil service director in five different sections, including conflict prevention, planning, civilian response operations and strategic communications, and resource management.

But S/CRS faced fierce resistance from other parts of the U.S. government and, indeed, from within the Department of State. USAID, for many years, had an Office of Transition Initiatives (OTI) in its Bureau for Democracy, Conflict, and Humanitarian Assistance. OTI's mission was "to provide fast, flexible, short-term assistance targeted at key political transition and stabilization needs." And USAID's Office of Foreign Disaster Assistance (AFDA), while focused primarily on responding to natural catastrophes, also included in its mission providing assistance during post conflict situations.

Not surprisingly, USAID saw S/CRS as not only encroaching on what it viewed as one of its core missions but also competing for scarce reconstruction and stabilization funding from Congress. Similarly, the Bureau of Political Military Affairs (PM) at the State Department looked at us with a wary eye. PM was the principal liaison with DOD, and its leaders viewed S/CRS as potentially competing for influence with the military and, worse still, as a competitor for congressional funding.

Although Carlos Pascual had offered me the deputy position, he later decided to leave the State Department for a think tank job. The new S/CRS coordinator was none other than Ambassador John Herbst. Given the excellent relationship we'd established in Uzbekistan, it was a pleasure to work with him again. After Uzbekistan, Herbst served from 2003 to 2006 as ambassador to Ukraine. This was a time of great ferment there, culminating in the Orange Revolution that resulted in sweeping democratic changes.

During my first meeting with Herbst, a rather formal man whom I always addressed as "ambassador," we talked about his expectations of me as his deputy. He outlined the bureaucratic challenges noted above that S/CRS was facing. The ambassador said policy issues and turf battles would occupy much of his time as he led the organization. My job would be much the same as a Deputy Chief of Mission (DCM) at an embassy. He needed me to oversee all operational aspects of the office, assuming personnel and budget oversight while also being prepared to step in as acting coordinator in his absence. I replied that I welcomed the opportunity to serve him in this role. I was about to walk out the door when he said in his customary quiet voice, "Oh, Mark, there's just one more thing."

I turned and said, "Yes, Ambassador, what's that?"

He smiled somewhat mischievously. "Well, in this office, we're very much involved with operations in African countries like Sudan, Liberia, and Zimbabwe. They're important to us. As you know, neither of us is an African hand, but one of us needs to become one. And I think that's going to be you!"

At this point, I'd never set foot on the African continent, let alone been posted there. But I knew the foreign service was full of surprises, and there was just one answer. "Of course, Ambassador. I'll make learning about Africa one of my top priorities."

And thus, I began what would prove to be a sharp career turn toward Africa. I read as much as quickly as I could about African history, politics, and culture. From the beginning, S/CRS needed to go beyond reconstruction/stabilization theory and engage as soon as possible in field work that would demonstrate what we called proof of concept.

One of the first opportunities for such engagement was in Sudan. In early 2003, a brutal conflict broke out in Darfur, the western region of the country. It pitted settled black African farmers against semi-nomadic Arabized African livestock herders and included disputes over access to water and land for grazing. Both groups practiced Islam; and their disputes, which soon escalated, were focused not on religion but rather on ethnicity and competition for scarce resources.

What might have remained a localized conflict became an outright brutal war in Darfur when rebel groups, including the Sudan Liberation Movement (SLA) and the Justice and Equality Movement (JEM), claimed the government in Khartoum was waging a war of ethnic cleansing against Darfur's non-Arabs. In addition to deploying its ground forces and aircraft, which indiscriminately killed hundreds of civilians, the government armed and deployed what came to be known as the Janjaweed. These were lawless militias of Arabized indigenous Africans who committed appalling atrocities, including gang rape as a weapon of war, mass murder, and terror tactics that destroyed entire communities.

The spiraling waves of increased violence during 2003–2004 led to worldwide attention and condemnation of Sudan's ruthless dictator Omar al-Bashir, who would be indicted in 2009 by the International Criminal Court (ICC) for crimes against humanity. In response, the

African Union sent poorly equipped and ineffective peacekeepers in what was called the African Mission in Sudan (AMIS) to Darfur in 2004. It was supplemented and expanded by the United Nations Mission to Darfur (UNAMID) in 2006. The Save Darfur Coalition, supported by celebrities including George Clooney and Mia Farrow, plus other U.S. non-government human rights groups, demanded Washington intervene to stop what Secretary of State Powell described as acts of "genocide" in Darfur.

The Bureau of African Affairs (AF) in the Department of State and the U.S. embassy in Khartoum were heavily involved in diplomatic efforts to bring an end to the bloodshed. Both were only too happy to accept S/CRS's offer to send members of its new Active Response Corps (ARC) to Sudan to assist in these and other efforts connected with Darfur.

By the summer of 2006, an ARC team had already been deploying to Sudan for extended periods. Working with embassy officers and other U.S. officials, they had recently helped broker the Darfur Peace Agreement between Sudan's government and the major SLA faction led by a charismatic warlord named Minni Minnawi. Sudan was our largest and most important deployment, with Washington staff coordinating with USAID and others in "whole of government" initiatives. During my two-year tenure, we would also have other successes with projects in Haiti, Lebanon, and Liberia.

On a personal level, my time at S/CRS proved to be yet another important turning point in my career. Much to my surprise, I was promoted in 2008, making me far more competitive for a future ambassadorship. My two years as deputy coordinator awakened in me a desire to serve in Africa. I finally traveled to the continent in 2007 to attend a weeklong United Nations Peacekeeping conference in Accra, Ghana. It was an amazing experience, and I was hooked.

In late 2007, I went to see Linda Thomas-Greenfield, the principal deputy assistant secretary in AF, to discuss the deputy chief of mission opening at our embassy in Khartoum, Sudan. I had come to know Linda well. I began by saying that although I'd never served in Africa, she knew how passionate I was about Sudan. Based on this and my having previously been a DCM, I asked if she would consider me for the Khartoum job. Linda, now the U.S. ambassador to the United Nations, has a commanding presence. She sat back in her chair and with a big smile said, "Well, Mark, if you were asking me about becoming DCM in Pretoria, South Africa, the answer would be a definite no. But we don't have that many people interested in Sudan. I certainly know and appreciate the excellent job you're doing at S/CRS. So, yes, I will definitely support your bid on Khartoum!"

That was great news. Now I just had to convince the person I'd be working for in Sudan that I was the best person for the job. And this brings up an interesting aspect of U.S. relations with the country.

The pro-Islamic government of Sudan headed by President Omar al-Bashir, a former general, had come to power through a bloodless military coup in 1989. During 1991–96, it provided a base of operations for Osama bin Laden and supported international terrorist groups before and after that. Accordingly, the United States put Sudan on its state sponsors of terrorism list in 1993. This resulted in crippling economic sanctions and our diplomatic relationship with Sudan being downgraded. Starting in 1997, a chief of mission (COM) rather than a U.S. Senate-confirmed ambassador would lead our embassy in Khartoum. The same became true at Sudan's diplomatic headquarters in Washington.

In 2007, the chief of mission at our embassy in Sudan was a fellow USIA veteran known for his fluent Arabic. He was also someone with a highly controversial reputation. Several years earlier, as a U.S. government media spokesperson, he'd publicly criticized U.S. policy in Iraq as "stupid," which nearly ended his career. In addition, few who'd previously worked for him had anything good to say about his leadership style or treatment of subordinates. I bid on the DCM position because I believed, naively as it turned out, that I'd get along fine with this person, whom I will refer to as the COM. After several telephone conversations and an in-person meeting, he offered me the job. Jane and I were delighted to be going to Africa; but unbeknownst to us, we had some incredibly rough times ahead of us.

Sudan

While the conflict in Darfur had by no means ended when I arrived in Khartoum in the summer of 2008, the U.S. foreign policy focus on Sudan had already begun to shift elsewhere. The most pressing issue during my two-year tour was whether semi-autonomous southern Sudan, with its capital in Juba, would vote for independence and become a new sovereign nation. Given the complexity of this issue, I need to provide some historical background before moving ahead with my personal story.

Historians of Sudan have argued that those living in the southern part of the country are distinct from the north because of being racially and culturally black Africans as opposed to "Arabs." Those living in the south were victims of frequent slave raids by Arabs from the north, something that continued to shape the relations between northerners and southerners. During the 1899–1955 colonial period, Great Britain pursued a policy of administering the north and south separately. Northern elites, especially those living in and around Sudan's capital, Khartoum, became known as Riverine Arabs.

Although they often were not fully ethnic Arabs, they embraced the Arabic language and Islamic identity. The British encouraged the isolation of the south by restricting northern travel there as well as promoting the development of an indigenous African identity dominated by the two majority tribes, the Dinka and the Nuer. Missionaries, mostly from Norway, introduced southerners to Christianity, which often coexisted with tribal religious beliefs and values. The use of local languages continued, with instruction in English being favored over Arabic.

One result of this was that while the north—with its better-educated, Arabic-speaking population—was favored by the British and accordingly benefited from the economic development of the northern portion of the country, the south remained economically undeveloped and politically and militarily marginalized.

Much of the recent history of Sudan, starting with its independence from Great Britain in 1959, has been characterized by the south's resistance against the northern majority's attempts to enforce an Islamic and Arab identity on it in the name of national unity. Sudan's 1955–1972 civil war between the north and south was ended by the Addis Ababa Agreement, with the north's military government, under the rule of General Gaafar Nimeiry, allowing limited autonomy to the south. In 1983, after Nimeiry attempted to impose sharia law on the southerners, the two sides went back to war in a conflict that would cost over two million lives and last until 2005.

The 2005 Comprehensive Peace Agreement (CPA), brokered by the United States with Great Britain and Norway as junior partners, finally ended the war. It provided a six-year transition period during which the semi-autonomous government of southern Sudan, headed by military officers from the Sudan People's Liberation Army (SPLA), exercised power through the Sudan People's Liberation Movement (SPLM) political party. The south was granted considerable regional autonomy, exempted from sharia law, allowed to keep a standing army, and granted a 50 percent share of oil revenues.

John Garang the U.S. college-educated Dinka founder of the SPLA who led the second civil war, was killed in a plane crash shortly after the signing of the CPA agreement. Garang was an advocate for a "new Sudan," bringing together both the north and south in what he said would be a democratic government at the end of the six-year period. Fellow Dinka, General Salva Kiir became president of the SPLM after Garang's death and, unlike him, favored independence for the south. While the CPA's stated goal was to make the unity of Sudan attractive, the agreement also included the key provision of guaranteeing southerners self-determination through a 2011 referendum on continuing unity or separation and nationhood.

As I mentioned earlier, Omar al-Bashir led a 1989 military coup that overthrew Sudan's democratically elected government. Through the 1990s, his dictatorial regime provided refuge for Islamic terrorists. al-Bashir would rule Sudan until 2019, when the military and a coalition of civilian prodemocracy groups forced him from power and jailed him on charges of corruption.

MARK L. ASQUINO

On August 7, 1998, Al-Qaeda—sponsored terrorists bombed the U.S. embassies in Nairobi, Kenya, and Dar es Salaam, Tanzania, resulting in the deaths of 224 people, including 12 Americans, and more than 5,000 injured. It was later shown that the al-Bashir government sheltered the terrorists who attacked our embassy in Nairobi, providing them with passports and allowing them to cross Sudan's border into Kenya.

In retaliation, President Clinton launched a highly controversial cruise-missile attack on the Al-Shifa pharmaceutical factory in Khartoum, killing one employee and wounding eleven others. At the time, the United States claimed the factory was producing a nerve agent, but subsequent reports cast serious doubt on the intelligence used to justify the strike. Some alleged the attack was a diversion by Clinton for the then-unfolding Monica Lewinsky scandal.

It was in this context of past ties to terrorist groups that in the early morning hours of January 1, 2008, two U.S. embassy Khartoum employees, USAID project officer John Granville and his Sudanese driver Abdel Abbas Rahama, were ambushed by gunmen as Granville was being taken back to his apartment after a New Year's Eve party at the British embassy. Rahama died immediately, and Granville passed away the following day in a Khartoum hospital. Two terrorist groups, Al-Qaeda in the Lands of the New Niles and Ansar-al Tawhid (Supporters of Monotheism), separately claimed responsibility for the barbarous murders.

While still in Washington, I received the terrible news on New Year's Day 2008. I learned that John Granville was single and just thirty-three, while his driver, Abdel Abbas Rahama, thirty-nine, left behind a widow and young son. Shortly afterward, five men were arrested for the crime, although their trial would not occur until the following year.

As I prepared for my assignment in the months that followed, I learned that the State Department's Bureau of Diplomatic Security had ordered enhanced security measures at the embassy. American employees could no longer drive or travel in their personally owned vehicles. Instead, they were required to be transported for both official and private business by embassy drivers in a fleet of newly acquired official armored vehicles. Both the COM and DCM were assigned armed bodyguards who were Sudanese embassy security section employees who accompanied them outside the embassy. The COM and DCM also had round-the-clock Sudanese military and armed embassy guards at their residences.

In the absence of an American doctor, a local-hire Scottish nurse at our embassy had valiantly tried to save Granville's life in the hours after the attack. Because of Khartoum's limited medical facilities, the State Department decided to assign to the embassy a full-time American medical officer who was a foreign service physician. All newly assigned personnel headed for Khartoum were required to take the one-week-long foreign affairs counterterrorism (FACT) training, which had previously been reserved for those assigned to Afghanistan and Iraq.

FACT was informally known at the State Department as the "crash and bang" course. In addition to providing emergency medical training, students were required to learn high-speed, evasive driving skills that included successfully crashing through blocking vehicles. In addition, we were given a day of weapons familiarization training.

I was also required to take once again a week-long course for DCMs at the Foreign Service Institute. It included updated training on supervisory skills, financial management, and interpersonal relations. In my case, it was a good "brush-up." I learned something new and important from our "mentor," Ambassador Prudence Bushnell. She had been the ambassador at our embassy in Nairobi when it was attacked on August 7, 1998.

Although Pru, as she asked us to call her, did not have a formal teaching role in the course, she was there to answer practical questions and provide us with advice. One day, she told the class that she had done everything she could to make the Nairobi embassy, an older building, as safe and secure as possible before it was attacked. Had she not done so, she added, she could never have faced the grieving relatives of those killed on that terrible day.

She told us that during the first week we were at the embassy, we should walk from the basement to the top floor with our management and security officers. We needed to look for any hazardous or insecure areas and check emergency doors, lighting, and exit routes. We should demand that the problems be fixed immediately and then follow up with an inspection of the work.

I took this advice to heart and inspected our embassy buildings not only as DCM in Sudan but also as an ambassador in Equatorial Guinea. It's something I recommend not just for those running an embassy but for anyone responsible for the welfare of employees, especially those working in older buildings.

Just before Jane and I left for Khartoum, I was invited to attend a memorial service for the two slain embassy employees at USAID's Washington headquarters. There, I met John's mother and Abdel's widow and child. It was a moving ceremony with poignant tributes. When it ended, some senior USAID officials took me aside. They said they expected me, as DCM, to oversee the judicial proceedings against the alleged murderers and make sure that justice was done. The tone of their voices was tinged with anger, which surprised me. I would learn why soon after arriving in Sudan.

Khartoum, sitting at the spectacular confluence of the Blue and White Nile Rivers, is a majestic city with stately buildings from the colonial period. Omdurman, a historic section of the city across the Nile, has a labyrinth-like market (souk) with exotic merchandise from Africa and the Middle East. Omdurman is also the site of a Sufi shrine where members of the Qadisiya Sufi order meet every weekend. There, they perform African rituals and dances open to the public that are very different from those of Turkey's Sufi "whirling dervishes."

While Khartoum is a fascinating city, it proved to be an extremely restrictive one for me because of security requirements. One of the first people I met after my arrival was my personal bodyguard. A fit-looking Sudanese man, he was wearing a khaki vest with a distinct bulge below the top left-hand pocket, where I learned he had a loaded Glock handgun. I would have a number of different embassy employee bodyguards over the next two years, all wearing such vests and similarly armed. Each would sit in the passenger side of the embassy's fully-armored Toyota Land Cruiser, with me seated behind him in the backseat.

Near the vehicle's front console was an M3 assault rifle, just like the one I'd practiced shooting during the FACT training. Should the driver and bodyguard be disabled or killed in an attack, the plan was for me to take the M3, get out of the vehicle, and defend myself with it. Fortunately, terrible shot that I am, I never had to do so! After a short time, I stopped thinking about possible threats. Despite John Granville's murder a few months earlier, Khartoum seemed like a relatively safe place. But the security rules were that my movements always had to be planned in advance.

Jane and I would eventually move into an uncomfortable two-story bunker-like residence with iron bars and metal plates on all its windows and doors. My new boss had moved from it into a charming smaller house where past DCMs had lived previously. At our first meeting at the embassy, he said to me with an arrogant smile, "I see no reason why you should have the nicer house!"

I had no objection to his taking the better place to live, but as it turned out, this was his view of everything in our working relationship. Thus began what would be a long unhappy year for me as his subordinate.

The U.S. embassy was in a run-down eight-story building that once had been a second-rate hotel. It faced directly onto a major street that, following the murders of John Granville and his driver, had been closed to vehicular traffic. However, the road's closure did little to make the embassy truly secure. It was less than twenty feet from the sidewalk where hundreds of people passed by every day.

Even worse, Sudanese police regularly allowed entry by "essential" vehicles, including delivery trucks, which could have been laden with explosives. As had been the case at the former embassy in Kazakhstan, the regional security officer in Khartoum and his staff constructed a high sandbag barrier in the space between the building and its outer iron fence to reduce the effects of a blast. We knew, though, that this was unlikely to prevent the old building from collapsing on top of us.

My greatest concern about the building was addressing its many safety hazards. I asked the security and management officers to accompany me on a walk up the eight stories. We started from the basement, climbing the emergency stairway to the roof, stopping at each floor to inspect offices. What I found was appalling. In the basement, where a number of local staff worked, the emergency exit had a rusty lock. No one could find the key to open it.

The same was true of the exit to the emergency stairway on the eighth floor, where Americans had offices. There were no stairway lights with backup batteries that would come on if the building's power failed. Old furniture blocked some of the landings; and many of the concrete stairs on the emergency stairway were broken, making them hazardous to walk down, especially in the dark. I found offices with homemade overloaded extension outlets, hot plates, and fuse boxes with worn, exposed wiring.

I made a list and told my colleagues they needed to take immediate action. For starters, we should install proper crash-bar emergency door locks with alarms on each floor, starting with the basement. Emergency lighting, stairway repair, and electrical upgrades needed to follow. I checked up on repairs to make sure all this got done in a timely manner.

During my first week on the job, the COM told me he was in charge of all policy matters and that I should focus exclusively on administration. While DCMs are, indeed, chief operations officers, they also need to be familiar with policy issues when called upon to become acting chiefs of mission. That had certainly been the case when I was DCM in Kazakhstan.

As I began to have introductory meetings with the embassy's agency chiefs and State Department section heads, it became clear few people in the embassy either liked or respected the COM. This was especially true for the USAID mission director. He told me that the COM had been on Christmas holiday leave in the United States when John Granville and his driver were murdered on January 1. Upon getting news of their deaths, the COM refused to cut short his vacation and return to Khartoum.

The AID director was understandably bitter about this, saying he was sure that if terrorists had murdered a State Department officer and his driver, the COM would have immediately come back. Instead, the COM ordered his relatively inexperienced subordinate to handle grieving, traumatized embassy employees. Although I avoided any direct criticism of the COM, my sense was that the director was absolutely right. As chief of mission, you are responsible for all your employees, not just those who happen to work for the State Department. It was now clear why USAID officials in Washington had seemed angry toward me when I attended the memorial for John and his driver.

I assured the mission director I understood how he felt, adding I couldn't change what had happened before my arrival. I promised him, as I had his Washington colleagues, that I would do everything I could to make sure those who committed the vile USAID murders were brought to justice. It took time, but the director and I developed a strong professional relationship. In an odd twist, when he came to dinner at our house one night, he and Jane began to chat and soon discovered they had been grammar school classmates in California!

During my first year on the job, one of my major accomplishments was overseeing the construction of our new embassy complex (NEC) on the outskirts of Khartoum. The NEC project had quite a history. Well before I arrived, the al-Bashir regime had refused to renew visas for its construction workers as well as for the entry of building materials. This was due to the conflictive relationship between our two governments.

As a result, the State Department had been forced to shutter the partially completed complex, which, in addition to a chancery, included a building for USAID and quarters for a marine detachment. Given the dangerous security conditions at our old embassy, the Department of Defense refused to assign marines there. To many, it seemed as if the NEC would never be completed. But Under Secretary of Management Patrick Kennedy saved the day. He set aside $50 million to start up again and finish the project.

Before I left Washington, Kennedy asked to meet with me, which was a highly unusual request coming from an undersecretary as senior officials normally meet just with outgoing ambassadors. Kennedy told me the safety and security of our employees depended on the completion of the NEC. He said that he would always be available to help me and that I shouldn't hesitate to reach out directly to him if needed.

The COM had no interest in the NEC project and was only too happy to have me oversee it. When I arrived in Khartoum, the project had just begun again, but the State Department construction manager told me he was still having trouble getting workers' visas and clearance for construction materials. I turned for help to Ambassador Nasreldin Wali, head of the Americas Desk at Sudan's Ministry of Foreign Affairs (MFA). A decade my junior, Wali was a courtly man who always began our meetings by serving sweet tea and refreshments. We would then make small talk about our families before launching into difficult discussions of serious administrative issues. My chief priority was getting assistance from the Sudanese government to complete our new embassy.

Wali was open to working with me on how we could help each other. During my two years in Khartoum, ours would become a remarkably constructive relationship, with each of us ably representing our respective governments. We eventually would get to know each other's family on social occasions. Without Ambassador Wali's assistance, the United States would never have completed and moved into the NEC, which we did in early 2010.

During that first year as DCM, I frequently traveled to Darfur. Because of deteriorating security conditions there, we limited the amount of time our staff could spend at our lodgings. I agonized every time I had to approve Darfur travel for embassy staff to do political reporting or supervise USAID programs, as I knew how dangerous it was.

Much the same was true in Juba, the capital of semi-autonomous southern Sudan, where we had a large compound, including housing, which had originally been constructed by USAID many years earlier. Being out at night in Juba could be perilous. Drunken former soldiers often set up illegal checkpoints, where they demanded money to let cars pass. On more than one occasion, these armed men stopped our official vehicles but fortunately let them proceed without incident.

As staff increased in the south, many of our employees wound up living in cramped converted shipping containers. Given the hardships of working and living in Juba, which had only a few miles of paved roads and few diversions, U.S. employees served there for only a year. They were also not allowed to be accompanied by family members.

As my year with the COM drew to a most-welcome end, we had a final blow-up. In early 2009, following Israel's military incursion into Gaza, there were large threatening demonstrations in front of our embassy. As Sudan had no diplomatic relations with Israel, protesters targeted the United States because they saw us as complicit enablers of Israel's war with the Palestinians. The demonstrations grew larger and louder, and Assistant Secretary of State for Africa Johnnie Carson called the COM. As a precaution, Carson said we had to reduce our staff by at least 10 percent of all nonessential American employees and their spouses in Khartoum. No accompanying children were allowed at the post, so this was not an issue.

Employees were to leave the capital as soon as possible in a voluntary "authorized departure" back to Washington for two to three months. The COM immediately told me it was my job to get enough American employees to volunteer to meet that goal. I had forty-eight hours to do so before the State Department, he said, would declare an ordered departure, which meant up to half of our staff would be forced to leave.

While being sent off for several months with little to do in a temporary DC job might sound appealing, almost no one ever wishes to be declared nonessential. For starters, this doesn't look good on your performance evaluation. For more altruistic reasons, many employees simply don't want to abandon their colleagues during a challenging time.

Gathering the American staff together, I said that the COM's spouse and Jane, with our two cats, would soon be leaving. I then asked for volunteers, but no hands went up. In fact, it took me several follow-up meetings to persuade the requisite number of employees to leave. It was neither an easy nor a pleasant task. As I recall, several employees burst into tears after agreeing to leave.

Near the end of having our staff on two months of authorized leave, the State Department informed us that then-senator John Kerry would be visiting Khartoum in the coming weeks. As I've mentioned, such high-level official visits are called CODELS (congressional delegations) and are always labor intensive. With less than a full staff in Khartoum, trying to support Senator Kerry, his wife, and a senior congressional assistant was going to be daunting. I reached out to Under Secretary of State Kennedy and asked that our nonessential employees be allowed to return. The decision was Kennedy's, and I pointed out that the demonstrations in Khartoum had now ended. I argued that if it was safe enough for John Kerry to be in Khartoum, the same should hold for our staff. I was pleased when Kennedy agreed, and with a full embassy complement, the visit went well.

Jane had not returned immediately after the authorized departure was lifted but began her travel back to Sudan shortly after the Kerry visit. She was flying to Khartoum via an overnight stop in Amsterdam with our cats, Chessie and Pasha. Jane was already airborne and on her way to Khartoum when I received a call from the embassy's senior Sudanese local employee who was at the airport awaiting her. Because of the H1N1 swine flu in nearby Egypt, he told me Sudan's government had just banned all animals, including domestic ones, from entering the country. He noted sadly that when Jane arrived, our beloved cats would be seized by customs officials and then killed.

As the embassy had received no advance notice of this new policy, and cats were not known to carry swine flu, it seemed grossly unfair to me that our vaccinated and healthy felines would be denied entry. I went into the COM's office to ask for help. He listened impatiently and then said curtly, "I'm sorry, Mark, but there's nothing I can do."

I was flabbergasted by his refusal but decided perhaps Ambassador Wali at the foreign ministry could help. I called, and he said he would do everything he could to resolve the issue. When Jane arrived at the airport a few hours later, I gave her the bad news. I reassured her that I thought there must be a way to resolve the problem. To prevent the cats from being seized by local authorities, we remained with them in the airport's arrival hall. Ambassador Wali called and said apologetically that he'd spoken with the foreign minister, who refused to allow the cats to enter.

It was now getting late at night, and I called the COM at home to explain our situation. If the Sudanese refused to let Jane and the cats enter, she would have to return to the United States with them on a flight leaving the next day. We were unwilling to lose our much-loved pets. He was obviously annoyed to hear from me and told me in a loud voice that he was not willing to reach out to one of his contacts in the presidency on such a "personal" issue. The conversation grew heated, and the COM shouted at me, "I don't give a damn about your cats!"

When angry, I've never been one to lack a quick comeback, "Actually, you don't give a damn about me, Jane, or anyone else in the embassy, do you?"

With that, he slammed down the receiver of his landline telephone. As the U.S. chief of mission, a phone call from him would have immediately resolved the problem. But without his intervention, Jane was forced, with little sleep, to board a flight with the cats the next day and return at our expense to Washington.

The month before the COM departed, the two of us had only brief frosty discussions about work issues, avoiding each other whenever possible. I would dare say there were few in the mission who were unhappy when he left and I became the chargé d'affaires. It would be close to two months before Bob Whitehead, the new COM, arrived at the post. It proved to be not only a busy time but also a dangerous one for me as acting head of the U.S. embassy.

A few weeks into my chargé tenure, one of the political officers noticed what appeared to be young men surveilling the embassy from an adjacent building. She reported what she'd seen to me, and I informed our security officer. He, along with others in the embassy, began working with the Sudanese police and intelligence officials and discovered there was a small group of men conducting surveillance of my movements. One of the first security precautions I'd learned in the foreign service was to vary my times and routes to and from overseas embassies. It was important, no matter where you were posted, not to leave and return home at the same times each day and not use the same routes. Most overseas kidnappings and killings of American diplomats occur during their departures from or arrivals at home.

Mission employees were reminded to take this daily precaution seriously and not be predictable in their daily routes as well as in their after-hours activities. After John Granville's murder, our American staff was not allowed to have private cars; all traveled in armored embassy vehicles, which added to their safety. The real threat appeared to be against me, as members of the terrorist cell were also observed surveilling Jane's and my residence. Accordingly, security was increased there, and my departure and arrival times were significantly varied. As the acting chief of mission, I not only had a bodyguard in my vehicle but also was followed by a "chase car" directly behind me, which had three heavily armed Sudanese guards from our embassy security office.

In due time, Sudanese security forces arrested the six-man terrorist squad surveilling me. Police confiscated and showed me spreadsheets in which the men had meticulously documented my every movement and the routes my driver used. It was chilling to see this despite the fact that between the security professionals in the embassy and Sudanese authorities, Jane and I felt protected at all times.

Not long after this incident, Sudan's Ministry of Justice announced it would begin the trial of the five men accused of killing John Granville and his driver, Abdel Abbas Rahama. As John was from New York State, and his murder was a federal crime, the FBI had sent an Arabic-speaking agent from its New York City office who would observe the trial. He was accompanied by a New York City police detective.

Although our security officer recommended against my doing so, I was determined to attend the opening of the trial. The acting USAID country director said she wanted to join me. For my part, I'd promised USAID officials in Washington to do everything I could to bring these men to justice, and I felt it was important to make my presence known in the courtroom. On the first day of the trial, my USAID colleague, the FBI agent, the NYC detective, a security officer and several embassy bodyguards and I stood in a plaza in front of the courthouse. Family members and supporters of the accused men standing near us began to murmur. I asked the FBI agent what they were saying. While it was fairly nasty stuff, it didn't seem to us that we were in any danger. A few minutes later, he whispered in my ear, "Sir, we should go inside."

When we got to the entrance, we were escorted into the courtroom by a uniformed Sudanese official. The USAID director and I sat in the front of the room with our companions in the row behind us. The wood-paneled courtroom was surprisingly small. Soon the five accused terrorists entered with their hands and feet shackled. The judge's raised tribunal faced a dozen wooden benches, with front rows reserved for defense and prosecution lawyers.

The youngest in the group, Mohamed Makawi Ibrahim Mohamed, short and slightly built, was the ringleader and alleged gunman who had fatally shot John and the driver. Makawi and the others wore dark-green prison garb and remained standing in the custody of two guards. What immediately impressed me was how Makawi smirked and casually chatted with the guards, who smiled as if hearing an amusing story. The room slowly filled up with the men's families and supporters. The black-robed judge came in last.

The defense attorneys, seated to our right, immediately requested that their clients be unshackled. The alleged killers were seated in an area directly facing the USAID director and me. With the FBI agent interpreting for us, the judge asked that the men's handcuffs be removed but not their leg restraints. Makawi fixed his eyes on me. I've never felt such hatred coming from another person; he knew exactly who I was and why I was there. It occurred to me that with his hands free, it wouldn't have been difficult for this accused murderer to grab one of the inattentive guards' loosely holstered pistols and shoot me. Despite this, I continued to stare defiantly back at him.

Scanning the front bench in front of us, the judge announced there was no one present from Sudan's State Prosecutor's Office. Makawi was from a prominent family; and along with his co-defendants, he was represented by well-known Sudanese attorneys. *Where are the prosecutors?* I thought. If they hadn't come to prosecute the case, then the Ministry of Justice must not be intending to try the men.

The judge declared the trial in recess, saying it would reconvene only if he had assurances that prosecutors would appear next time. Looking toward my companions and me, he said in fluent English that we would be allowed to exit the courtroom before others left. I was furious because it appeared charges against the men would simply be dropped.

The following day, I requested a meeting with the minister of justice. I'd met him previously; and once again, he greeted me cordially in his office, providing the customary refreshments. He acted as if nothing was amiss and expressed surprise that I'd urgently wanted to see him. I cut directly to the chase. "Mr. Minister, the failure of your government to prosecute this act of terrorism against the United States will negatively affect all aspects of our bilateral relationship. There will be immediate consequences unless Sudan vigorously prosecutes the charges against these men."

As acting chief of mission, I was greatly exceeding my authority. To begin with, rather than protesting through the foreign ministry, the normal diplomatic channel, I'd gone directly to the minister of justice and issued an ultimatum on behalf of the U.S. government. I'd done this after initially reporting to the State Department what had happened at the opening of the trial and had received no instructions on how to proceed. Since I wasn't told to stand down and do nothing, I took a chance. I opted to confront Sudan's government and then inform the department afterward. It was a risky gambit and could have failed badly, especially if the Sudanese had called my bluff. In this case, it was successful. After a few weak excuses, the minister offered his apologies. He assured me that state prosecutors would be present when the trial resumed.

The acting USAID director and I went to the next session, and this time, the prosecutors were there. It was obvious they had come prepared to make the case against the men. With the trial now underway, I felt no need personally to be there for future sessions. Instead, I had an Arabic-speaking political officer attend and report on the trial's progress. In June 2009, four of the men, including Makawi, were sentenced to death for the murders. The fifth man received a two-year sentence for providing the weapon used in the attack. USAID, plus the Granville and Rahama families, was satisfied that justice had been served. I too was pleased John's and his driver's killers would be punished. Such satisfaction for all of us would be short-lived.

Just a year later, the four men sentenced to death "somehow" escaped from Khartoum's high-security British-era prison where they'd been confined. The embassy immediately requested that the foreign ministry provide us with information on how they had managed to flee. We were told the convicts had tunneled their way out of the prison. But when we asked to see the tunnel, Sudan's government changed its story, saying that the men had inexplicably obtained a weapon, killed a policeman, wounded another, and then successfully escaped, presumably out the front door. Of course, this was ridiculous. It was obvious that Sudan had let the men go free. One was recaptured, returned to jail, but subsequently pardoned.

In 2013, the State Department designated two of the other fugitives as U.S. global terrorists," but they remain at large to this day. Makawi reportedly joined the Al-Shabaab terrorists in Somalia, where he was subsequently killed. It's not clear if the United States was involved in his death, but that mattered less to me than the fact he had met a violent end.

Jane had returned to Sudan after finding someone in Washington to take care of our cats. In the late spring of 2009, we went to the airport to greet Bob Whitehead, the new chief of mission, and his wife. Bob knew Sudan well, having served previously in Khartoum and opened our consulate in Juba. He'd spent most of his career in Africa, spoke fluent French and some Arabic, and had been a DCM several times. This was his first posting as a COM. His elegant and beautiful wife, Agathe, originally from Rwanda, was outgoing, energetic, generous, and absolutely delightful.

Like me, Bob had an academic background and had been a Fulbright lecturer in Zaire. Thin, wiry, sharp-witted, and keenly intelligent, Bob and I hit it off from the start. Unlike his predecessor, he wanted me to work with him on policy issues. Given Bob's previous experience in Sudan, I learned a great deal about the country from him. He had excellent contacts from his prior tours, which gave him almost immediate access to political circles.

Bob was also open and fair with the staff, which was a major change from his predecessor. He and I complemented each other in working effectively as a front-office team. Of all my bosses, he was one of the absolute best for whom I'd worked. The positive transformation of Embassy Khartoum in a short time under Bob's leadership was nothing short of amazing.

Just when Jane's and my final year in Sudan took a major turn for the better, her parents' health went into a sudden decline. In late 2009, Jane's mom, Mary Alice, who was eighty-six, became gravely ill. Jane flew back to Wyoming and was there with her two sisters when Mary Alice passed away peacefully at a hospice. Three months later, Jane's dad, Frank, succumbed to lung cancer at the same hospice. Once again, Jane returned to be with him in his final days. I was fond of Jane's parents and saddened by their passing.

During one of Jane's absences, former president Jimmy Carter and his wife, Rosslyn, arrived in Khartoum. The Carter Center has been involved in Sudan since 1986 and, following the 1989 coup that brought Omar al-Bashir to power, actively promoted peace and a return to democracy. The purpose of their April 2010 visit was to monitor elections for local, state, and national offices throughout Sudan, plus separate polling in the ten states in South Sudan. The elections there were part of the 2005 Comprehensive Peace Agreement (CPA) and would be followed by a January 2011 referendum on unity or separation for the south. South Sudanese president Salva Kiir's ruling Sudan People's Liberation Movement (SPLM) won 93 percent of the vote in the south's ten states, all but assuring the referendum would favor independence the following year.

During the elections, President Carter personally visited dozens of polling stations, and the Carter Center announced the election had met international standards. Jimmy Carter, at eighty-six, and Rosslyn, just three years younger, demonstrated amazing stamina and commitment to promoting democracy.

A month earlier, I had overseen our move to Khartoum's New Embassy Compound (NEC). Under Secretary Pat Kennedy would arrive shortly afterward for the formal inauguration of a building that never would have been completed without his support. In those final months, I also spent a fair amount of time in Juba.

Chris Datta, the highly competent consul general, had recently departed, and I needed to provide supervision and support for the series of acting consuls general who replaced him before his permanent successor arrived. With the local election results in the south overwhelmingly supporting Salva Kiir, who favored independence, it was time for us to begin the expansion of the consulate compound. We started construction work on the existing main office building, which would soon become our new embassy's chancery in South Sudan.

By then, I realized I would not get an ambassadorship as my next assignment. I'd had a number of discussions with the deputy in AF, and Bob had been extremely supportive of my getting my own mission, but nothing was available. However, my detested first boss in Khartoum was now ambassador to Equatorial Guinea and would be leaving in two years. Clearly, what I needed to do was return to Washington and lobby hard to be his successor.

CHAPTER 12

On the Road to Becoming an Ambassador

CAREER FOREIGN SERVICE officers seeking an ambassadorship often return for a Washington assignment to lobby. Certain jobs at the State Department, including working for an under or assistant secretary, provide excellent launching pads. That's because these officials are the ones who make nominations and, in some cases, sit on the committee that chooses ambassadorial candidates.

I returned to Washington after Khartoum to begin the lobbying process. However, after two stressful and sometimes dangerous years in Sudan, I wasn't ready to jump quite yet into a senior State Department job. Following so many trips to Darfur, where I often saw horrific conditions in its internally displaced-persons camps, I was emotionally burned out and needed a break. That's why I applied for and got a year-long State Department fellowship to teach at George Washington University (GWU).

The State Department has a number of what are called "billets," or non-departmental assignments, which allow foreign service officers to study or teach for a year or more. Such billets are at U.S. universities and military command headquarters where the State Department pays your full salary in what amounts to a government fellowship.

For many years, GWU, just a few blocks from the State Department, had had a senior diplomacy fellow teach undergraduates at its School of Media and Public Affairs (SMPA). The position opened in the summer of 2010. I arrived at the media school in the late summer of 2010 and was surprised to learn that I was not expected to teach until the second semester. This allowed me time during the first semester to prepare for the course and make small changes to my predecessor's fine syllabus.

My course was entitled U.S. Government Public Diplomacy and began with an overview of the establishment of the first government information program, the Committee on Public Information or Creel Committee (1917–19). Next was a discussion of public diplomacy during World War II, including the founding of the Voice of America (1942). This was followed by a deep dive into the politics of the Cold War, legislation creating the Fulbright program (1946), and the establishment of the U.S. Information Agency in 1953. After the demise of the latter in 1999, I traced how public diplomacy was incorporated into the State Department.

In the thirty years that I had been away from teaching, there had been enormous changes in the classroom. For one thing, almost all of the students arrived with small laptop computers, used presumably to take notes but, in many cases, to surf the Internet during class. They no longer were assigned articles placed on reserve in a library reading room. Instead, this assigned material was online, where they could access and download it at any time. Class attendance, submission of assignments, and grading were all done via computer platforms like Blackboard. Initially, the technology baffled me. Fortunately, GWU assigned two excellent graduate student assistants to help me.

What I said during the first class was that I was not there to prepare students for careers in the foreign service. Although the course might be useful for that, my intention was far broader. The public affairs tools we'd discuss would be equally useful and applicable in business and other professional pursuits.

My secondary goal was to provide them with a historical context for understanding U.S. diplomacy. Given my American Studies background, I integrated a great deal of history into the revised syllabus. The semester went by quickly, and I found myself looking forward to classes. Of all the teaching I've done, this was without a doubt the most rewarding.

In early 2011, I was offered a second year at GWU, but by then, I was sixty-two years old. The mandatory retirement for foreign service officers is sixty-five, and I knew I needed to take a senior job at the State Department the next year if I were to have any chance of obtaining an ambassadorship.

II

After my year at GWU, I was pleased to get the job of chief of staff for the State Department Under Secretary for Civilian Security, Democracy, and Human Rights. When I interviewed for the position with Undersecretary Maria Otero, she told me she was looking for someone with strong management and leadership skills who could supervise a front office staff of twenty, including both foreign and civil service employees. She stressed that her chief of staff would be responsible for personnel issues and overall administration.

The chief of staff job was not an especially challenging one for me. Having previously been the deputy coordinator in the Office for Reconstruction and Stabilization (S/CRS), which had a far larger staff, I was already experienced in carrying out the full range of management tasks required by the job. Of greatest value were the working-level contacts I developed with key senior officials, which provided me with an understanding of how the State Department an on a daily basis, including who had resources in which offices. These contacts would prove invaluable to me as an ambassador.

Early in my tenure, Otero asked me to help political appointee Ronan Farrow, the son of Mia Farrow and Woody Allen, set up an office for youth affairs in her undersecretariat. Ronan had previously worked for Special Representative for Afghanistan and Pakistan Ambassador Richard Holbrooke. When Holbrook died in December 2010, Secretary Clinton suggested that Ronan, who was just twenty-three years old at that time, might carry out a youth outreach initiative for the State Department.

The major problem was that beyond the salaries for Ronan and several Foreign and Civil Service assistants, there was no budget for the new youth office. Any funding for travel and programs had to come from the undersecretary's front office, which put me in the position of holding the new office's budget strings. Thus, I became Ronan's paymaster, not the easiest of roles.

Anyone who has ever met Ronan comes away dazzled by his brilliance and charm. By the time he started at the State Department, he'd already received a law degree from Yale, passed the New York Bar Exam, and worked for a leading New York City law firm. But for all of his accomplishments, Ronan had never hired a staff and set up or run an office.

Kathy Giles-Diaz, the veteran public affairs officer in the front office, and I did all we could to assist Ronan in establishing what was called the Office of Global Youth Issues. We worked hard to counsel and share our experience with him.

That said, it was a difficult year for Ronan. Despite his overseeing some promising programs, he found it challenging to run an office and supervise staff. He would leave the State Department in the spring of 2012 for a year at Oxford on a Rhodes Fellowship. In recent years, Ronan has established himself as a top-flight Pulitzer Prize-winning investigative journalist.

But getting back to my experience, working for Undersecretary Otero gave me a great deal of face time with those who would help me secure an ambassadorship. The most important of these was Assistant Secretary for the Bureau of Africa Affairs (AF) Johnnie Carson, whom I'd met when I served in Sudan. With strong support from my good friend and former boss in Khartoum Bob Whitehead, Assistant Secretary Carson was the key person in my being nominated as U.S. ambassador to Equatorial Guinea. In the fall of 2011, he put me at the top of AF's short list of three candidates for the job. I now needed to line up support for the Equatorial Guinea job with members of what is called the D Committee, composed of senior State Department officials who choose nominees.

The first person I approached was Undersecretary for Management Patrick Kennedy, whom I'd gotten to know well from working with his office on the construction of our new embassy compound in Sudan. He was on the D Committee and had enormous influence in the selection of ambassadors. I met Pat in his spacious suite on the State Department's seventh floor. After some initial small talk, I came to the point, asking if he'd support me to be ambassador to Equatorial Guinea. With a bemused expression on his face, he replied, "Well, Mark, you're the first person to come and ask me for support on the embassy in Malabo. And

I have to tell you the truth. I don't expect many others will be interested in Equatorial Guinea, given what a tough place it is. But I'm sure you and Jane know what you'd be getting into. So yes, you have my full and enthusiastic vote for the job!"

I thanked him and as I was leaving his office, I heard him call out, "Are you sure you want to go to Equatorial Guinea?"

I turned and saw him smiling as he closed the door.

I also made the rounds to speak with other undersecretaries, but I knew that Assistant Secretary Carson's and Pat's support would likely be sufficient to have the D Committee vote for me as ambassador to Equatorial Guinea. After the committee met in early November, I got a call from personnel congratulating me on having gotten the initial nod.

However, this was only the first step in actually getting an ambassadorship. Until the White House publicly announces your nomination, you are sworn to secrecy as you go through the various vetting processes. At the most, if someone asks about your next assignment, you are allowed to say, "I'm being considered for a mission," but forbidden from divulging where that might be. I was allowed to tell Jane but cautioned her not to breathe a word to anyone else. I did make one exception, though, and that was with my father, Louie.

After almost five years of being in an independent-living apartment, followed by several more in another with assisted-living services at his retirement center, my dad moved in 2010 to the nursing wing of the facility. At age ninety-seven, he began a long final descent into dementia.

After returning from Sudan, I visited him every month. Jane and I were always there to celebrate the holidays and his birthday. At first, he seemed forgetful and occasionally confused about where he was, but by 2011, there were times when he didn't recognize me. Nevertheless, my dad was always cheerful and happy to see me, even when he wasn't quite sure who I was. While it was difficult to watch him decline both physically and mentally, I treasure the time I spent with him in his final years.

I went to see him at the beginning of December 2011, just a few weeks after the D Committee voted to give me an ambassadorship. When I arrived at his private room, Louie was alert and clearly knew who I was. He seemed particularly intent on inquiring about how I was doing. He asked if I had enough money and if Jane and I were happily married. Louie had always been extremely fond of Jane, as she was of him, and so he was pleased when I told him we had no financial worries and were happy together.

He then looked at me with a somewhat troubled look in his hazel-brown eyes. "But how are you doing in your job, Mark? Is everything okay?"

"Well, Dad, I'm doing extremely well. Actually, I want you to be among the first to know that I'm going to be an ambassador."

There was a long pause as if my dad was slowly taking in what I'd just told him. And then his face lit up. "Ambassador! That's good, Mark. That's very good!"

It was the happiest I'd seen him in years. As I later thought back on my visit, it was as if he knew he could now depart peacefully in the knowledge that everything would be well with me.

As I was leaving, my father and I embraced. Then he did something unusual. An orderly had just entered, and Louie asked for his help in standing and walking to the room's door. As I went to the elevator, I saw my dad standing there in his favorite tan cardigan sweater and an old black cap he liked to wear, even indoors. He smiled and waved goodbye. It was the last time I saw my dad before his passing. That endearing mental image of him will remain with me for as long as I live.

Shortly after this, he entered hospice care at the retirement center. He passed away peacefully on the evening of December 11 before I could get back from Washington to be with him. When Jane and I returned to make final arrangements for his funeral, the nursing staff gave me my father's shiny old black worn leather wallet. They put it for safekeeping in a locked cabinet at the front desk. Inside, I found a few dollars, photos of my mother and me, and a folded yellowed news article.

It was a story written by a journalist from my hometown newspaper, *The Providence Journal*. We'd met in Uzbekistan after 9/11 when I was the public affairs officer, and he was one of the dozens of reporters I came to know. The journalist asked if he could mention he'd met a fellow Rhode Islander in a story he was filing, which I said was fine.

My father saw the piece, cut it out, and carried it in his wallet for the next decade. People in the retirement center told me afterward that he would often take it out and say to them proudly, "Read this! It's about my son in Uzbekistan."

There isn't a day that passes that I don't think about and miss my extraordinary father.

III

In January, I took the required two-week-long ambassadorial seminar that is known as "Charm School" by foreign service officers. In theory, it's meant to teach you everything you might ever possibly need to know to be both a charming and effective ambassador. Of course, that's quite a lot to pack into a ten-day course! For those of us who were career officers, it had some useful information and guidance but hardly prepared us for the many things we would soon confront in leading an embassy.

There were only ten of us in the January course: nine career officers and a genial political- appointee on his way to the Netherlands. My former boss and good friend Bob Whitehead had been nominated to be ambassador to the West African nation of Togo. I was glad he was one of my classmates. The "star" of the class was Chris Stevens, who was slated for the important post of ambassador to Libya. Chris was handsome, intelligent, personable, and self-deprecating.

Still in his early fifties, he grew up in California, where he attended Berkeley as an undergraduate and received a law degree from Hastings School of Law in San Francisco. A former Peace Corps volunteer in Morocco, Chris had a meteoric foreign service career. Entering in 1990, he served in Israel, Egypt, Saudi Arabia, Syria, and Libya, where he returned in 2010–2011 as the U.S. special representative to the National Transitional Council during the civil war there. He was widely regarded as an expert on Libya and the ideal choice to be an ambassador in Tripoli.

I don't recall much from Charm School except for one class in particular. It would come back to haunt me on September 11, 2012, the day Chris was killed in Benghazi along with three other Americans from his embassy. We were told by the lecturer that, as ambassadors, our highest responsibility was for the well-being and safety of those in our mission. In addition, we were tasked with assisting and protecting American citizens living and working in our assigned countries. The buck literally stopped with us. Had Chris lived, he would have taken full responsibility for what had happened. After carefully weighing the pros and cons of going to Benghazi, he decided to make the visit knowing full well the risks.

The months after Charm School were busy ones for me. They were mostly filled with submitting final paperwork to the Department and the White House, including financial disclosures and highly detailed security background information, even though I already had a high-level clearance. During this time, the State Department's Bureau of African Affairs asked our embassy in Malabo to secure what is called in diplomatic parlance *agrément*, a French term indicating approval by the host government for an incoming ambassador.

After a series of delays, the Equatoguinean government granted me agrément. On March 16, the White House formally announced President Obama had nominated me to be the next U.S. ambassador to Equatorial Guinea. I was finally able to talk about the nomination, including gathering information from those in the U.S. government who were knowledgeable about Equatorial Guinea. However, I was an "ambassador designate" until confirmed by the Senate, and I was not allowed to consult with experts outside of government, including those in academia and think-tanks.

The next hurdle was getting a date to testify before the Africa subcommittee of the U.S. Senate's Foreign Relations Committee. My hearing before the Senate subcommittee on Africa was set for May 17, 2012, and I threw myself into preparations. I practiced with Jane delivering my five-minute opening statement. She quizzed me on a range of issues I thought might come up. We both worked incredibly hard. In addition, the AF Bureau arranged what in diplomacy is called a murder board. This included Africa experts at the State Department who grilled me in a simulated hearing. Finally, I took a one-day course at FSI on Testifying Before Congress, as this was the first time I would be questioned at a hearing.

Despite all that preparation, I was still nervous as Jane and I arrived at the Senate Dirksen Office Building for my hearing in room 419. We entered an ornate chamber with beautiful dark-paneled wood, stately columns, warm indirect lighting, and a raised dais where the senators sat. It was all rather intimidating. The two other nominees also headed to Africa, and I each had what seemed like very small tables in front of us with looming video cameras on each side of the room to record the event. Jane, along with the other nominees' families and well-wishers, sat in the row immediately behind us.

On the floor facing us was a set of three lights: green, yellow, and red. We'd been told that we had just five minutes for our opening statements and that the lights would indicate when we were close to that mark, with red indicating we were out of time. Jane and I had practiced the length of my presentation, which was just short of the maximum.

I was the second to give my opening statement in which I spoke of my previous experience, the challenges Equatorial Guinea presented, and the three policy areas that would be my priorities if confirmed. The first was promoting good governance and democracy in a country ruled by the same authoritarian leader for nearly four decades. The second was related and focused on upholding U.S. foreign policy to advance respect for human rights. Finally, I said I would protect the welfare of those in my mission and the five hundred Americans living and working, mostly for U.S. petroleum companies, in Equatorial Guinea. In that connection, I would promote U.S. business interests by working to safeguard maritime security in the Gulf of Guinea. That was a lot to cover in just five minutes!

I then took questions for the next twenty minutes. Nothing I was asked was unexpected, and I answered each question by drawing on the detailed information I knew by heart, rarely needing to look at my notes on the table. I spoke about everything from Equatorial Guinea's Spanish colonial past to post-independence politics and its sad history of brutal dictatorial rule.

Senator Chris Coons, who chaired the subcommittee, came up afterward to congratulate Jane and me, saying I would have no trouble being confirmed by the Senate. Indeed, the Foreign Relations Committee quickly approved my nomination. It was then sent to the full Senate, which confirmed me in a unanimous voice vote on June 29. Now all that remained was the ambassadorial swearing-in ceremony at the State Department. Then, I would officially be Ambassador Mark L. Asquino.

I chose to have my July 16 swearing-in ceremony take place in the grand Benjamin Franklin Ballroom on the eighth floor of the State Department. I asked my friend and mentor Undersecretary Pat Kennedy to administer the oath of office. In addition to foreign service colleagues, family members attending included Jane's sister Ann and her husband, Tom; my then-eighty-five-year-old aunt Betty and her daughter Cheryl; plus my cousin Lynn, who came with her friend Kelly Stuart; and my cousin Michael. I was delighted that several of my Brown University classmates traveled to Washington to attend the event. These included Mollie Sandock, who came with her husband, Jim Brokaw, as well as Chris and Judy Hunter.

Before administering the oath of office on a raised platform in the center of the vast room, Undersecretary Kennedy spoke at times humorously about my long foreign service career and ability to perform well in challenging places. Jane held the Bible on which I placed my left hand, raising my right as I solemnly swore to defend the Constitution of the United States against all enemies, foreign and domestic.

After signing a document officially making me an ambassador, I spoke briefly about how my parents had always been there to guide and help me. I told the story of the last time I'd seen my dad and told him I was going to be an ambassador. I then turned to Jane and said that I would never have become an ambassador without her constant love, encouragement, and support.

There were two guests at the ceremony who would come to loom large during my ambassadorial tenure. Tutu Alicante was an outspoken critic of the Obiang regime, and as a young man, he was forced to flee the country into political exile in the United States. Eventually becoming an American citizen, he received law degrees from the University of Tennessee and Columbia and focused as an attorney on labor law and international human rights. In 2010, he founded EG Justice, a U.S.-based nongovernment organization dedicated to denouncing human rights violations and corruption in his homeland.

Tutu and I spoke on the phone after my confirmation, and he asked if he could attend my swearing-in with Equatorial Guinea's leading human rights lawyer Fabián Nsue. After the ceremony, Tutu and Fabian came up and introduced themselves. A short baldheaded man with an intense manner, Fabián spoke no English, so we conversed briefly in Spanish. I learned that he was on a visit to the United States and would soon return to EG. As it turned out, our brief acquaintanceship would lead to one of my first major confrontations with EG's government.

CHAPTER 13

Equatorial Guinea:
A Culture of Fear

I T WAS LATE on an August evening when our flight began its approach to Malabo International Airport on tiny Bioko Island, which is just twelve miles across the water from the eastern coast of Cameroon. Looking out the window, I saw in the distance a smokestack-like structure flaring a bright-orange flame that shot high into the starless sky. It cast an eerie infernal glow on everything around it. Next to it was the Marathon Petroleum Corporation's vast liquefied natural gas processing plant, with its twisting tubular metal structures and twinkling off-white lights. Both were on Punta Europa, a spit of land jutting out into the sea. It was the site not only of the industrial complex but also as I would later learn, of a U.S.-style housing compound with well-kept bungalows and numerous amenities for American employees. From the air, Punta Europa seemed surreal. Indeed, this would prove an apt introduction for Jane and my next three years in Equatorial Guinea.

During my first week at the embassy, one of the American employees used the phrase "a culture of fear" to describe what life was like for the million-plus inhabitants of this Spanish-speaking authoritarian country. They were words that I would recall time and again as ambassador. In the introduction and earlier chapters of this book, I've written briefly about Equatorial Guinea's unusual and tragic history. Before I continue my personal story, it's now time to elaborate briefly on this history.[7]

As I've noted previously, from the late fifteenth to the late eighteenth centuries, what someday would become Equatorial Guinea was under

---

[7] Much of my historical discussion is drawn from Randall Fegley's *Equatorial Guinea: An African Tragedy* (New York: Peter Lang Publishing Inc, 1989).

Portuguese sovereignty. In 1777, Portugal signed a treaty with Spain, giving it not only Fernando Po Island but also adjacent possessions on the Central African mainland. Spain showed little interest in this new African possession.

And so, enter the British. After legally abolishing slavery in 1807, Great Britain took a keen interest in Fernando Po, seeing it as a well-located waystation in the Gulf of Guinea to resettle slaves the British Navy had freed from other nations on the high seas. To this end in 1828, Great Britain formally leased the island from Spain and established the first permanent settlement on Fernando Po.

Their capital was named Port Clarence after the Duke of Clarence, and the small outpost had a large natural harbor. The British made peace with the indigenous Bubi tribe, settled the now-free slaves on Fernando Po, and in 1837 offered to purchase it from Spain along with the island of Annobón, off the coast of Angola.

After several years of negotiations, Great Britain finally agreed in 1841 to Spain's high asking price. But in a surprising move, the Spanish Parliament (or Cortes) decided it didn't want to sell the islands after all. However, after turning down the sale, Spain told the British they were welcome to remain on Fernando Po and continue appointing the island's governors. It was not until 1858 that Madrid finally sent its own representative to govern Fernando Po.

The Berlin Conference, convened in 1884 by Germany's Otto von Bismarck, would become known by historians as the Scramble for Africa. It allowed the European countries attending to divide the African continent among themselves and infamously colonize and commercially exploit its people and resources. The "victors" emerging from the conference were Great Britain, France, Belgium, and Germany, with Spain largely pushed aside as others seized its holdings. Eventually, Spain was left with only Fernando Po and several other small islands, plus a greatly reduced Rio Muni territory on the mainland.

In 1898, having been defeated in the Spanish-American War, Spain lost most of its remaining empire, including Cuba, Puerto Rico, and the Philippines. It was only then that it saw the commercial potential of Fernando Po and Rio Muni, or Spanish Guinea, as it was known. The

Spanish established a thriving plantation economy in their tiny African colony. Cacao and palm oil became major cash crops in Fernando Po while timber and coffee were exported in large quantities to Spain from the Rio Muni mainland.

In need of a larger workforce on Fernando Po, Spain moved Fang tribe members from the mainland. The Fang gradually marginalized the indigenous Bubi tribe, treating them as second-class citizens. As the plantation economy grew in the early twentieth century, Spain still lacked sufficient local labor for its plantations. This led to their bringing in large numbers of indentured plantation workers, mostly from British-ruled Nigeria and, to a lesser extent from Liberia and Sierra Leone.

During the decades that followed, Fernando Po boasted a robust commercial infrastructure, including coffee processing plants, fish-canning factories, and warehouses crammed with locally produced cacao. Parts of the island became vacation spots for Spanish tourists. Meanwhile, Rio Muni on the mainland developed but at a far slower pace.

In 1936, at the start of the Spanish Civil War, Generalissimo Francisco Franco's Nationalist forces easily defeated the Left-leaning Republican government's military regiment stationed on Fernando Po. Following World War II, Spanish Guinea continued to have economic importance for Spain. These years witnessed various indigenous, political, and social movements begin to call for the colony's autonomy, if not outright independence. When Spain was finally admitted to the United Nations in 1955, Franco came under increasing international pressure to decolonize Spanish Guinea. The Franco regime fiercely resisted losing the lucrative economic benefits derived from this colony.

Despite this, there continued to be a push for independence, with two opposing camps competing over the colony's future. The Bubis strongly advocated for their own, independent nation on Fernando Po Island, leaving a Fang-ruled country in Rio Muni on the mainland. But the Fang and the Franco regime favored a union of Fernando Po and Rio Muni as a single independent nation. Not surprisingly, it was this option that prevailed.

MARK L. ASQUINO

In one of history's ironies, Franco's authoritarian government supervised the drafting of a democratic constitution for the new country. Predictably, many of its provisions granted strong powers to the chief of state. Nevertheless, the constitution paid lip service to create a multiparty, multiethnic democratic state. In an August 1968 referendum supervised by the United Nations, 64.3 percent of the colony's inhabitants, including a slim majority of Bubis, approved the new constitution.

In the September presidential elections that followed, Francisco Macias, a former minor colonial bureaucrat, won in the second round of voting. As mentioned in the introduction, although democratically elected, Macias would soon become a tyrannical despot during his eleven-year reign of terror.

Born in 1924 to an Ensangui-clan Fang-tribe family in a village near the mainland city of Mongomo, Macias had what were decidedly undistinguished and unpromising beginnings. He was a notoriously poor student who failed the Spanish colonial civil service examination three times. Finally, on his fourth try, he passed the test but was relegated to the lowly job of being an orderly in the forestry service. In 1950, using his Fang language skills, he secured a court interpreter position. From there, despite his limited education, Macias rose steadily in the Spanish colonial bureaucracy. He was reportedly seen by his supervisors as someone who was not very bright but completely dedicated to advancing Spain's interests.

The Spaniards, though, were in for an unpleasant surprise. Beneath the surface, Macias harbored deep-seated resentment and anger toward Spain. And quite unexpectedly, he proved to be a talented orator in his native Fang, using emotional nationalist rhetoric to move local audiences. Macias also was a shrewd politician whose skills went far beyond his fiery oratory. To win the 1968 presidential election, he formed an alliance with a former Bubi rival, which allowed Macias to triumph in the second round of voting.

Soon after becoming president, Macias turned on his former Spanish masters, denouncing Spain and threatening its citizens who were still working in the country. By early March 1969, hundreds of

Spaniards, many with much-needed technical abilities, were evacuated by the Spanish government from its former colony. Macias also raged and threatened the Nigerian plantation workers, forcing most of them to leave as well.

But the worst was yet to come. Macias used a March 1969 coup attempt by his foreign minister as a pretext to clamp down manically on anyone he perceived to be an enemy. He declared a state of emergency and rounded-up dozens of the country's most prominent politicians, including members of his own party as well as his erstwhile Bubi allies. He had most of them summarily executed, and those who escaped immediate death were imprisoned and tortured at Malabo's colonial-era Black Beach Prison.

It's estimated that between fifty to one hundred thousand Equatoguineans were executed or simply disappeared during Macias's eleven years of savage rule. Another one hundred thousand fled, including many of the country's most educated and capable citizens. Equatorial Guinea became known as the Auschwitz of Africa. To stop his countrymen from escaping by sea, he burned the country's fishing fleet, destroying what was left of a once-lucrative industry. Thus began a culture of fear in Equatorial Guinea that would continue long after Macias was gone.

Macias dismantled the country's fundamental institutions. He replaced the 1968 constitution with one giving him absolute power and making him president for life. Creating a cult of personality, he declared himself Equatorial Guinea's "unique miracle" and "grand master of education and culture." His was the only political party allowed, and initially, it was called the Unique National Party (Partido Unico Nacional).

Teodoro Obiang Nguema Mbasogo was one of the president's nephews. Born in 1942 to a poor family in a village near Mongomo, Obiang joined the colonial military guard as a young man. In 1961, he was one of a small select group of promising young soldiers chosen by the Spanish to attend a two-year officer training course at Spain's General Military Academy in Zaragoza. Obiang graduated as a lieutenant in

1963 and returned to Spanish Guinea, where he began to rise through the military ranks.

By the early 1970s, Obiang was a lieutenant colonel and became the military commander of Fernando Po Island. Having gained his paranoid uncle's complete trust, Obiang was named deputy defense minister and commandant of Fernando Po's notorious Black Beach Prison. He became Macias's brutal henchman and the second most powerful person in Equatorial Guinea.

But that was all about to change. By 1979, Obiang feared his increasingly insane uncle would turn on him. It was time to act, and on August 3, Obiang led a bloody coup. After ferocious battles on the mainland, Macias's troops, aided by Cuban and North Korean soldiers, were finally defeated. Macias was soon captured. After a brief military trial, the former president was found guilty of numerous crimes, including mass murder and embezzlement. He was executed by a firing squad on September 25, 1979.

After the coup, Obiang assumed leadership of the Supreme Military Council. One of his first acts was to pay the back salaries of all those in the armed forces. He reopened churches and schools throughout the country, which had been closed by Macias. In a conciliatory gesture toward its indigenous tribe, Obiang changed the name of Fernando Po to Bioko Island in honor of a precolonial Bubi king. As head of the military junta, Obiang reestablished diplomatic relations with Europe and the United States.

For many, the August 3 "freedom coup" (El Golpe de Libertad), as it came to be known, was little more than changing one authoritarian regime for another led by a member of the same family. Many of those who had served in Macias's government shifted to new positions. In August 1982, after four years of military rule, Obiang held a referendum for a new constitution stipulating that, if it was approved, he would be elected as president for a seven-year term. In what would be the first of a series of rigged votes, Obiang claimed 95 percent of the population approved the constitution that made him president. He was reelected unopposed in 1989 with 99 percent of the vote. With underfunded and harassed opponents, he has won every election since then, most recently in 2022.

In October 1987, Obiang founded the Democratic Party of Equatorial Guinea (PDGE), which became the country's sole political party. It was only after considerable domestic and international pressure that he allowed other political parties to exist as stipulated by the 1991 constitution. But registering a truly independent political party in Equatorial Guinea is exceptionally difficult. Aside from "pseudo-opposition" parties that vote in lockstep with the PDGE, the only registered, true opposition party is Convergence for Social Democracy (CPDS). The latter has been constantly attacked and undermined by the government, and from time to time its leaders have been imprisoned.

In 1995, because of Obiang's increasing authoritarianism and harassment of U.S. Ambassador John Bennet, a strong proponent of human rights, Washington decided to close its embassy in Malabo. American interests in EG were covered once again by the U.S. Embassy in Yaoundé, Cameroon. Ironically, the embassy shutdown came shortly after a small Texas-based petroleum company, Walter International, discovered enormous offshore oil and gas reserves north of Bioko Island. This led to a boom in petroleum production in EG, with Mobil becoming a major investor in 1995 and other well-known American petroleum companies soon following.

What ensued was the transformation of Equatorial Guinea from a poor African country to one of the continent's richest nations. By the early 2000s, it had become the third largest oil and gas producer in sub-Saharan Africa, with U.S. companies as its largest investors. But that did little to benefit the country's citizens. EG's newfound wealth was siphoned off through the massive corruption of President Obiang, his family, and the regime's Fang ruling elite. As mentioned earlier over 70 percent of the country's population struggled to live on less than $2 a day.

However, as a direct result of the growing role of U.S. petroleum companies in EG, there was pressure on the U.S. government to reopen the American embassy in Malabo for the convenience of the oil workers and their families. In 2003, an acting chief of mission plus a handful of

American diplomats arrived to restart embassy operations on a limited scale. In 2006, Washington appointed its first resident ambassador since John Bennett's 1994 departure. Arriving in 2012, I became the third resident ambassador following the 2003 reopening.

With that historical overview, it's time to get back to my story. Malabo, with its old city center perched on a cliff overlooking an expansive, deep-water harbor, has a certain charm. Although dilapidated, many of its remaining 1920s Spanish colonial buildings have elegant wooden balustrades and decorative iron grills. During our first weekend on the island of Bioko, formerly Fernando Po, Jane and I visited the picturesque seaport town of Luba. We also saw Moka, a small village in the cool highlands near the caldera of an extinct volcano. Despite mariner Fernando Po originally naming the island Formosa, which means "beautiful" in Portuguese, Bioko is anything but a tropical paradise.

Its coastlines are rocky, with rainforests often descending close to the shoreline. There are few bathing beaches, except for remote, dramatic volcanic ones in the south of the island. And apart from the gaudy mansions and vast estates in Malabo and elsewhere, which are owned by members of the Obiang family and the elite, what we saw on our tour were mostly modest cement dwellings and numerous squalid shacks. There were also run-down, one-story schools with no indoor plumbing.

Occasionally, we'd pass colonial-era Catholic churches, whose lofty spires dwarfed everything around them. Every now and again, there were also small latticed open-air "houses of the word" (casas de la palabra). These were gathering places where only male elders were allowed to enter and discuss tribal affairs. Hardest to look at were the rickety wooden roadside stands where villagers hung freshly killed bushmeat carcasses from metal hooks. In addition to selling large-pouch rats, they offered higher-priced endangered species like pangolins, drill, and colobus monkeys. For several decades, Drexel University in Philadelphia has run a conservation project, the Bioko Biodiversity Protection Program (BBPP), which seeks to protect these and other unique animals.

And so, on our first weekend, we got to see all of the rustic "attractions" of the island, which was to be our home for the next three years. You could drive on well-paved roads around Bioko in about three hours. You might decide to stop for lunch, as we'd done, at a so-so restaurant in Luba. Eating anywhere else on the island outside of Malabo was definitely not a good idea. This was not going to be a place where you could drive very far. It was clear that Jane and I had quite an adventure before us.

The U.S. embassy in Malabo, not far from the city center, was in a rented two-story art-deco-style villa in an undistinguished residential neighborhood with the misleading name of El Paraiso (Paradise). This former private dwelling was surrounded by high whitewashed walls, which the State Department's diplomatic security bureau had topped with ugly barbed wire. The house had a large yard in front where we flew the U.S. flag. Embassy vehicles were parked off to one side in a long driveway, as we used the converted garage for office space and storage. In the early years after reopening, the embassy had only three American officers and a small number of local employees.

In 2012, there were nine Americans were assigned to the Malabo embassy, and supported by a couple of dozen local employees. The "consular section" consisted of a narrow corridor with a window looking out onto a semi-covered porch. Here, Equatoguinean visa applicants and American citizens alike waited for services from a lone U.S. consular officer. It tended to get wet on the porch because of Malabo's perennial rainy climate. I was embarrassed that we had no indoor consular waiting room for our clients.

Our Equatoguinean staff worked in small cubicles wedged into common areas. The American staff—except for the consul, who had an "office" in the corridor—had desks on the second floor. I was fortunate to have a spacious office there. We had only unclassified communications with Washington, as there was no secure space within the building for classified equipment.

All of the Americans lived in rented housing not far from the embassy. Jane's and my two-story house, about ten minutes away, had a small swimming pool and adequate space for entertaining. Each night

MARK L. ASQUINO

at dusk, Jane and I watched as a flock of majestic white herons gradually appeared on our lawn. While far from the high standards of a chief of mission's residence, it was comfortable, and we were happy during the year we lived there.

The half-finished embassy complex was several miles away in a new part of the city called Malabo II. It included not only a chancery, or office building but also spacious residences for the ambassador, DCM, and townhouses for the rest of the American staff. There was a tennis court and swimming pool with a multipurpose cabana on the 12.5-acre compound. The construction site had been carved out of the dense rainforest.

All the government ministries were gradually in the process of being relocated to Malabo II. Everything there was meant to impress. With its rows of huge, largely-vacant, multi-story ministry buildings, it had the air of a tropical Potemkin village. And right in the middle of everything was the anomalously small one-story U.S. embassy, overshadowed by its hulking neighbors. The ongoing construction needs of the compound sparked my first knock-down battle with the government.

We were expecting via air cargo, a sealed diplomatic container needed at the construction site. Under the Vienna Convention, not only small diplomatic pouches but also larger shipments are exempted from host country inspection. They cannot be opened or x-rayed. The container was protected under these provisions. It held highly sensitive equipment that would be used for classified communications at the new chancery.

The shipment was set to arrive on the evening of September 19 on a Lufthansa flight from Frankfurt. We sent a team of American officers to the airport. They had official permission to meet the plane on the runway and then load the container directly into an embassy truck. From there it would be taken to a secure area at the new embassy site. As with all embassy construction projects, Malabo had a State Department security officer assigned to the site. He was an energetic young Yemeni-American named Khalid Hafez, whom everyone called K. A former marine who'd served two combat tours in Iraq, K had extensive knowledge of security measures, having worked on previous construction projects. So, when K called me at home that night, saying I needed to come to the airport immediately, I knew something had gone drastically wrong.

As soon as I got there, I learned that the airport customs officers refused to let the team load the container onto the truck. They demanded that it be opened for inspection. When K and the American officers refused, airport authorities called the vice minister for national security who soon arrived at the airport. This official was told the same thing and became livid. Before leaving, he ordered the customs officers that under no circumstances was the container to leave the airport or the tarmac for that matter.

When I got to the airport, I spoke first with K, who explained that if the container's seals were broken or the embassy lost custody of the shipment, it would have to be sent back to Germany. Should this happen, it would take months for new communications equipment to arrive, delaying the completion of the new diplomatic compound. The container was still sitting on the tarmac. The airport manager offered to let us move it to Lufthansa's airport warehouse, where it would be safe overnight until I could work out its release with the foreign minister on the following day. That sounded like a good solution to me, but K pulled me aside and said that unless someone was allowed to have eyes on the container all night, we would have no choice but to ship it back. He added this was needed to prevent its being x-rayed or covertly inspected. As the construction site security officer, K said it was his job to guard the container.

We moved the shipment to the warehouse, and K was allowed to remain with it overnight. The next morning, I called the office of Foreign Minister Agapito Mba Mokuy, whom I'd met briefly a few days earlier. During that meeting, I'd presented him with a copy of a letter from President Obama to President Obiang stating that I was the new U.S. ambassador and asking to be "fully accredited" in his country. In diplomatic parlance, such ambassadorial documents are known as credentials. As was customary, by providing a copy of the letter to the foreign minister, I was allowed to begin work while waiting for a date to formally present my credentials to the president.

MARK L. ASQUINO

Much to my chagrin, I learned that Foreign Minister Mba Mokuy was already in New York with President Obiang, where they were both representing Equatorial Guinea at the annual opening of the United Nations General Assembly. I left an urgent message for his deputy, Pedro Ela Nguema Buna, who was the acting foreign minister. After repeated tries, my office assistant Christine was able to reach the deputy foreign minister. Ela Nguema proved to be a reasonable man but informed me that the problem with the container was the embassy's fault. He explained that my staff did not properly apply for and received a *franquicia* from the Foreign Ministry required for such a shipment.

This document authorized customs officials to release it directly to the embassy. Absent this documentation, the airport was obliged to inspect the shipment. The deputy concluded with regret in his voice that the container must therefore either be opened or returned to Germany on the Lufthansa flight that evening. I told him this was not acceptable to the embassy and that between the two of us, we needed to find a way to resolve the situation.

When I checked with my administrative section, it turned out the Foreign Ministry was right. The embassy had dropped the ball and not obtained the franquicia. This was a problem I needed to address but not right then. For the moment, I had to find a way to get the container released to us. I called the deputy back and offered profuse apologies over what had happened. I added that we had corrected the error, and the proper forms were now on their way to the ministry so that a franquicia could be issued. Surely, I concluded this would be sufficient for him to release the shipment. There was a long pause on his end of the line, and then Ela Nguema said that this would be "highly irregular" for him to do. It would require getting approval from the foreign minister in New York. We agreed to speak again after he'd consulted with his superior.

By then, it was close to noon, and embassy officers were on shifts guarding the container while K got some rest. It was midafternoon when the deputy minister called me back. His voice was animated as he told me he and his boss had found a "solution." The government would release the shipment if we allowed its bomb-sniffing dogs to check for drugs and/or explosives. I had all I could do to keep from losing my temper. Did he think we were a bunch of drug-smuggling terrorists? How insulting! However, I held my tongue and said I would share his proposal with Washington.

I spoke with my desk officer at the State Department and then with the director for African affairs. All of us agreed EG was offering an absurd face-saving gesture to resolve the problem. However, I admitted that the embassy had been at fault for not submitting the proper paperwork. That being the case, my Washington colleagues said it was entirely my call on whether or not to let the dogs have at the container.

In the meantime, we got informal word that the Foreign Ministry had received our paperwork and was preparing to release the shipment once the dogs sniffed it. So, I called Ela Nguema, thanked him and the foreign minister for their assistance, and said we were fine with the dogs being deployed under our watchful eyes. As we expected, the dogs had no interest in what for them was just a big box. Our team was then allowed to load the shipment onto our truck and take it to safekeeping at the construction site. Problem solved.

There had been much emotional grandstanding on both sides during the day-long standoff over the container. I learned this was how things often worked in Equatorial Guinea. I also came to understand that resolving a problem sometimes would require accepting what appeared to be a ridiculous face-saving gesture.

Following the president's and foreign minister's return from New York, I was scheduled to present my credentials during a formal October 4 ceremony at the presidential palace. I was in a group of other new emissaries, and each of us would present our credentials separately to President Obiang. There was no schedule for the order in which we would present our credentials. We all waited at the hotel for two hours before the Nigerian ambassador, with whom I'd struck up a pleasant conversation, was called to present his credentials to President Obiang. After a half hour or so, two military honor guards motioned to me from the lobby, and along with Jane and my DCM, Rafael Foley, I was escorted out of the hotel. There in the portico, we saw an elegant dark-green official Mercedes sedan, which we were invited to enter, with Jane and me in the back and Rafael in front.

We were then taken on a short slow ride around Independence Square, passing Malabo's imposing cathedral and stopping in front of the presidential palace's black-and-gold metal gates. After a few minutes, they were opened. Jane and Rafael were directed by an aide to a waiting area inside the building. Another aide escorted me to a red carpet as an Equatoguinean military band, decked out in dress uniforms, made a valiant attempt to play "The Star-Spangled Banner."

While this was happening, another elegantly arrayed soldier slowly raised the U.S. flag next to that of Equatorial Guinea's, which was already at full mast. Both flags flapped gently in what was for me a most welcome breeze. I stood at attention, my right hand covering my heart, and in a low bass voice, I sang the lyrics of the U.S. national anthem. Meanwhile, state media photographers and cameramen scampered around me to record the event.

And I have to say that after more than three decades of serving as a diplomat overseas, I never felt more proud or more patriotic than I did in those few special moments. Once the anthem had concluded, I walked along the red carpet to the front of the building as members of the honor guard stood at attention and saluted me.

The Presidential Palace is a relatively new four-story building. Once inside, I met up with Jane and Rafael again. The presidential head of protocol escorted us on an elevator to the top floor. With my wife and DCM off to one side, I was told to stand in front of tall gold-trimmed white wooden doors. After about ten minutes, the doors suddenly opened inward and someone inside whom I couldn't see announced in beautifully elocuted Spanish, "El Excelentisimo Señor Don Mark Louis Asquino, el Embajador Extraordinario y Plenipotenciario de la República de los Estados Unidos de America!"

Across the room, I saw a distinguished-looking man wearing an exquisitely-tailored charcoal suit. He had a distinctly military bearing and kept his arms closely aligned against his thin frame. The unseen announcer again intoned in the same deep baritone voice, "El Presidente de la República de Guinea Equatorial, Su Excelencia, Teodoro Obiang Nguema Mbasogo!"

As I'd been instructed beforehand, I then walked to the middle of the room and stopped. With a stern look on his face as if sizing me up, the president remained where he was, flanked to his right by a row of solemn-looking ministers. After what seemed like a long time, President Obiang finally approached me. Once we were standing face-to-face, I extended from my right hand a formal-looking envelope embossed with the White House crest in one corner and addressed in black calligraphy to President Obiang. Placing it in Obiang's outstretched hands, I then said that it was my great honor to present to His Excellency my ambassadorial credentials from President Barack Obama.

Jane and Rafael were in the back of the room as all of this was happening while state media once again were filming away at what I would shortly learn was a live broadcast on national television. President Obiang said a few words of welcome, and an aide motioned to Jane that she should join me. The three of us moved to nearby gold-upholstered chairs. I could see that the media had left the room as well as the ministers, except Foreign Minister Mba Mokuy. He sat in a less-grand chair as a notetaker for my thirty-minute meeting with the president.

With the formal ceremony over, Obiang now seemed relaxed and smiled graciously as I introduced Jane to him and the foreign minister. After saying how pleased Jane and I were to be in Equatorial Guinea, I delivered two prepared talking points.

The first was related to my meeting several weeks earlier with the foreign minister. Mba Mokuy had told me Equatorial Guinea was considering ending its decades-long practice of allowing Americans to enter the country without a visa. He noted this had been a courtesy originally extended to U.S. petroleum company workers in gratitude for their discovery of oil and gas in the country. However, the foreign minister added that the U.S. government had never shown reciprocity on this issue. After all of these years, Equatoguineans, including students, were still required to obtain visas to enter the United States. During that earlier meeting, I'd pushed back with the minister, noting that both of our countries greatly benefited from visa-free entry for the workers of U.S. petroleum companies and other Americans who came to Equatorial Guinea.

I now raised the same point with the president. I told him that as the American ambassador, one of my primary responsibilities was to promote U.S. business in his country. Accordingly, I very much hoped that His Excellency would not change the visa-free regime. Obiang listened carefully but remained absolutely noncommittal.

I then launched into my second point. During President Obiang's recent visit to Washington, Assistant Secretary of State for Africa Johnnie Carson had arranged for him to meet there with U.S. human rights groups. At the time, I had not been confirmed by the Senate, so I did not attend the meeting. I was briefed afterward that the groups had called on Obiang to respect human rights in EG. The president replied they were misinformed on the subject and that his country fully respected human rights. He then invited them to visit Equatorial Guinea to see for themselves that this was the case.

As a follow-up, Carson had sent the president a letter reminding him of his invitation and asking when the groups could come. But months had passed with the letter going unanswered. I asked Obiang about this, to which he answered that, of course, the human rights advocates were most welcome. Glancing toward Mba Mokuy, the president evenly said that his foreign minister would soon be replying to the assistant secretary and conveying invitations to the groups.

Now, this seemed to me like quite an unexpected opening. As I noted earlier, one of my major priorities as ambassador was to promote respect for human rights and the rule of law in Equatorial Guinea. Had the president been serious about what he'd just said? Before I departed, the foreign minister told me we should meet as soon as possible to discuss the two issues I'd just raised.

Following the meeting, the protocol chief escorted Jane and me to the official Mercedes sedan, which was awaiting us for our return to the U.S. embassy. Rafael had not been invited to my tête-à-tête with the president and had already returned to the office. Jane and I sat in the backseat of the Mercedes as it drove slowly, with a motorcycle escort of white-helmeted police in the lead and to both sides of the vehicle. As we proceeded, their sirens made an unforgettable shrill, high-pitched whine.

Now back at the embassy, I asked Denise Taylor, my lone political officer, to prepare a diplomatic note requesting a meeting with the foreign minister as a follow-up to my discussion with the president. With uncharacteristic alacrity, we received a diplomatic reply the next day, saying the foreign minister would see me on October 5.

There was a certain ritual that always accompanied my meetings with Mba Mokuy. Climbing the Foreign Ministry's massive wooden stairway to the second floor, usually with either Rafael or Denise as my notetaker, I was met on the landing by a protocol officer who led us to a small waiting room. As with the president, I usually had a long wait to see Mba Mokuy. But on this occasion, I was called by the protocol official rather quickly and ushered into the minister's spacious office. Rafael and I sat on a couch to the right of Mba Mokuy. He took a seat at the head of a large glass coffee table that separated us. The minister, always dapper and extremely formal was a decade younger than me. An experienced professional diplomat, he had previously spent close to a decade in Paris as EG's ambassador to the United Nations Educational, Scientific and Cultural Organization (UNESCO) there. He spoke flawless French as well as fluent English, but our initial meetings were in Spanish.

The foreign minister began by saying the president appreciated my having been respectful in presenting the two issues I'd raised. Obiang had been pleased that while focused on outcomes, I was not demanding. Mba Mokuy concluded that as a result I'd made a good impression on the president. I thanked him for this feedback and then moving directly to the reason I was there, I asked how he proposed to proceed on the visa issue for Americans as well as invitations to EG for U.S. human rights organizations.

On the former, the foreign minister replied that in return for Americans not being required to have visas, Equatoguineans should, as he'd told me previously, have visa-free entry to the United States. I replied that, unfortunately, this was not possible. No other African country had this status, and I knew the State Department would not agree to it for EG. However, I had a counterproposal.

As he was aware, U.S. visas issued to the citizens of neighboring Gabon and Cameroon were valid for five years as opposed to just two for EG. Similarly, students from those nations were issued multiyear visas while Equatoguineans studying in the United States had to renew their visas every year. I said I thought this was unfair, and that I would do my best to change the situation. My goal would be to guarantee EG equal treatment for visas with these countries. EG was forever gauging itself in comparison with its neighbors, and I could see Mba Mokuy saw value in my alternate proposal. He said the Foreign Ministry would hold off on imposing visa requirements for Americans subject to improvements in the visa regime for Equatoguineans.

We then turned to the far more difficult of the two issues. Mba Mokuy suggested that the U.S. human rights groups might come in December as part of a planned Africa-Caribbean symposium hosted by Equatorial Guinea. I said such timing for the groups would be problematic. If there was to be any significance in the president's inviting U.S. human rights representatives, their visit should be separate from the symposium.

Mba Mokuy reluctantly agreed that a stand-alone visit for the human rights groups in mid-November might be possible. He added that in the letter he planned to send to Assistant Secretary Carson, he preferred not to specify which groups EG was willing to invite. I noted that my understanding was that President Obiang had invited "all of the human rights groups" to the meeting. But the foreign minister was adamant that his country would decide on who was invited, and this would be just one or two groups. It was clear this was all I was going to get on the visit, so I didn't push the matter any further. We agreed to continue working together on both issues.

As I was on my way out of the ministry, I spotted a small group of state media journalists, including a TV cameraman, waiting near the downstairs exit. They moved toward me, and I knew I would need to say something about the meeting. In fact, I welcomed doing so. My only chance to speak directly to a large public audience in EG would be through such brief media encounters. Having spoken Spanish as a second language for much of my adult life, I was able, when needed, to add nuance and sometimes oblique messages in speaking with journalists.

As was to be expected, the journalists asked what I'd discussed with the foreign minister. I spoke in general terms about the two issues, noting I'd also raised them with the president after presenting my credentials.

I was pleased with the meeting's outcomes. With the United States as the only country granted visa waivers, American companies in EG had an enormous competitive advantage over their oil industry rivals. But I would need to get concessions from Washington to preserve these visa waivers.

As I'd expected, the issue of obtaining invitations for U.S. human rights groups to come to EG had been challenging. Still, I felt my discussion with the foreign minister had been positive, and I thought I was off to a great start. But in just a few weeks, a human rights case would lead to my near expulsion from the country.

CHAPTER 14

Off to a Rocky Start

ON OCTOBER 10, I made my first trip to Rio Muni, the mainland portion of the country. Jane accompanied me, and we arrived via an hour-long flight on a local carrier from Malabo to Bata, Equatorial Guinea's largest city. With some 250,000 residents, Bata has roughly a quarter of the country's entire population. The embassy kept an official vehicle there, and we were met at the airport by my driver Gabriel, who had arrived a day earlier.

The Rio Muni region borders Cameroon and Gabon, where the majority speaks French although English is also spoken in the former. Bata is located in continental Africa, and it's common to hear French spoken there and throughout the region. Compared to Malabo, there was a feeling of openness in this seaside city.

I had traveled to the mainland primarily to attend EG's annual October 12 Independence Day celebrations. This year, they would take place in the Fang heartland city of Mongomo, near the border with Gabon. All ambassadors were expected to attend this observance, which included an hours-long review by the president and his cabinet. There would also be a religious service attended by the First Couple at Mongomo's Basilica of the Immaculate Conception, the second-largest Catholic church in Africa. It was built between 2006 and 2011 in honor of Pope John Paul II's historic 1982 visit to the city.

This year, the government was providing a special October 11 flight to take diplomats to the celebrations. I informed the Foreign Ministry, much to its displeasure, that I would be traveling to Mongomo on my own. I added that as a new ambassador, I wanted to spend time additional time on the mainland.

Before heading off the next day on the three-hour drive to Mongomo, I met with a well-known opposition party member, Dr. Wenceslao Monsogo Alo. An accomplished physician, he found it hard due to government harassment, to run his private practice. This culminated in trumped-up malpractice charges being brought against him, leading to his imprisonment for several months before being granted a presidential pardon.

Dr. Monsogo told me about the horrible conditions at the Bata prison. There was no medical care for those with injuries, sanitation was terrible, and friends and relatives had to provide food for the inmates. Worst of all, men and women were often kept together for a period of time in large unsupervised holding cells. He'd initially been confined to one and spoke of how a young woman had been gang-raped every night by men who were hardened criminals. The men threatened him and others who tried to intervene to stop the brutal attacks, and the guards simply ignored what was happening.

We then spoke at length about municipal and parliamentary elections expected to take place in the spring. He said that the opposition had not been allowed to participate in an electoral census to determine those registered and qualified to vote. This would certainly lead as it had in the past, to voting fraud by the government. Further, the ruling PDGE had the lion's share of financial and other resources to campaign, including complete control of the media. He added the government would call elections at the last minute. The authorities also resorted to obscure legal and technical pretexts to prevent opposition candidates from holding public rallies.

Dr. Monsogo provided me with a dark, depressing portrait of his country. Yet he somehow retained hope about the future despite his recent imprisonment and the continuing restrictions placed on him.

Jane and I left for Mongomo right after lunch. Unlike in Sudan, we had no bodyguard in the embassy vehicle or a security detail following us. For all of its drawbacks, Equatorial Guinea was a relatively safe place to be an ambassador. When on official business though, we were required to travel with our driver in an armored embassy vehicle.

The vegetation we passed on the road to Mongomo was more verdant and appealing than that on Bioko. Once again, extreme poverty was evident as soon as we left Bata. The landscape was dominated by wooden huts, naked children, and roadside bars with blaring music. Every twenty or thirty kilometers, there were police checkpoints. As our vehicle had diplomatic plates, we were waved through, but other motorists were stopped by the heavily-armed soldiers, who demanded small bribes.

As we approached Mongomo, we began to see substantial houses, which Gabriel told us belonged to the Ensangui clan, the Fang tribe's ruling elite. All of a sudden, the rural two-lane road we'd been traveling on became a well-paved four-lane highway.

Soon, we saw in the distance the Mongomo Hotel, where we would be lodged along with other ambassadors. It was a large, light-green, two-story building, and on the upper floor, there were balconies decorated with white-painted crenelated wooden railings. Gabriel parked, and we entered the lobby, which was adorned with Louis XIV–style furniture and faux French landscape paintings.

It turned out that the flight with my ambassadorial colleagues had not yet arrived, which was fortunate for us. The hotel was quickly filling up with government officials, and Jane and I were given a two-room suite. But by the time the other ambassadors tried to check in, there were only a few rooms left. Consequently, many of them wound up being bused off to a third-rate hotel in another town.

That evening, we were able to get a quick meal in the hotel restaurant before an officious young protocol officer came into the dining room and announced that in five minutes, he would take us to the Basilica of the Immaculate Conception. Jane and I, along with a handful of the other ambassadors, followed the fellow on a short walk to the immense church. From time to time, he would wave his arm forward over his head in a hurry-up gesture as if we were a bunch of dawdling school kids.

Like St. Peter's Basilica in Vatican City, this basilica had an enormous square in front of it, with an elliptical forecourt encircled by a Doric colonnade on each side. Unlike the papal edifice, its Mongomo cousin had a rather small dome flanked by two spires. On December 7 of the previous year, Obiang formally opened the Mongomo basilica, which was named in honor of the Immaculate Conception of the Virgin Mary.

Obiang had said after Pope John Paul's brief, 1982 stop in Mongomo, that he would build a great basilica in the city dedicated to the pontiff. Having overthrown Macias and installed himself as an authoritarian leader, Obiang had good reason to be grateful to this pope. Much to the disappointment of those who'd listened to John Paul's remarks in Mongomo that year, the Roman Catholic pontiff said nothing about human rights or democracy. Instead, he praised the new government for supporting Catholicism, which under Obiang was on its way to becoming the country's de facto state religion.

As we entered the softly lit basilica, Jane and I were impressed by how cavernous it was. There were long rows of red marble columns leading to the altar, which in addition to a statue of the Virgin Mary, was adorned with a huge gold-leaf Vatican seal. After being seated by our handler, we waited for over an hour until the president and first lady arrived.

The evening mass to celebrate Independence Day then began. The papal nuncio, the Vatican's official representative to Equatorial Guinea, entered from a door off to one side of the altar. He wore resplendent green vestments and was flanked by two Equatoguinean bishops. There were a dozen priests and just as many altar boys who followed.

The high mass was celebrated with a great deal of incense and chanting of verses. We finally reached the part of the ceremony in which the celebrant delivers a sermon. The papal nuncio, a short, compact Italian in his early fifties, walked to the pulpit and calmly surveyed the VIP congregation. Speaking fluent Spanish with a faint Italian accent, he spent the next forty minutes praising the Obiang regime. He spoke of how the president had brought liberty, peace, and "allegría" to his nation after more than a decade of "darkness." He admonished that no one should be "misled" by those who "exaggerated" Equatorial Guinea's problems. The government had begun delivering on its promises of prosperity for all and showing just how wrong its critics were. The new generation of Equatoguineans enjoyed the sort of freedom unknown by their parents and grandparents.

MARK L. ASQUINO

He then shifted to praising the Catholic Church for running most of the country's schools, hospitals, and orphanages while also addressing the spiritual needs of its people. The papal nuncio's voice rose to something of a crescendo, which I hoped was an indication he was about to finish. He proclaimed that the Roman Catholic clergy would always show great respect for the country's leadership and feel deep gratitude to President Obiang, who had built this great basilica.

The papal nuncio had given a political speech having nothing to do with religion. Even after Macias had closed churches, Catholic bishops, priests, and nuns continued to try to help people and criticized the president's insane abuses. For this they paid a high price with many being murdered, imprisoned, or forced into exile. Under Obiang, the Catholic Church had been completely co-opted and obediently served his regime. As I sat there in this opulent basilica, it was clear to me the Roman Catholic hierarchy was completely on the side of the ruling class and not an advocate for the country's vast majority, who lived in poverty and fear.

On the following morning, the same obnoxious protocol officer was in the hotel lobby at 9:00 a.m. to herd us in the direction of several small white vans that would take my fellow diplomats and me to the Independence Day celebration. Jane wisely decided to sleep in and spend the day reading near the hotel swimming pool. Once in the VIP reviewing stands, we sat for two hours awaiting the arrival of the president who had been preceded by members of his cabinet. Obiang and the first lady were seated in the same ornate chairs I'd seen at the basilica and occupied a special area apart from the rest of us.

What followed was a three-and-a-half-hour parade or better described as a "spectacle." It began with uniformed members of the armed forces and military vehicles, including tanks, armored personnel carriers, and trucks, passing by the reviewing stand. The president, dressed once again in a dark suit, stood at attention as wave after wave of those in the military saluted him. Two athletic-looking armed Israeli bodyguards, young men wearing earpieces and microphones to communicate with each other, stood several feet away to the right and left of the president. Other bodyguards were stationed around the reviewing stands. All of them looked intently as the soldiers marched by, vigilant for any false move. It seemed odd to me that Obiang would be reliant on this foreign security detail of white men to protect him against his own people.

At the end of the military portion of the parade, several French Mirage jets soared overhead. They were flown by Ukrainians as EG did not have its own pilots. Obiang—who had been standing unflinchingly straight for over an hour, a rather impressive feat for a seventy-year-old—then sat down. After a fifteen-minute pause, contingents from the regime's ruling Democracy Party of Equatorial Guinea (PDGE) marched down the parade route. Many were dressed in brightly colored shirts bearing the likenesses of the president and first lady. Others held banners praising them, and there were chants by some repeating the president's name. Members of the dozen or so political parties that always voted in lockstep with PDGE in the country's parliament came next.

Toward the end of the event, a red-and-yellow Massey Ferguson tractor, with a sign indicating it was from a state-run agricultural enterprise, noisily rumbled down the road, its diesel engine spewing black fumes. It was pulling a trailer in which there were two of the largest hogs I'd ever seen in my life. The poor penned-up creatures appeared to be as unhappy as we diplomats were. Suddenly, all of us burst out in spontaneous laughter and applause. The bodyguards glared at us, and several ministers turned around. They looked in our direction with expressions of withering disapproval that seemed to say, "This is a solemn occasion! How dare you treat it with levity?"

Thankfully, the spectacle was soon over. We got back in the vans and were taken to a nearby pavilion where an elaborate government-hosted VIP reception awaited us. I greeted the president and first lady, munched on some of the food, and then left discreetly. Gabriel and the embassy car were nearby and took me back to the hotel. Once there, Jane and I hurriedly packed our bags and were soon on the road back to Bata.

Before returning to Malabo, I met with a Canadian evangelical missionary named Roland "Rollie" Grenier. Rollie and his Colombian wife, Cristina, a skilled medic, had lived in Bata for almost nineteen years. When I called to introduce myself, he kindly invited Jane and me to have dinner at his and Cristina's place.

Their modest small home was in a working-class neighborhood outside of Bata. During his time in EG, Rollie built a church and a small adjoining Bible study seminary not far from where he and Christina lived. They told us how Bata had been nothing more than a village with a dozen or so cars when they first arrived. They marveled at how it had become the country's largest city in less than two decades. Theirs was a virtual open house where those not only from the neighborhood but also living in surrounding villages were welcome at all hours. Rollie said that many people came to discuss marital problems with him, while Cristina provided first aid and health advice to others.

In addition to Spanish, Rollie spoke fluent Fang and had a deep understanding of Fang tribal traditions, beliefs, and customs. He offered me advice that proved to be invaluable on how to deal with the Fang governing majority. He explained that given their tradition of having been hunters and trappers, the Fang often found working in business and the government challenging. They tended to focus on the needs of today and for this reason, found it difficult to set long-term goals. The idea of public service also did not come easily for them. Rollie advised me to take care not to make commitments to the Fang that I was unlikely to be able to fulfill. As he said this, I thought of what I'd told the foreign minister about trying to obtain better U.S. visa terms for his citizens. I made a mental note that I had to find a way to deliver on what the regime now considered a commitment.

Rollie continued that the Fang were deeply distrustful of outsiders, fearing that they were full of trickery and deception. However, given their own cultural background as trappers, the Fang were adept at ensnaring unsuspecting foreigners. The best policy, he told me, was to be straightforward with the Fang while also taking care not to fall into their subtle snares. He also spoke of the need to respect their animistic religious beliefs, as well as to acknowledge their fear of witchcraft, especially the conviction that disease was the result of evil spells.

As foreigners, Rollie and Cristina quite understandably steered clear of politics, and neither praised nor condemned the government. Instead, they remained focused on doing what they could as missionaries to help those in need. In that sense, after visiting their sparsely furnished home and later seeing Rollie's simple wood-frame church and seminary, I couldn't help but contrast their work with what I'd just seen and heard at the grand basilica in Mongomo.

I had been back in Malabo for less than two weeks when I learned that the country's leading human rights attorney, Fabián Nsue, had gone missing. He had last been seen near Black Beach Prison, where he'd gone to meet a client being held there. As I've written in an earlier chapter, I briefly met Fabián when he attended my ambassadorial swearing-in ceremony at the Department of State. He was a member of the unregistered Popular Union opposition party. I learned that Fabián's client was a French language teacher from Bata named Agustin Nsono who had been arrested with his brother Juan Manene and Irene Adjomo, a woman acquaintance of theirs.

Nsono and Manene belonged to an illegal fringe organization called The Movement to Fight the Dictatorship in Equatorial Guinea (MLCD). It apparently had few members and posed no real threat to the regime, but in its literature the group obliquely called for violence. The government claimed that the prisoners had been planning to launch a coup against President Obiang during the October 12 Independence Day celebrations in Mongomo. They were detained in Bata and then transferred to Black Beach Prison, where Fabián Nsue had an appointment to see his client Nsono.

According to Fabián's wife, who'd contacted us, he'd driven his car to the prison's security checkpoint and been allowed to enter and park. He was last seen heading to the prison's visitors' entrance and then disappeared. His wife said she could not reach Fabián on his cell phone and that prison authorities denied any record of him having entered the facility. Although Fabián's car remained in the prison parking area, they insisted they had no idea what might have happened to him.

Given Fabián's prominence in the human rights community, the ambassadors from Spain, France, and Germany, all of whom I'd just met in Mongomo, contacted me. They said they were worried the government could have harmed him. We decided to send the Ministry of Foreign Affairs a joint diplomatic note expressing the concern of the European Union and U.S. embassies over Fabián's welfare.

The foreign minister was traveling, but his deputy, Pedro Ela Nguema, whom I knew from the shipping-container episode, replied that the government had no information about Nsue's whereabouts. Despite this, there were rumors that he had been detained upon entering Black Beach Prison and was now being held incognito. Human Rights Watch issued an international alert on social media accusing the government of having kidnapped him and holding it responsible for his well-being. Within a matter of days, the disappearance of Fabián Nsue became a cause célèbre with human rights organizations around the world.

By pure coincidence, I was scheduled shortly after Fabián's "disappearance" to have an introductory meeting with Minister for National Security Nicolas Obama Nchama. It's customary for new ambassadors to have individual initial meetings with the cabinet members of the country to which they are assigned. As a courtesy, I sent the minister of foreign affairs a list of all of the ministers I was planning to see and then had my staff set up meetings.

During these courtesy calls, a new ambassador has the chance to introduce himself or herself to the ministers, and normally, nothing of substance is ever raised. Despite this, I had every intention of using the meeting with Obama Nchama to speak to him about Fabián's case. I was well aware that his ministry was in charge of national penitentiaries, including Black Beach. I made a copy of a Human Rights Watch alert in which Minister Obama Nchama himself was named as being responsible for Fabián's disappearance.

My driver took me to the Ministry of National Security, which had a detention center in its basement with the chilling nickname of Guantanamo, where prisoners were said to be interrogated and tortured. I had decided to do the meeting alone and without a notetaker, knowing it would be confrontational and be best done one-on-one. Black-uniformed heavily-armed security police, who also guarded Black

Beach, were at the entrance. Two of them escorted me to the minister's office on an upper floor.

When I entered, Minister Obama Nchama came from behind his desk and gave me a firm handshake. He was a short, heavy-set man in his forties and had a large round face. Obama Nchama wore gold-rimmed glasses and had his hair shaved close to the scalp. Despite his reputation as one of the most brutal men in government, he seemed quite cordial, smiling broadly as he welcomed me. I surmised there would be just the two of us in the meeting.

We sat face-to-face across a small round table. I began by telling him about myself. He told me how much he admired the United States, adding he had children studying at a college in Pennsylvania. It was all pleasant until I changed the subject.

I began by saying that I realized it was customary not to raise specific issues at an initial meeting, but I felt I had to regard the case of Fabián Nsue. I then outlined the facts surrounding his disappearance, noting the U.S. government was deeply concerned about his well-being. I added that the lack of a response by EG's government on this matter raised questions for the United States about his country's respect for human rights and due process. As I was saying this, the minister frowned.

I continued by noting that international human rights groups had sounded the alarm in social media over the unknown whereabouts of EG's leading human rights attorney. I told the minister that he had specifically been identified as one of the officials responsible for what was being termed a kidnapping. Holding Amnesty International's "urgent action" alert in front of Obama Nchama, I called his attention to a box that included not only his name but also his contact information, with a request that people demand information from him on Nsue's disappearance. I said that unfortunately this was something his children in the United States might learn about from their classmates, and I felt it important for him to be aware of it.

This last bit infuriated the minister. He yanked the notice from my hand and immediately began reading it, becoming increasingly agitated. Finally, he slammed it down on the table. He said angrily that the claim of his involvement in Nsue's disappearance was an outrage, insisting that he knew nothing about it. He continued that his ministry's security forces played no role at Black Beach Prison, concluding such dastardly calumnies against him were intolerable.

I knew he was lying about the ministry's role at Black Beach. I also believed he'd ordered Fabián's detention there. However, I realized that this suddenly volatile man, who had been all smiles and charm just minutes earlier, could easily "disappear" me if I was not careful. And for this reason, I chose my words carefully, "Mr. Minister, I completely understand and agree. I'm sorry to have had to bring such information to your attention. But for this reason, I would like to suggest that you investigate what might have happened to Mr. Nsue."

He stared at me with cold, calculating eyes, as I was sure he did during interrogations. He then asked why he should do that.

"Well, Mr. Minister, I think it would allow you to clear your good name, given what is being said about your alleged role in Mr. Nsue's disappearance."

Minister Obama Nchama said nothing, and there was an uncomfortable minute or so of silence. I imagined he was weighing what I'd just proposed and determining if I was trying to trick or otherwise ensnare him. Finally, the minister told me he would get to the bottom of the whole affair.

I then took out one of my cards, wrote my cell phone number on it, and suggested that he might let me know when he discovered something. It was late on a Friday, and I didn't expect to hear anything very quickly. It was apparent though that our meeting was over. He went to his desk, called someone on an intercom, and said I should be escorted out of the building. I very much hoped I was not about to be taken to the basement.

The minister shook my hand, this time in a perfunctory fashion. The same two guards who'd led me to the minister's office then appeared. We got on the elevator, and I was relieved when one of them pressed the ground floor. Gabriel drove me back to the embassy. As Rafael was on leave, I briefed political officer Denise Taylor, who was my acting deputy, on what had happened, and then I went home.

About an hour later, I got a call on my cell phone from a blocked number. When I answered, it was the minister, and his voice returned to its previous amiable tone. He said that I'd been absolutely right. It turned out that Nsue, his client Esono, and the two other alleged coup plotters were all being held at Black Beach Prison. The minister continued that he'd immediately ordered their transfer to his custody, and they were now confined at the National Security Ministry's detention center. It was his intention to find out exactly what had happened.

I thanked Obama Nchama for his decisive action in solving the so-called mystery of Nsue's disappearance. I then asked if Nsue's family members and a lawyer could visit him over the weekend. I added that as I understood it, this was a right that was guaranteed to prisoners under EG's constitution. The minister replied that he would consider the question and provided me with a telephone number at the detention center that family members and an attorney could call for a possible visit.

I then contacted Denise, who relayed the information to Fabián's family as well as informed the Spanish, French, and German ambassadors. She also called another prominent human rights attorney, Maria Jesus Bikene Obiang, who agreed to visit the prisoners over the weekend. On Sunday, I got another call from the same blocked telephone number. Not surprisingly, it was the minister who said that he'd spoken with President Obiang, and all was resolved. He told me that Fabián would most likely be released during the afternoon of the following day. However, when this did not happen, I placed a call to the minister's office but was told he was not available.

That afternoon, Obama Nchama called and said he needed to see me right away. This time, it was hard to read from the tone of his voice exactly what this meant. I asked if, when we met, he would have "good news" for me regarding Fabián. I said I'd been disappointed that he had not already been released. The minister hedged, saying only that I would find out during the meeting but that he thought I would be pleased.

Dropping everything, I told Christine I needed to go to the Ministry of National Security. But this time, I decided to take along Denise, as well as the desk officer for EG from the Department of State, who was visiting Malabo. My intuition told me there was something suspicious about this snap meeting, and it seemed like a good idea to have others with me.

When we arrived at the ministry, we were escorted to the minister's office. Upon entering, I saw six men, some in uniform, who rose and introduced themselves as senior national security officials. The minister then said hello quite brusquely, and we all sat down.

As he began the meeting, there was no affability in Obama Nchama's voice. He picked up a large black binder bulging with papers inside. Reading from one of them, he announced that Fabián and the three other prisoners—Agustin Esono, his brother Juan Menene, and Irene Adjomo—had all been involved in an October 12 coup plot to overthrow the president. In addition, there was evidence they were guilty of other grave offenses against the state.

Then the minister abruptly stood and walked to a set of double doors leading to another room. He knocked hard, the doors abruptly opened, and security police led Fabián and his three alleged co-conspirators into the room. It was all very dramatic. Obama Nchama gestured toward them, announcing in an officious tone of voice that these were the four dangerous criminals who had been arrested and detained by his government.

Before I could say anything, Agustin Esono, Fabián Nsue's client, rushed toward me. He held up his arms and showed me deep red welts and bruises on his wrists.

"Ambassador! I was tortured in Black Beach Prison. Look at my wounds! They hung me from chains and beat me!"

The minister said nothing in response to this allegation but motioned for the police to make the prisoners sit down in nearby chairs. Addressing them, he said he'd shared damning information with me about their crimes and asked each to respond to the charges.

Fabián turned toward me. Looking haggard, tired, and angry, he protested loudly that he'd been illegally detained and should be released immediately. He'd simply been visiting his client when he'd been seized and imprisoned with no charges brought against him.

No sooner had he spoken than his client Esono proclaimed his innocence, noting that he was just a French language teacher in Bata and had nothing to do with any coup. His brother, Menene, chimed in, saying he had no idea why he'd been arrested.

Looking frail, Irene Adjomo, the last detainee, sat silently with downcast eyes. She said nothing until the minister demanded that she speak up. The terror on her face was palpable. Unlike her companions, who were eager to protest their innocence, she seemed drained of energy and emotion. Without looking up at anyone, she said in a low, weak voice she was a friend of Esono's. They'd been together when the police burst into his apartment and arrested both of them. She'd done nothing wrong and wanted to go home.

Thinking of what Dr. Monsogo had told me in Bata a couple of weeks earlier, I could only imagine the terrible abuses she'd experienced at Black Beach.

Without allowing me to ask the prisoners anything, the minister told the guards to take them away. He then turned in my direction and said he needed my advice. What would I recommend that he do with the prisoners?

He'd laid his trap and ensnared me. There was no right answer to his question, but I knew there was certainly any number of wrong ones that I needed to avoid.

"Mr. Minister, neither my government nor I in any way questions your right to conduct investigations of your citizens, particularly regarding the national security issues you've raised. However, Equatorial Guinea is obliged to comply with its national laws as well as its international commitments to respecting the rule of law. As you know, Mr. Minister, according to your constitution, anyone detained must be charged within seventy-two hours or released. Unfortunately, this has not happened in the case of Fabián Nsue and the other prisoners. And there was no warrant for Mr. Nsue's arrest when he was taken into custody at Black Beach. So respectfully, Mr. Minister, I would suggest either you bring charges against him and the others or release them."

The minister looked at me with the same interrogator's hard eyes I'd seen during our previous meeting. He asked if I was telling him to release Nsue and his companions. Raising his voice, Obama Nchama demanded to know what made me think I was qualified to lecture him on Equatorial Guinea's laws.

It was a swift return volley. "No, Mr. Minister. I'm sorry if you misunderstood me. Of course, the decision is entirely yours regarding the release of the prisoners. As a foreign diplomat, I have no say in such matters. Regarding Equatoguinean laws, I simply raised certain provisions based on my understanding of them. I would never presume to question your knowledge of such matters."

Minister Obama Nchama seemed pleased with my deferential answer. He then did something that caught both me and my two colleagues completely off guard. Turning to the six national security officials, he asked if they thought the prisoners should be released.

What had been Kafkaesque political theater was now turning into a kangaroo court. Each of the officials dutifully opined on the merits of either releasing Fabián and his companions or prosecuting them. Much to my surprise, they were more or less evenly divided on which of the two options the minister should choose.

It was just about then that the double doors suddenly opened again. This time, it was one of the minister's aides telling him he had an urgent phone call. Obama Nchama rose and disappeared into the adjoining room but reemerged seconds later, announcing the call was from the president, concerned about what we'd been discussing. He concluded by thanking me for coming on such short notice to meet with him and his officials.

With that, he closed the doors behind him. Whether this was a ruse to get rid of us or an actual call was not clear to me. But it was time to go, and we bade farewell to the officials. Two policemen appeared and escorted us out the front door.

When we got back to the embassy, I told Denise we should hold off writing a cable about what had happened until we saw if anything came out of the meeting. But as it turned out, we did not have to wait long. Within an hour, the Spanish ambassador, a strong advocate for human rights in EG, called me to say he'd heard that Fabián, Juan Menene, and

Irene Adjomo had all been released from Guantanamo. Fabián's client, Agustín Esono, however, was still in custody for now.

It was great news, and I was hopeful that it would be merely a matter of days before Esono would be free. However, he would face over a year more of imprisonment and never be charged with any crime. I went home feeling I'd truly accomplished something in getting three of the four of them out of jail.

But my celebration was to be brief. The following day, the embassy received a stiffly worded diplomatic note from the Foreign Ministry. It said Minister Mba Mokuy was immediately summoning me for a meeting.

Now, being "summoned" as an ambassador to the foreign ministry of a country is never a good thing. Arriving at EG's Foreign Ministry, I was immediately ushered into Mba Mokuy's office. I could tell by his stiff posture and the scowl on his face that this was going to be unpleasant. After asking me to sit down, he launched into a litany of complaints. He said that when I had a bilateral issue to raise with his government, the Vienna Convention required I do so through his ministry. Why then had I raised a matter with the minister of national security that had nothing to do with the bilateral relationship between our two countries?

Without giving me the opportunity to answer, Mba Mokuy asked rhetorically how the Department of State would react if Equatorial Guinea's ambassador to Washington went directly to the U.S. attorney general to complain about the imprisonment of a U.S. citizen. That, he claimed, was exactly what I had done in talking with the minister of national security about the whereabouts of Fabián Nsue, an Equatoguinean with no connection to the United States.

I had to give him credit. The foreign minister was eloquent, forceful, and impressive in the way he presented his points. Having paused, he gave me the chance to jump in. "Well, Mr. Minister, I appreciate your candor in sharing these views with me. But, of course, I must respectfully disagree with you. I previously sent the Foreign Ministry a diplomatic note stating I would be making courtesy calls on fellow ministers. My meeting with Minister of National Security Obama Nchama had been scheduled long before the disappearance of Mr. Nsue, and his whereabouts were still unknown when I met the minister. Further, his disappearance was of concern to my country. A key policy of the Obama administration is the promotion of human rights and respect for the rule of law around the world. So, when Equatorial Guinea's leading human rights attorney mysteriously disappears, that concerns my government. He's just not any private Equatoguinean citizen. Finally, I met Mr. Nsue when he attended my swearing-in ceremony at the State Department, so I was personally concerned about his welfare. This was another reason that I raised his disappearance with Minister Obama Nchama."

Mba Mokuy shifted in his seat and then insisted on knowing why if the matter was so important, I hadn't raised it directly with him. Had this been chess, he would have said, "Check."

The next move was mine. "Mr. Minister, as you're aware, you were traveling outside the country when all this occurred. Beyond that, given the Ministry of National Security's role in guarding Black Beach Prison and the fact Mr. Nsue was last seen there, I believe it was perfectly appropriate for me to raise his disappearance with Minister Obama Nchama. Certainly, you're not suggesting that I have to receive the Foreign Ministry's approval beforehand for topics I raise with other ministers?"

The foreign minister gave me a rather sour look, apparently miffed by that provocative question. He then began by saying that many years earlier, one of my predecessors had constantly complained to EG's government about human rights. As a result, he was an unsuccessful ambassador who had a difficult tenure. Looking at me, Mba Mokuy admonished that it would be most unfortunate should the same thing happen to me.

Of course, I knew Mba Mokuy was referring to Ambassador John Bennet, who'd served in Malabo from 1991 to 1994. He'd received death threats, been accused of witchcraft, and nearly been thrown out of the country as a persona non grata. I greatly admired Bennet's courage and principles.

"Mr. Minister, I'm quite aware that you are referring to my colleague, Ambassador John Bennett, whom I regard as someone who did an outstanding job here. That said, these are different times, and no two ambassadors are alike. What I can assure you is that as the representative of the United States, I will speak out on human rights and other issues whenever necessary to support my country's foreign policy priorities."

It had been a tense, tough exchange. I was not sure where it might lead. Barely two months into my tenure, I wondered afterward if this would indeed be a short ambassadorial assignment for me.

There was also another unanticipated result of my meetings with Minister of National Security Obama Nchama. He called to say that he would no longer be able to meet with me. The minister said he'd been told by Second Vice President Teodoro Nguema Mangue, the president's oldest son and heir apparent, that he was not to see me ever again.

Teodorin—as he is known, which means Little Theodore in Spanish, a nickname he detests—is a notoriously corrupt playboy, but he wields considerable power. However, he is unpopular with the general public as well as some members of the Fang tribal elite in the mainland city of Mongomo. Viewing him as unqualified, they argued at the time that he was not ready yet to be in the direct line of succession. He had been made second vice president for defense and national security, with an old party stalwart as the figurehead first vice president, who would, at least in theory, succeed Obiang in case of the president's death or disability.

However, there was no provision in EG's constitution for a second vice president. And as Teodorin was not in a constitutionally authorized position, other Western ambassadors and I refused to meet with him. Doing so would have lent our countries' recognition of his assumed role. Consequently, I had no plans to pay a courtesy call on Teodorin. I'm sure this was one of the reasons that he told Obama Nchama to avoid me.

But there was an odd spin to this. Apparently, Obama Nchama genuinely liked the United States and for whatever reason, seemed to have enjoyed our back-and-forth discussions on Fabián Nsue. As a result, he proposed a back-channel manner in which I could reach him without our having a meeting whenever I wanted to raise a national security matter with him.

What a bizarre arrangement, I thought. It was one of the many morally ambiguous choices I would have to make in Equatorial Guinea. If I agreed, I'd be establishing a murky means to contact a man who was notorious for cruelty. At the same time, being able to communicate with the minister could be extremely useful, as I'd already seen. After considerable thought, I decided to go along with what Obama Nchama proposed. I would have occasions in the coming months to use this channel. About a year later, the second vice president decided to end his meeting ban against me, which allowed me to see the minister again. The "moral grayness" I'd first learned to accept in Romania would also apply in EG.

After the "excitement" of my first two months, those that followed were relatively calm. EG's government authorized two members of the U.S. human rights group Freedom House to visit the country. It was a far cry from President Obiang's open invitation for all such groups he'd met in Washington to come to Malabo. But allowing such observers from even one group to have open access to reporting on the country was a first. The public report the two Freedom House staffers released after leaving the country was frank and fair in documenting the Obiang regime's denial of civil and human rights to its people.

Not long afterward, I informed the foreign minister that the United States had agreed to extend the validity of tourist and business visas for Equatoguineans from two to five years. Students would now have two- rather than one-year visas. The embassy's consular section had gathered data showing the State Department as well as Homeland Security that the instances of visa fraud and the number of those overstaying their visas were far lower in Equatorial Guinea than in neighboring Gabon and Cameroon. Therefore, we had a strong argument that EG should have the same longer visa durations as these countries.

With this new visa regime for his country, Minister Mba Mokuy never raised again requiring visas for American citizens. The next time I saw President Obiang, he thanked me for arranging longer validity of U.S. visas for Equatoguineans. I was back in the government's good graces, at least for the time being.

And this brings me to a brief discussion of the U.S. petroleum industry in EG, which included, when I was there, representatives from Exxon-Mobil, Noble, Marathon, Hess, and Vaalco. They were happy to learn that the Foreign Ministry was no longer threatening new regulations that would have required their U.S. employees to apply for EG visas. With that said, my relationship with these oil majors was a complicated one.

The companies wanted the status quo in EG to continue and had little interest in issues such as democracy and human rights. In fairness to them, if you were in the oil and gas extraction business, what was most important was that the government respect the sanctity of its contract with your company. In return, you provided the country with its stipulated profit share. It didn't matter whether the government was democratic or authoritarian. As one of the American executives once said to me, "Where we go to pump oil is based on geology, not politics."

The oil companies were quite satisfied with Equatorial Guinea's geology and their relationship with Minister of Mines, Energy, and Industry Gabriel Mbaga Obiang Lima. He was the U.S.-educated, hardworking younger son of President Obiang. Fluent in English, Gabriel (as everyone called him) thoroughly understood the oil and gas industry, respected the sanctity of contracts, and most importantly was supportive of the U.S. oil majors, who were his country's largest investors.

However, as it was widely known, Gabriel stood little chance of succeeding his father to the presidency. This was because his mother was not Equatoguinean. She was one of the polygamous president's many "tribal wives" who came from the nearby former Portuguese colony of São Tomé and Principe, now an independent island nation. Accordingly, given his mother's nationality, Gabriel was not seen as a full-blooded Fang, and this was a major drawback in EG.

In contrast, his older half-brother, Teodorin, was the son of First Lady Constancia Mangue de Obiang. Born to a family in the upper echelon of the Mongomo Fang tribe elite, Doña Constancia, as she was known, was Obiang's sole canonical wife, whom he'd married in the Catholic Church. In her view, Teodorin, whether qualified or not, was the "first son" whom she was determined to see succeed her husband. Not surprisingly, the two siblings disliked each other. Despite this, the president relied on his capable son Gabriel to run the country's complicated oil and gas industry.

While I suspected the U.S. oil and gas executives were not particularly pleased with my advocacy of human rights and democracy, we got along quite well. They were well-educated professionals who had decades of experience in the petroleum business and working overseas. One of my priorities was to support and promote U.S. business and on occasion when the oilmen believed their companies were being treated unfairly by the EG government, I would meet with Minister Gabriel to ask for his assistance.

I enjoyed occasionally visits to the oil companies' "Little America" enclaves, as well as going to a luxurious new part of Malabo called Sipopo. As host of the 2011 African Union Summit meeting, the Obiang regime built a multimillion-dollar deluxe "city" to accommodate African leaders. Each was housed in one of the fifty-two luxury presidential villas built just for that event. There were also new conference centers in Sipopo, plus a state-of-the-art Israeli-run hospital for the elite, an artificial beach, the five-star Sofitel Hotel, and the country's first 18-hole golf course. Sipopo was constructed at enormous expense over two years to host a one-week-long summit. The presidential mansions and conference centers remained empty unless there were international meetings. Only members of the government and foreigners could afford to use Sipopo's golf course, clinic, hotel restaurant, pool, and other amenities.

I decided early on that I was not going to spend much of my time among the privileged in such "bubbles," while the majority of EG's citizens were impoverished. The best way to convey this message, I thought, would be to make high-profile visits to Campo Yaoundé, Malabo's worst slum, as well as to the city's wretched, Spanish-era "General Hospital." The embassy's security officer thought that my going to Campo Yaoundé was dangerous and a bad idea. After I insisted, we agreed I would go to the slum accompanied by one of our Equatoguinean security guards, who'd grown up there. I wore casual clothes, left the embassy car several blocks away, and walked into Campo Yaoundé with the guard.

Entering the slum, I saw and smelled raw sewage running through open channels on both sides of its muddy streets. There were nests of tangled wires overhead taking "free" electricity from outside utilities, and inhabitants lived in run-down wooden shacks with no running water. Visiting Campo Yaoundé was a reality check for me and also a political statement to the regime.

About a week later, I went to see the General Hospital. After being given a tour of the newer portions of the medical campus, I asked to visit the multistory Spanish-colonial-era hospital where most of the patients' wards still were. Unlike the newer air-conditioned buildings, the old hospital had windows open to catch a breeze in the torpid heat. Blood splats stained the floors, and the corridors and sick bays reeked of feces and urine. The shelves in the hospital's pharmacy were virtually bare, with fewer medicines and supplies than those in our tiny embassy infirmary. There was hopelessness in the faces of the patients I saw, who were sitting forlornly in the overcrowded waiting rooms. There seemed to be few medical personnel.

What a contrast, I thought, to the new Israeli-run La Paz Clinic in Sipopo, with its highly trained foreign physicians, spotless operating theaters, high-tech equipment, and comfortable hospital rooms for patients. It was rare for any ordinary Equatoguinean citizen to be admitted to La Paz. The clinic's prices were on a scale with those found in the United States.

When foreign delegations came to the capital, the regime immediately whisked them from the airport to Sipopo on Malabo II's six-lane highway. There, they were lodged at the luxurious French-operated Sofitel Hotel. The last thing the government wanted such visitors to see was the squalor and misery of Campo Yaoundé or the horrible conditions at the General Hospital. For that matter, few diplomats ever saw either, as it was far easier just to pretend that they didn't exist. For me, it was important to see both despite how hard it was to do so. They were shameful reminders of how people were treated in a country that had Africa's highest per-capita income.

I also made another provocative move that I suspected the government wouldn't like. To celebrate African History Month, I planned a late-February roundtable to discuss the many contributions of African Americans to U.S. society and to link this with a discussion of African history and culture. I invited as our keynote speaker, Michael Battle, who was the U.S. ambassador to the African Union in Addis Ababa

A political appointee, Ambassador Battle was an ordained minister with a doctorate from Howard University. He'd taught theology courses and held senior administrative positions at several historically black universities. In addition, he'd been a U.S. Army chaplain for two decades, retiring with the rank of lieutenant colonel. Given his impressive background and accomplishments, I thought he was an ideal choice and was delighted when the ambassador accepted my invitation.

To round out the panel, I invited Minister of Culture and Tourism Guillermina Mekuy, a young woman who had published several novels in Spain. Finally, I asked the South African ambassador to speak. The program was held in the large conference room of a hotel not far from the national university. At the last moment, the South African canceled. In his place, we added State Department employee Otis Pratt, who was working as a construction specialist at our new embassy compound. Otis was an African American who'd spent most of his professional life working in Africa. He brought a fascinating perspective to the roundtable's dual themes.

On the night of the program, the conference room was packed, mostly with students. Local television taped the roundtable for later broadcast. Minister Mekuy spoke on African culture and how she incorporated cultural themes into her writing. Ambassador Battle, a polished presenter who spoke in a resonant voice, traced the history of the U.S. civil rights movement and the importance of civil society organizations. Otis reflected on his personal experiences in both the United States and Africa. Everything went smoothly until the question-and-answer period.

The students began by asking the ambassador a number of excellent questions about the continuing civil rights struggle in the United States, as well as racial discrimination there. He had thoughtful, candid answers. The questions for the minister of a culture focused on what audience members said were restrictions on students' free speech.

Mokuy was combative and attacked the questioners. She was unprepared, as it was exceptionally rare for an Equatoguinean official to be challenged in a public forum. I was pleased with what I took to be a lively, informative discussion on civil rights. Of course, that was not at all a view shared by the Foreign Ministry.

For the second time in less than a year, I was called in by Minister Mba Mokuy. He began our meeting by saying the government was "not pleased" with the roundtable. One had to be "careful" in discussing themes with young people for which they were "unprepared." I needed to understand this could be "dangerous." The minister then charged that I had "misled" the government with a diplomatic note requesting the minister of culture's participation. My program, he said, had not been about culture at all but rather "political" in nature.

I replied that culture and politics were often inseparable in the United States, especially for African Americans in their struggle for civil rights. I added that Ambassador Battle was not a political activist but rather a distinguished African American educator and administrator who had first-hand knowledge about the U.S. civil rights movement. I concluded that the minister of culture had given an excellent presentation on African culture, and the program, in my view, had been a balanced one. Needless to say, that did little to assuage the minister, and state media never broadcast the roundtable.

Unlike on the previous occasion, the foreign minister didn't issue a veiled threat to expel me. But he let me know that I'd once again deeply displeased his government by raising democracy and civil rights. To say he was personally unhappy with me would be an understatement. However, things were about to get even worse in our relationship.

A visiting senior State Department official had raised the possibility with President Obiang of the United States providing electoral experts to advise the government and all of the political parties on improving upcoming municipal and parliamentary elections. The president seemed open to the proposal, so I arranged a follow-up discussion with him to make a specific offer. I asked if the president was interested in having a U.S. organization like the "International Federation of Electoral Systems" (IFES) come to EG before the elections. Obiang seemed to welcome such U.S. electoral assistance, and I saw this as an opportunity to help ensure more competitive and fair elections scheduled just a couple of months away.

I contacted IFES, which said it could not come to Equatorial Guinea on such short notice. Not deterred, I was able to secure an early-May visit of an election expert from the Organization of American States and a political science professor who'd previously worked at the Carter Center. In April, the embassy sent a diplomatic note to the Foreign Ministry referring to my meeting with President Obiang and informing the government of the experts' upcoming visit. Everything appeared to be set.

But in a subsequent meeting with Minister of Interior Clemente Engonga, I was told having the electoral experts come before the elections was a bad idea. He suggested it was too late for the specialists to come, suggesting they might visit at a later date. I replied that President Obiang had personally approved this visit, but the minister insisted that I should "reconsider."

Minister Engonga was a high-ranking member of the ruling PDGE party and at the same time served as the longtime head of the national electoral commission. The opposition had told me that he controlled all aspects of the electoral process and was at the center of rigging elections. When I asked him if he thought there was a conflict of interest for him as a government official and PDGE member to be overseeing elections, he smiled broadly and said absolutely not. He claimed he was completely neutral as head of the electoral commission.

Shortly after seeing Engonga, I received a terse diplomatic note from the Ministry of Foreign Affairs, saying that the government did not want or need the two election experts and they should not come to Equatorial Guinea. By coincidence, President Obiang was in the United States about this time and was scheduled to see the acting assistant secretary for African affairs. I decided to ask my colleagues in the Bureau of Africa Affairs to have this senior State Department official ask the president to allow the election experts to come.

But when the issue came up during their meeting, Obiang was adamant, telling the acting assistant secretary that his country already had its own American electoral experts. He also complained that I was too much of a hard-charger when it came to democracy and human rights. Much to my surprise and disappointment, I learned from the bureau that the acting assistant secretary did not push back but instead assured the president the embassy would cancel the speakers.

I was left with no other option but to follow Washington's orders and scrap the program. When I informed my staff the following morning, my office manager Christine asked me how this would affect my "personal prestige" and standing as an ambassador, given that I'd been thwarted not only by the EG government but also by the Department of State. She wondered how the opposition parties and non-government organizations in the country would react and if it would impact my future dealings with the EG government. I appreciated Christine's candor, as they were all good points. There was no doubt that I'd been given the double whammy by both governments.

I replied that I had a clear mission as U.S. ambassador to promote democracy and electoral transparency. With the next major elections in EG not scheduled until 2016, after I'd completed my tour, the upcoming polls offered the best opportunity to pursue these goals. I added that I was confident EG's opposition and others would understand that I had done everything I could to promote free and fair elections, which turned out to be the case.

What was most interesting from this episode was learning about the so-called U.S. elections experts mentioned by President Obiang at his State Department meeting. Obiang was referring to International Decisions Strategies (IDS), a U.S. for-profit consulting company run by R. Bruce McColm, former director of the International Republican Institute (IRI). Both IDS and McColm had checkered histories. During the 2002 presidential election, EG's government had paid McColm and his company over a half million dollars for "monitoring services."

It was an election in which all opposition candidates dropped out, and President Obiang was reelected with 100 percent of the vote.

Given this background, it was no surprise that during the May 2013 elections, McColm and IDS were completely at the service of the EG government although they once again claimed to be monitoring experts. Of course, when President Obiang told me he welcomed U.S. electoral experts, he meant IDS's being in EG to make sure the PDGE won.

With IDS's assistance and the regime's enormous resources, including control of the media, the legislative and local elections turned out much the same as all previous polls. The PDGE won all of the seats in the Chamber of Representatives and the newly created Senate, except for one delegate in each body awarded as a token to the Convergence for Social Democracy (CPDS) opposition party. In local elections, the PDGE claimed victory in all of the races. Democracy had once again lost.

In early June, Jane and I flew back on paid leave to the United States for what the Department of State calls "rest and recreation" (R&R) for its diplomats. In my case, it felt more like rest and recovery as I approached the first-year mark in Equatorial Guinea. Despite setbacks and some missteps, I'd stood up for what I believed in and felt I'd accomplished a great deal.

CHAPTER 15

Under the Volcano

L ET ME EXPLAIN this chapter's title with a bit more history. British settlers in the late 1820s were the first Europeans to climb the majestic, nearly ten-thousand-foot volcanic peak on what was then Fernando Po Island. In preparing for my assignment, I sometimes wondered how the indigenous Bantu-speaking tribes who had inhabited the island long before the arrival of the Europeans thought about this soaring peak. I imagined they must have regarded it with a mixture of fear and reverence.

For there was something mysterious about Pico Basilé, as the Spanish named it, with its summit almost perpetually cloaked in dense clouds and mist. The Obiang regime had established the seventy-thousand-acre Pico Basilé National Park on the volcano's slopes. At least in the country's official tourist literature, this huge park offered visitors the opportunity to see diverse high-altitude plants and other vegetation. The government also claimed the refuge provides a habitat for endangered primates, which are protected from illegal hunting.

But as with many other aspects of life on Bioko Island, things were not quite what they seemed. Far from being a vast, welcoming national park where people could hike, camp, and enjoy nature, all of Pico Basilé was a closed-off national-security-restricted zone. There was a large military barracks near the road leading to the peak, and soldiers guarded the entry gate. And members of the military were often the ones engaged in the illegal hunting of primates and other endangered species.

It took time and effort, but before Jane and I left Bioko, we were finally able to secure a special permit allowing us and a number of the embassy's American staff to visit Pico Basilé. After negotiating with the guards, who suspiciously examined our permit before allowing us to enter, our caravan of several private vehicles slowly ascended the steep, winding, narrow road built by the Spaniards.

It was fantastic to spend time near the summit of Pico Basilé, but doing so raised the question of why this incredibly scenic part of the island was closed off to virtually all Equatoguineans and just a small number of foreigners. Was it because of the danger of volcanic activity? The last major eruption, which had devastated the city, occurred almost a century earlier. However, there were signs that Pico Basilé was far from inactive.

In 2012, just before our arrival, steam vented from fissures near the summit. And there would be no seismic monitors installed on the peak until 2017. Therefore, the danger of such an event could not be ruled out. Nevertheless, I soon would learn that it was the regime's paranoia rather than the threat of lava flows, which led to Pico Basilé being declared off-limits because of "national security" concerns.

Equatorial Guinea is a place where there are constant rumors of possible coups to overthrow the country's authoritarian government. Some of these, such as the alleged October 2012 plot shortly after my arrival, were fabricated by the government and had no basis in reality. The Obiang regime used them to stifle dissent and impose new repressive measures on the population. But some of the threats were quite real. Recent attacks included one in February 2009 when heavily armed mercenaries in small boats landed near Malabo's presidential palace. Their intent was to kidnap President Obiang and hold him for ransom. The president was not actually in Malabo at that time, and after a fierce gun battle, presidential guards successfully repelled the attackers.

The most famous attempt to overthrow Obiang occurred in 2004. Called the "Wonga Coup," using an African slang word for *money*, it included a motley band of international mercenaries led by former British Special Air Services (SAS) officer Simon Mann. The goal of Mann's coup was to replace President Obiang with Severo Moto, an exiled political opponent living in Spain who had gone to the Canary Islands. According to the plan, he would await word of a successful coup there and then be flown to Malabo. Moto had already signed exclusive deals for rights to oil and other resources to the plotters, which would have made Mann and others rich. But the plot fell apart when a rented Boeing 727, with Mann and sixty-four former soldiers recruited in South Africa onboard, landed in Harare, Zimbabwe, to pick up an arms shipment. The plane never took off for Malabo.

President Mugabe's government arrested the mercenaries at the Harare airport. He then tipped off Obiang about the coup, and the co-conspirators already on the ground in Equatorial Guinea were quickly rounded up. Mann and his companions were imprisoned in Zimbabwe, with those in Malabo were also jailed. Mann would eventually be extradited to EG and spend time in Black Beach Prison before being released. The coup had elements tantalizingly similar to the plot of Frederick Forsyth's 1974 thriller *The Dogs of War*.

However, on our return to Malabo from R&R in late June 2013, I was not focused on the latest coup rumor. My biggest challenge was the completion of the new embassy compound. Opening this new diplomatic facility would represent having a "real embassy" in Equatorial Guinea, and during the coming months, my all-consuming task was making sure everything went smoothly.

In early August, we got good news. After several delays because of quality issues, the Department of State finally certified that the new embassy compound, including the chief of mission's residence and other staff housing, was ready for occupancy. But in the year leading to its completion, there had been nothing but headaches. Unlike the on-site construction managers with whom I'd worked as the deputy chief of mission in Kazakhstan and Sudan, the one in Malabo could not have been more difficult and evasive when construction problems occurred.

Even while still in Washington, I realized there would be issues with some of the materials used in the construction of this fifty-three-million-dollar complex. Shortly before Jane and I flew to Malabo, I'd gone to the State Department's Overseas Building Office (OBO) to look at plans and sketches of what the completed embassy compound would look like. And there I saw an immediate problem: wood was being used in "rain screens" on building exteriors. As noted earlier, EG has one of the wettest climates in the world. I told OBO officials that, given these conditions, it seemed to make no sense to use wood. I was immediately assured by the staff there that this would not be a problem. Special "ipe wood" appropriate for tropical climates was being used.

A year later, I could see that I'd been right. The external wood on the buildings was already becoming discolored and beginning to buckle. When I brought this up with the project director, he said the rain screens would be repaired and receive a coating of waterproofing shellac. However, that did little to solve the problem. As it turned out, though, this would prove to be the least of our worries.

Despite this and other concerns, we went ahead with the move. Temporary staff from Washington arrived and helped us pack essential supplies and materials in well-coordinated sequences. As the compound had been supplied with new furniture, computers, and equipment already in place, these items in the old embassy went into storage for eventual sale. Prior to the move to the new chancery, all of the American officers had packed up their personal belongings and moved to the compound's housing, which was also fully furnished. On our last day at the villa that had served as our embassy for nearly a decade, we had a flag-lowering ceremony in the front yard.

Jane and I were delighted to be in the spacious two-story CMR, or chief of mission's residence. Through the privately funded Art in Embassies Program, the Department of State allowed ambassadors and their spouses to choose American art to display in the CMR. It came from a large varied collection of multimedia work on loan to the U.S. government. In keeping with our planned retirement to Santa Fe, New Mexico, we chose art that primarily depicted that beautiful state.

Upstairs, we had a wraparound outside veranda with breathtaking views of the Pico Basilé. The CMR seemed very close to that looming volcanic peak. In many ways, it became a metaphor for our life in Equatorial Guinea: while everything might seem calm, we never knew what was rumbling just below the surface and about to explode.

One of the areas in our new home that we enjoyed the most was a small screened porch on the ground floor, where we often read while listening to the chirping sounds of an array of colorful tropical birds.

But there were also snakes! One day, I noticed that our Maine Coon cat Chessie was fixated on something on the other side of our dining room's closed glass door. It proved to be a six foot long green mamba, a highly venomous emerald-hued serpent. After Jane and I watched it try unsuccessfully to slither up the exterior wall of the house, I called a local employee in the General Services section to ask for help. This brave staffer managed to get the green mamba into a large trash can with a hinged cover. Tender-hearted souls that Jane and I are, we didn't want him to kill it. Instead, he took it to a heavily wooded area and set it free. But that was not our only encounter with a snake.

One Sunday morning, I noticed that our other feline, Pasha, appeared to be playing with a string on the dining room floor. When I took a closer look, I realized it was a small green mamba he'd captured on our downstairs porch. Jane was in the kitchen when I announced rather calmly, "Hey, Jane, come look. Pasha's just brought a green mamba into the dining room!"

Of course, that was the wrong thing to have said. Alarmed, Jane rushed into the dining room. I could tell she thought that somehow the six-foot green creature had made a return visit and was now inside the house. As this was a Sunday, there was no one at the embassy to call for help. Miraculously, the small viper had not bitten Pasha, which certainly would have done him in. Our first task was to get this curious feline away from the snake without our being bitten in the process.

With great care and no absence of tense communication, we accomplished this. Then Jane had an inspired idea. She put a wastepaper basket over the serpent to trap it, and then retrieved a cookie sheet from the kitchen, sliding it carefully beneath the snake. And now came the really hard part: still in our pajamas, we picked up the basket, firmly holding it against the cookie sheet and trash can securely, and gingerly carried both outside. We took our quarry to the farthest edge of the perimeter wall and released it. Whether out of gratitude or fear, neither the green mambas nor for that matter their relatives ever visited us again.

Besides those visits by the inquisitive vipers, everything seemed to be going along just fine. But then, the metaphoric volcano erupted, and I was confronted with a completely-unanticipated crisis. This time, rather than involving EG's government, it came from within the embassy itself.

As I've mentioned previously, the recently completed embassy was in Malabo II, the new part of the city. Our former headquarters had been close to public transportation and near where many of our local employees lived. There were also inexpensive restaurants and food stands where they could eat in the old neighborhood. Malabo II was far from the city center and a virtual ghost town with little more to offer beyond mostly empty government buildings.

Soon after our move, Rafael, my DCM, departed for a new assignment. My acting DCM, Aye Okojie, told me that the Equatoguinean employees were not happy. Finding transportation to the new compound was expensive, as taxis charged more to go to Malabo II. Unlike the previous embassy building, where there had been a kitchen used by local employees to make lunch, there was no such area in our new digs. Additionally, the new embassy lacked a cafeteria. Even worse, it had been years since the State Department had provided worldwide raises for its overseas local staff. On top of all this, the meager transportation allowances our local employees received was inadequate to get them to and from the new embassy. They wanted to know how they would pay for their increased transportation costs.

When informed of this, I asked Aye to gather data from the employees on these unexpected costs, including the average increase in distance they had to travel from their homes to the new facility. Based on this information, we requested that the State Department provide a significant increase in the transportation allowance. Aye also identified space in the chancery to create a kitchen and eating area for our employees. Finally, he inquired about the possibility of having local vendors come to our compound at lunchtime to sell inexpensive food to our staff.

I felt we were not only listening to our local employees' legitimate complaints but also doing everything we could to address them. Accordingly, I was flabbergasted one Monday morning in early September when the head of the local employees' association came to my office to present me with a petition. Signed by most of our national staff, it said that unless I found a "fast solution" to getting them an adequate transportation allowance, virtually all of the local employees would go "on strike" the following Monday. The petition ended by asserting that this was their "peaceful right."

Without having to consult either Washington or Peji Khan, my regional human resources officer (HRO), I knew it was against the law for federal workers to go on strike. I asked Aye to contact a local attorney who sometimes did legal work for the embassy, and he told us that Equatoguinean law also prohibits employees from walking off the job. Clearly, the embassy was on firm, legal ground regarding the illegality of a threatened strike. I knew that when it came to increasing allowances, the State Department never moved quickly. And if the local staff broke both U.S. and EG law by refusing to come to work, there was no way I could run the embassy with just nine foreign service officers.

The first thing I did was provide the local employees with copies of the cables we'd sent to the Department requesting an increase in the transportation allowance. There were also replies from Washington that I shared with them indicating the request was under review. I then sent them a memo noting provisions of U.S. law prohibiting strikes by federal workers, both Americans and local overseas employees. I wrote that I wanted to have a productive, cooperative relationship with them and a partnership between management and embassy employees. Finally, I convened an all-hands meeting of local employees for that Friday.

The embassy had an all-purpose conference room large enough for the entire local staff. HRO Peji Khan was based at the U.S. embassy in Nigeria and joined the meeting via a conference call. Aye sat next to me at the head of the conference table, but as ambassador, I was clearly front and center in delivering a tough message. I looked around the room at the unhappy faces of my entire local labor force. I'd studied all of the relevant regulations and terms of the workers' contracts and was fully prepared.

I started my presentation by taking a legalistic approach, detailing the prohibitions against strikes in both U.S. and EG laws. I then spoke of what Aye and I had done to address the workers' legitimate concerns, especially regarding their increased transportation costs. In addition to the cables they'd already seen that had asked for a higher allowance, I told them I'd spent a great deal of time on phone calls with Department of State officials urging a quick resolution. Changing my tone somewhat, I said that I'd come from a blue-collar, working-class family and understood the sorts of financial issues they'd raised. But I continued, returning to a harder line, I regarded loyalty as a two-way street. I believed that I could get them the increased transportation allowance, but it would take time. In return, I expected they would support me by remaining on the job.

I then hit them full force, saying that anyone who went on strike would be subject to losing his or her job. This was U.S. law, and I had every intention of following it to the letter. Peji joined the conversation and described the process for terminating the employment of workers who went on an illegal strike.

It was now the turn of the head of the local employees' association to respond. He accused me of being undemocratic and oblivious to the legitimate rights of the local workers by presenting them with a "take it or leave it" choice. I pushed back vigorously, restating the legal constraints I was under, my expectations of them as workers, and my commitment to continue doing everything I could on their behalf. But I was also resolved to begin firing those who went on strike.

There was silence until the deputy of the local employees' association, a soft-spoken employee in the political section, stood up. He was the exact opposite of his fire-brand colleague and began by thanking me for explaining my position on the proposed strike. He said it was now time for all of the local employees to go into a separate session to discuss what I'd just shared with them. They nodded in agreement around the room. I said I appreciated his and everyone's understanding of the situation and pledged once again to do what I could to obtain the transportation benefit for them. With that, the meeting ended.

Later that day, Aye told me that cooler heads prevailed during the follow-on employees' meeting. He'd learned that many of them said they had not understood the consequences of signing the petition threatening to strike. In the end, they all agreed among themselves not to strike, and two months later, the department, at long last, informed the embassy that our requested increase in the transportation allowance had been approved.

The session with the employees was one of the toughest things I would have to do as an ambassador in Equatorial Guinea. In speaking with them, I'd been hard-edged and unrelenting as I pursued one objective: stopping the employees from going on strike. My chief responsibility as ambassador was to run the embassy. I was relieved that in the end, it had all worked out for both them and me.

In mid-September, my new deputy chief of mission, Joyce Namde, arrived at the post. As helpful as Aye had been, it was great to have a full-time DCM again. I'd personally recruited Joyce, who was a highly knowledgeable Africa hand with years of administrative experience running consular sections. Her husband, Basile, originally from Chad, worked remotely as a consular specialist for the State Department's Bureau of Consular Affairs. Both would prove to be invaluable in the months ahead as we settled into the compound.

Shortly after her arrival, I put Joyce in charge of organizing the embassy's inauguration ceremony, which was scheduled for October 17. I was delighted that Undersecretary for Management Patrick Kennedy had accepted our invitation to come to Malabo as the State Department's representative for the event.

Those plans were thrown into disarray when the U.S. federal government shut down on October 1 after Congress failed to appropriate funds for the fiscal year 2014. Negotiations broke down between the Obama administration and the House and Senate Republicans to pass a continuing resolution providing stop-gap funding. Fortunately, the shutdown ended in mid-October, when the political impasse was broken. But Undersecretary Pat Kennedy's visit and the inauguration were postponed until December, and this proved to not necessarily be a bad thing.

Starting in late September, the compound began to have one mechanical breakdown after the next. For the first year, we limped along with frequent power outages. And then, there were the water main breaks throughout the compound. The U.S. construction company had cut corners by using substandard pipes, and we wound up having to replace much of the defective system. My new deputy Joyce performed superbly in dealing with these constant problems.

Most of the short-term construction glitches had been addressed by the time Undersecretary Kennedy and Heather Townsend, one of his senior staffers, arrived in Malabo for the December 11 inauguration. President Obiang had accepted my invitation to come to the event but subsequently canceled to attend the funeral of Nelson Mandela. The first vice president, prime minister, and minister of foreign affairs represented the government at the inauguration.

My DCM Joyce was also its master of ceremonies and introduced the speakers. Pat went first, followed by First Vice President Ignacio Milam Tang. I said a few words, mostly thanking everyone who had made the new embassy possible. Our remarks were all mercifully brief. Pat and the vice president next unveiled a black granite plaque attached to the outside wall near the embassy's entryway. It was inscribed with Secretary Hillary Clinton's name and mine as U.S. ambassador, along with the date of the inauguration. There was a ribbon cutting, and Joyce invited guests to a reception in the embassy's multipurpose room.

The rest of Pat's visit went smoothly. Joyce briefed him on the many construction flaws we were experiencing, and he promised to provide whatever assistance we needed. That evening, Jane and I hosted a dinner for Pat that was attended by members of the opposition, diplomatic colleagues, and U.S. petroleum company representatives. The following day, Pat met with the American and local employees before departing.

But as with the passing of all such momentous events, I felt a let-down after the inauguration. During downtime in late December and January, I thought about what I hoped to accomplish before I left Malabo. During the first half of my tour, I'd frequently taken an "in your face" approach to advocating democracy and human rights with the government. I had no regrets about this, but doing so often led to my slamming into a proverbial brick wall. While I had no intention of ceasing such direct advocacy, I decided that occasionally changing tactics might be more effective in getting across important messages in these areas. Looking ahead, I had a useful example of how several months earlier, I'd effectively used "cultural diplomacy"

Although Equatorial Guinea did not have theaters, the country had an outstanding independent theatrical company called Bocamandja. Its director was an accomplished poet and playwright who sometimes described himself as an "outraged artist." The company derived its name from two typical national dishes: bacao and mandijaa. Its repertoire consisted almost exclusively of works by Equatoguinean writers, many of whom had been forced to flee the country into exile. The themes of such works were frequently provocative, including the prevalence of domestic violence, gender discrimination, and the lack of AIDS education in EG's schools. But in presenting such works, the company also added humor and surrealism to their interpretations, which helped them avoid government censorship

Bocamandja usually performed at either the Spanish or the French cultural centers. I'd been impressed by the group's work. I was more than happy to have the U.S. embassy sponsor a visit by a U.S. theater professional to work with the company. Dora Arreola was a Spanish-speaking associate professor of theater at the University of South Florida. Tutu Alicante, director of the U.S.-based human rights group EG Justice, contacted me about doing a program in EG with her. We worked together to arrange for her to come to Malabo.

Part of the U.S. embassy's human rights agenda was advocating against gender violence and promoting the rights of women and girls. Dora worked with all of the company's members on acting skills and stage movements. But she spent additional time with its women, coaching them on how to project empowerment and strength in roles on subjects like domestic violence and gender discrimination. I went to a session and saw how Dora worked with the female members of the company. Dora's master classes accomplished far more on these subjects than my talking about them with government officials. It was cultural diplomacy at its best.

Following this program, I lined up other major artistic events in my remaining year and a half. Perhaps the boldest of these initiatives was inviting American journalist and filmmaker David France to come to

Malabo. France's 2012 award-winning documentary *How to Survive a Plague* was a chronicle of how political activists in the AIDS Coalition to Unleash Power (ACT UP) and the Treatment Action Group (TAG) demanded that the U.S. government do far more to develop effective HIV/AIDS drugs and treatments for the thousands of mostly gay men dying from the disease. Through large-scale highly vocal but peaceful demonstrations in the 1980s and 1990s, the HIV activists successfully pushed government officials and drug manufacturers into taking urgent action, including devoting more money to AIDS research.

France's documentary won critical acclaim and numerous awards, including a 2012 Academy Award nomination for Best Documentary Feature. During his October 2014 visit to Malabo, he was accompanied by an associate dean of the University of Southern California's School of Cinematic Arts and a Cuban American filmmaker and writer. On one level, France's and his colleagues' programs could be seen as sharing information with foreign audiences on U.S. documentary filmmaking. But from a public diplomacy perspective, his documentary's messages were far more important than how he made the film. *How I Survived a Plague* is about the power of protest by ordinary citizens and civil society organizations.

Getting Equatoguineans together to talk about the film's substance and the need for change in their own country was really my bottom-line objective. To that end, the night after *How to Survive a Plague* was shown, Jane and I hosted a large reception at our residence attended by government officials, local filmmakers, students, opposition party leaders, and those from the nongovernment organization community.

These were people from opposite ends of the political spectrum. They rarely, if ever, had occasion to speak with each other, let alone socialize. On that evening, they freely mingled, and undoubtedly a liberal supply of alcoholic beverages and good food helped with the conversation. Although not fluent in Spanish, David was quite comfortable informally conversing in the language. That meant he was able to speak about the film with a large number of the guests. Jane was the one who oversaw our receptions, and she deserves enormous credit for what proved to be one of the most productive official gatherings we hosted in Equatorial Guinea.

One of the hardest things about cultural diplomacy is the impossibility of measuring its short-term effectiveness. You are planting seeds. The rewards are seldom immediate, which was certainly true of the Bocamandja, David France, and other cultural programs I initiated in Equatorial Guinea. But I believed that doing them would have future positive results long after I left the country.

I greatly enjoyed supervising this work, which was ably arranged by my public affairs staff. However, that was only a small part of what I did as an ambassador. Embassies are expected to provide insightful political and economic reporting back to Washington. Denise Taylor and the two officers who followed her wrote insightful cables on these issues. At a small post like Malabo, I also drafted a fair amount of reporting cables, as did my deputies and others.

For those of us serving in Africa, 2014 was a special year because the U.S.-Africa Leaders Summit was scheduled in Washington that summer. My friend Michael Battle, who'd spoken in EG for Black History Month, had finished his ambassadorial tour at the African Union. He was now back in Washington as one of the chief organizers of this mammoth event.

In my view, during President Obama's two terms, the summit would be his most important foreign policy initiative for Africa. It involved meetings at the State Department during August 4–6 between the president and fifty sub-Saharan African leaders. The principal focus was on trade, investment, and security on the continent. The idea for the summit originated during Obama's 2013 three-nation Africa tour when he'd noted that America's annual trade with African nations was $85 billion compared to China's $200 billion. However, although trade and investment were the central themes of the gathering, the summit also included issues that were focused on Africa's new generation.

President Obama had a genuine interest in helping Africa develop the enormous potential of its youth. In 2010, he established the Young African Leaders Initiative (YALI), which was a program aimed at providing young African leaders with opportunities to network with their American counterparts. YALI fellowships to the United States were in business and entrepreneurship, civil society management, and public policy and management. In recognition of the continent's youthful population, the summit was organized under the rubric of "investing in the next generation" and went beyond economic issues by having sessions devoted to the importance of civil society, women, peace and prosperity, food security, and health care.

Several leaders of sub-Saharan African nations were not invited to the summit. Sudan's Omar al-Bashir was under an International Criminal Court arrest warrant for crimes against humanity; Zimbabwe's Robert Mugabe was excluded because of U.S. economic sanctions against his regime; and Eritrea's president Isaias Afwerk, sanctioned by the UN, also refused to fully accredit the U.S. ambassador in his country. Rounding out the list of the "uninvited" were the Central African Republic, recently suspended from African Union membership following a coup, and the Sahrawi Arab Democratic Republic (former Western Sahara), which was not recognized as an independent nation by the United States.

There were some in the U.S. government who maintained that President Obiang should also be excluded. They cited the fact that he was the continent's longest-serving authoritarian leader and that Equatorial Guinea had a terrible human rights record. I opposed President Obiang's exclusion from the summit for a number of reasons.

First, there were no U.S. or international sanctions against either him or EG. Second, we had full diplomatic relations with the country, and our policy was to engage with the government on democracy and human rights. Finally, U.S. oil majors were Equatorial Guinea's largest investors, and due to this, it made no sense to exclude the country from a gathering largely focused on increasing U.S. trade and investment in Africa. In the end, I was pleased that the State Department's Bureau of Africa Affairs supported Obiang's attendance, sharing my view that it was imperative we engage with EG's president to promote change.

Secretary John Kerry would have one-on-one side meetings at the summit with a small number of democratic African leaders whom the United States viewed as moving their countries in the right direction.

President Obiang was not going to be among that group. I argued, though, that he should meet with a senior State Department official who would deliver strong messages on the need for democracy and good governance as well as respect for human rights in his country. I requested that he meet with Undersecretary for Political Affairs Wendy Sherman, the third highest-ranking official at the State Department

During my year working as chief of staff for Under Secretary Otero, I'd had many occasions to see Sherman in action at meetings. She was smart, tough, and not someone who minced her words in stating U.S. foreign policy. I knew Sherman would speak the unvarnished truth to Obiang about democracy, human rights, and corruption. However, many at the State opposed the meeting for a very specific reason.

In 2006, Secretary of State Condoleezza Rice met with Obiang at the State Department. Addressing the press while standing next to EG's president, Rice said, "You are a good friend, and we welcome you." Given Obiang's horrible human rights record, her remark was a major embarrassment to the U.S. government. Nobody wanted to see that happen again. Consequently, it took strong support once again from the Bureau of Africa Affairs for me to get an agreement for an Obiang-Sherman tête-à-tête. The ground rules could not have been clearer: it would be a private meeting in the undersecretary's office with no press coverage and absolutely no photos.

The Department of State requested that all U.S. ambassadors to African countries travel to Washington to be present during the August 4–6 summit. Before leaving Malabo, I'd written a briefing memorandum with background and talking points to prepare Sherman for her discussion with Obiang. The messages I wanted her to deliver were the same tough ones I'd been making with the EG government for the past two years. They included telling the Obiang regime it was time it started using its vast oil and gas wealth for the benefit of its citizens by investing in education and health care for them. In addition, after close to four decades in power, Obiang needed to start preparing for a democratic political transition and allow opposition parties and civil society a greater role in governance.

MARK L. ASQUINO

Undersecretary Sherman was in her mid-sixties. She sported dark-frame glasses and wore her silver hair in a stylish cut. Her office was on the seventh floor, just down the hall from Secretary Kerry's suite. I sat in as the notetaker. Sherman got right down to business, forcefully making the points I'd outlined in the memo. She was respectful but clear in how she presented each. As his interpreter translated them, I could see the look of surprise on Obiang's face. It was one thing to hear all of this from me but quite another to be told the same thing by such an important senior official.

In response, Obiang launched into his usual speech about the tremendous progress Equatorial Guinea had made under his "benevolent rule." There was peace, stability, and prosperity in the country following the first disastrous decade under his predecessor. He maintained that EG was a multiparty democracy and that in addition to the ruling PDGE, the country's national assembly and Senate included opposition members from twelve different parties. Turning to security and defense, Obiang claimed that because of the threat of international terrorism, it was necessary for the police and armed forces to prevent the rise of extremism within the country. He ended by praising the role of U.S. oil majors in his country.

Undersecretary Sherman looked directly at Obiang and began by saying that they both had seen and achieved a great deal during their lives. But now they were approaching the end of their careers. She said it was time that Obiang thought about his legacy and how he wished to be remembered. Sherman said she hoped that in addition to bringing peace and stability to his country, Obiang would want to facilitate a smooth, democratic transition for his successor.

Pausing momentarily to let Obiang's translator catch up, she continued that she understood why the president was concerned about international terrorism and protecting his country from violent extremism. But she added that we now lived in an interconnected world very different from the one the two of them had known growing up. To be competitive in the global economy, she emphasized, the United States and Equatorial Guinea must engage with the rest of the world rather than trying to close their borders.

Sherman asked Obiang to think about the future of Equatorial Guinea and consider how he could benefit its people. Ideally, she concluded, he would leave them with the sort of society in which they could actively participate in the economic and political future for themselves and future generations.

The president kept a straight face as he followed the translation. He then smiled enigmatically, as I'd often seen him do, and thanked Undersecretary Sherman for the meeting. She said she was pleased he would be attending the summit. They then shook hands, and the president and his entourage left.

I told Sherman I appreciated her taking the meeting. I could tell she had no time for chitchat. I was grateful to her for laying down clear markers on what it would take for EG to improve its relationship with the United States.

Two days before Sherman's meeting with Obiang, I'd gone to Andrews Air Force Base with Equatorial Guinea's new ambassador to Washington, Ruben Maye and his wife. Along with a State Department protocol officer, we were there to greet President Obiang when he arrived on his official jet. After the summit began, I spotted Ambassador Maye several times, often in the corridors between sessions. He always seemed harried and too busy to talk. After saying hello, he would excuse himself, telling me he was late for some meeting.

It also seemed strange to me that Maye did not attend the meeting between Undersecretary Sherman and President Obiang. As EG's ambassador to Washington, he certainly should have been there. Finally, Maye and his wife seemed particularly nervous around the president after he had arrived at Andrews. I would soon find out what was going on.

On the last day of the summit, Foreign Minister Mba Mokuy sent me a note asking if we could speak briefly. I said I'd be pleased to meet with him. We found a place to talk not far from the EG delegation's office space. Mba Mokuy said that he didn't want me to be surprised by the fact that Ambassador Maye would soon be leaving Washington. He continued that Maye would be replaced by a younger diplomat. I said that this did surprise me, as Maye was only in his forties and had been in Washington for a short time. The foreign minister didn't dispute this, but added that his government had decided it was time to make a change. President Obiang would soon give final approval to this decision. I thanked him for letting me know.

Obviously, Maye had fallen out with the regime for reasons that were not completely clear to me. But several weeks passed, and Maye remained at his post in Washington. After I returned to EG, I decided that it was better not to ask the foreign minister about this. And then came a bizarre event that abruptly ended Maye's ambassadorial tenure in a way I never could have anticipated. Once again, the volcano erupted, and I found myself in the middle of a difficult situation, not of my making.

CHAPTER 16

Journey's End

I TRAVELED TO Washington alone for the summit and went back to Malabo immediately afterward. August was usually a quiet month in Equatorial Guinea with government officials and well-heeled locals taking a month-long vacation, turning Malabo into a deserted place.

When my EG tour ended the following summer or early fall, I would be sixty-six and one year over the normal age limit for foreign service officers. As an ambassador, I was allowed to stay until the end of my tour and then be required to retire. Therefore, I would end my thirty-seven-year diplomatic career in Equatorial Guinea. During these tranquil last weeks in August 2014, it seemed like an ideal time to start thinking about retirement. Obviously, I should have known this was too good to be true in such a "volcanic" place.

On the morning of August 27, I received a call from my desk officer. He told me that *ARL Now*, an Arlington, Virginia, newspaper, had run an attention-grabbing story. On the night before, local police were summoned to the suburban residence of EG ambassador Ruben Maye. He and his wife had leased a large house in Arlington to accommodate the several children who had accompanied them to the U.S. According to the news report, police had received a 911 call reporting that a young girl had been hit over the head "with a chair." The woman who called added, "There's someone going crazy at her house," referring to the Mayes' residence.

The victim was Ruben Maye's sixteen-year-old daughter. The ambassador allegedly had beaten the girl on the head with a chair leg, causing her to have a serious laceration. Bleeding profusely, she'd fled to a neighbor's house, where the woman who answered the door let her in and then called 911. Paramedics arrived and rushed Maye's daughter to the Virginia Medical Center, where she was treated and then kept overnight for observation. The girl told police that her father had hit her on the head several times. Based on this, they filed a report that she was the victim of malicious wounding and child abuse.

When the officers went to the Mayes' home, Maye came to the door, identified himself as an ambassador, and said he had full diplomatic immunity from any law enforcement action against him. Accordingly, the police didn't arrest Maye but informed the Department of State.

The Associated Press picked up the story and circulated it widely on its wire service. The incident was now running in the United States and overseas. In response, Washington issued a brief press statement, "The State Department has been in close touch with the local authorities regarding the welfare of the victim and possible charges against the alleged perpetrator."

The desk officer said the State Department t wanted me to send an urgent diplomatic note (DipNote) to the Foreign Ministry. I should request the EG government to formally waive diplomatic immunity so Maye could be arrested and prosecuted in Virginia. If EG refused, Maye should be immediately recalled and stripped of his diplomatic post in the United States. Unless the EG government took one of these actions, Maye would be declared persona non grata and expelled with his family from the United States.

Once the completed DipNote had been hand-delivered to the ministry, I asked to see Foreign Minister Mba Mokuy as soon as possible. The next morning, I was quickly admitted to the minister's office. He looked grim as we sat down at his low coffee table. While nothing had appeared in EG's state-run media about Maye's alleged assault, U.S. and international news reports had already become an embarrassment.

Mba Mokuy began by acknowledging the seriousness of the incident and told me he had forwarded my DipNote to President Obiang. The minister continued that until the president made a decision regarding the U.S. request, his ministry could do nothing. He then informed me that Maye was on his way back to Malabo. I asked if this meant that he had been officially recalled. Mba Mokuy hedged, claiming that

Maye's return had been planned before "the episode" with his daughter. I suspected this was not true, thinking to myself that the minister had ordered Maye to get on the first flight back to Equatorial Guinea.

I told Mba Mokuy that the State Department expected a reply to the DipNote in the coming days. I added it was in our mutual interest not to have EG's ambassador to Washington declared persona-non-grata and expelled from the United States. I said as diplomatically as I could that I was aware from our conversation in Washington that there had been previous issues with Maye. It was now up to the two of us, I added, to avoid having him undermine the American-Equatoguinean relationship. He agreed and promised to expedite a reply.

Several days passed, and I heard nothing. I called the foreign minister, who assured me he was in contact with the president's office but still did not have an answer. I then told him that I was under considerable pressure from Washington to get a formal reply to the DipNote about Maye. I'd been asked by the State Department to meet with President Obiang and had already submitted a request to see him. Normally, Mba Mokuy would have objected that I was going over his head. But on this occasion, he simply said that he understood.

I was also contacted by someone senior at the State Department's Office of Protocol who was concerned about the welfare of the sixteen-year-old girl, who reportedly had returned to the Mayes' residence. After being contacted by Washington media, the daughter recanted what she'd told the police. She now claimed he had never struck her but during an argument, that she'd fallen and hit her head against a chair leg. The girl now maintained she'd been "foolish" to go to the neighbor's house. She said the media had blown the story out of proportion and were unfairly slandering her father.

It was obvious, the protocol official said, that the girl had been pressured to change her story. There was concern at the State Department that once Maye and his family were forced to return to EG, he would retaliate against his daughter.

On the following Saturday, I was surprised to get a call on my cell phone from Ambassador Maye. He was in Malabo and needed to see me to clear things up regarding the allegations against him. I replied that

I was willing to meet him but suggested we do so at the Hilton Hotel near the airport. We agreed to have coffee the following morning in the hotel lounge. I arrived early, and ten minutes later, I saw my diplomatic counterpart enter the lobby. He was dressed in crisp, open-neck shirt and stylish slacks and wearing his customary gold Rolex. He smiled broadly when he saw me, and as he approached, he seemed like someone who didn't have a care in the world.

We sat down and ordered coffee, and he commenced to tell me his side of the story. Although fluent in English, Maye spoke in Spanish on this occasion. It was true, he said, that he and his daughter had had an argument over what he said was her rebellious behavior. She cursed him, yelling close to his face until he pushed her. He claimed the girl had fallen backward, hitting her head on a chair leg. Maye said he tried to help her, but she ran from the house to their next-door neighbor's place. Maye vehemently condemned both the Virginia police and U.S. news media, saying they had no right to intervene in a family matter. He had been completely justified in disciplining his daughter and was infuriated by the reaction in the United States.

I listened intently, keeping the same serious expression until he finished. I then told him that the accusations against him were deeply troubling. His daughter had initially told the police, his neighbors, and hospital staff that he had repeatedly beaten her over the head with a chair leg. The medical report confirmed that the girl had suffered blunt-force head injuries consistent with this. Every indication was he had forcefully hit his daughter, causing a deep laceration requiring medical attention.

I continued that child abuse in the United States was a serious criminal offense. He needed to understand that while a parent beating a child might be acceptable in EG, it was not in my country. I concluded the police, State Department, and media had acted properly in response to the serious allegations against him.

Of course, this didn't sit well with Maye. He denied repeatedly that he'd beaten his daughter, adding he was willing to return to Virginia to defend his reputation. I replied that in this case, EG's government should waive his diplomatic immunity, which would lead to his being arrested and charged with a felony. If convicted, he would be subject to likely imprisonment and a fine. The State Department, I told him, had requested that he be stripped of his ambassadorship. I added that he should not, under any circumstances, retaliate against his daughter. It would be better in fact, if he allowed her and his other daughter to remain in the United States to finish high school there. The State Department would assist them.

Maye said in a loud voice that his daughters' education was for him and his wife to decide and none of my or the State Department's business. He insisted that it was his "right" to discipline his children in any way he saw fit. In doing so, Maye came very close to admitting that he'd indeed beaten his daughter. I replied he had no such right in the United States.

The meeting ended with my informing Maye that I was awaiting a reply from his government on whether he would be recalled or stripped of his immunity to face criminal charges in Virginia. If the State Department didn't receive an answer in the coming days, he'd be declared persona- non- grata and expelled with his family from the United States.

Returning to the office the next day, I received word through the Foreign Ministry the president would receive me in Bata at Obiang's presidential palace there. I arrived in Bata without a notetaker, having decided to handle alone what could be my final diplomatic act in the country. If the United States expelled Maye, Equatorial Guinea would certainly respond in kind by forcing Jane and me to leave.

Bata's presidential palace is an ornate. multistory building near the seafront walkway. I was taken to a first-floor room, where I waited for a bit over an hour. A protocol officer then appeared, and we climbed a stairway, ascending several flights until I was told to remain on the landing near the top floor. After a few minutes, I was summoned to come and stand before the tall mahogany doors that I assumed led to Obiang's office. As during past meetings, the doors were suddenly flung open, I was formally announced, and I saw the president standing alone some distance away. Once I entered, President Obiang motioned for me to sit down at a table off to one side of the room.

The president looked serious and thanked me for coming to Bata. He said he had earlier met with the Council of Ministers, his cabinet, although I knew he was the one who made all the decisions. During the meeting, the ministers voted unanimously to relieve Maye of his post. The president said he had a copy for me of the presidential decree. Obiang then took a single sheet of paper embossed with the presidential seal from a folder in front of him and handed it to me. I quickly skimmed the decree's flowery language announcing Maye's removal. It was now my turn to say something, and I was relieved not to have to present the ultimatum I'd prepared. "Thank you, Your Excellency. I am pleased your government has made this decision and will immediately inform the State Department. Once you've named someone to succeed Ambassador Maye, I will do everything I can to expedite his or her appointment in Washington."

Obiang now seemed more relaxed and even smiled briefly. What he said next was completely unexpected. He explained that the Foreign Ministry had wanted to remove Maye for poor performance before the incident with his daughter occurred. The president noted that he had spoken with Ambassador Maye in Washington during the summit and had decided to give him another chance. Obiang then paused, as if for dramatic effect, and concluded this turned out to be a mistake, for which he was sorry.

It took me a few seconds to process Obiang's apology. But of course, he in no way acknowledged Maye's assault on his daughter. I thanked the president and said that there was just one other, related issue I wanted to raise. The U.S. government was concerned for the welfare of the Mayes' daughter and possible retaliation against her once she returned to Equatorial Guinea. Perhaps it might be best if she and her sister remained to finish high school in the United States.

Obiang's demeanor once again became serious. He assured me that there was no need for concern by the United States for the safety of the Mayes' daughter and her sister. I thanked the president for seeing me and for the swift action of the Council of Ministers. I returned to Malabo on the afternoon flight and immediately informed Washington of Obiang's decision.

I would see Maye one final time. The State Department had asked that we request he provide us with his passport so the consular section could physically cancel his U.S. visa. To my surprise, rather than having someone drop it off, he came in person to the embassy. Several weeks had passed since the presidential decree removing him as ambassador, but Maye seemed in good spirits. He informed me he was now engaged in various business ventures, and things were going well in his life. After numerous delays, his wife and the two teenage girls returned to Malabo. Early in the following year, a trusted regime insider arrived in Washington as EG's new ambassador. With the Maye problem resolved, it was time for me to return to normal business.

In early 2014, leaders from the country's only independent registered opposition party, Convergence for Social Democracy (CPDS), met with President Obiang to discuss convening a national dialogue with all of the country's political parties, including those in the diaspora. The purpose would be to discuss opening political space for a truly multiparty system. There had been four previous national dialogues with the ruling PDGE, which had produced little concrete change.

But Andres Esono, secretary general of the CPD, told me he was guardedly optimistic that the fifth national dialogue might produce positive results. In their discussions, the CPDS reached a number of preliminary understandings with the president. In principle, he agreed to issue an amnesty for all political prisoners currently being held in EG. There would also be a presidential amnesty for leaders of what the government deemed "illegal" political parties and formations, including those in exile. They would all be welcome to participate in the dialogue without legal consequences. There would be a discussion of a new electoral law and the possibility of registration for additional parties. Obiang said he was willing to discuss private media's eligibility for licenses, permitting them to operate freely in the country. Finally, international observers would be allowed to attend the national dialogue proceedings.

I thought that the upcoming national dialogue, scheduled for November 7–15, might provide initial steps toward significant political change. In helping to prepare CPDS for the dialogue, I thought that

Esono, who had never been to the United States, would greatly benefit from discussing democratization with Democratic and Republican Party counterparts there. And in May, I was able to obtain special funding from the State Department to allow him, along with two colleagues, to spend several weeks in America. They had meetings in Washington, New York City, and finally, Manchester, New Hampshire, where they were able to observe local elections. When the group returned, they told me it had been extremely valuable for them to meet American politicians and elections officials and that they'd learned much about the U.S. political system.

Before the national dialogue began on November 7, the CPDS put out a communique saying that President Obiang had not honored a number of commitments he'd made during their previous discussions. The party noted that few, if any, of the political prisoners in EG had been released, and it was questionable if the president would follow through on other reforms to which he'd agreed in principle. I encouraged the CPDS to attend the opening of the national dialogue and bring up these issues, which they did. But they withdrew on the afternoon of the first day, stating they were dissatisfied with the government's response. The government argued that the purpose of the dialogue was to discuss such matters, and there was no reason for the party to leave so precipitously.

I thought both sides had a point. But in my view, the CPDS had far more to gain by continuing to engage with the government in the dialogue than by boycotting it. The live, uncensored broadcasts of the sessions gave the party a unique opportunity to reach large audiences with their positions. But Andres and others in the party disagreed with me. At the end of the day, it was their decision, which I fully respected.

Although the CPDS refused to participate, a number of unregistered parties, many of which had gone into exile, were able to present their ideas to EG's public via the national media, which covered the summit live. Along with other diplomats, I silently observed many of the week-long discussions, and I found them indicative of what might have been, had Equatorial Guinea been open to new political directions. Many in the opposition saw it as nothing more than another regime "show," lacking in any substance.

But I was more positive, reporting to Washington that despite its failings, the Fifth National Dialogue had resulted in some minor improvements to the political system. It paved the way for the eventual registration of Citizens for Innovation (CI), a new, independent opposition party led by a former regime insider who'd returned from self-imposed political exile in Spain.

Jane and I spent the Christmas holidays in Paris, which was a nice change after what had seemed to us like a long year. I was excited, though, about returning to Malabo because we had several innovative public diplomacy projects scheduled for my final months there.

The first came about when Tutu Alicante, director of EG Justice, proposed that the embassy cosponsor a year-long rule-of-law program with a Mexican American attorney named Elsa Peraldi. She would spend six months in Bata and another six in Malabo to assist local civil society organizations in building their operational capacity. This was a challenging task because of the regime's hostility toward these groups, which made it essential that her project have U.S. embassy sponsorship.

Elsa arrived in January 2015 and began work in Bata with CEID (Center for Development Studies and Initiatives), one of the country's preeminent civil society organizations. There she helped set up a legal clinic and conducted human rights workshops for high school students. She also helped local attorneys document human rights violations and provided them with advice on drafting habeas corpus requests for their clients.

In Malabo, Elsa established a civil society youth group called Locos por Cultura (Culture-Crazy Folks), which used the arts as a way to advance an awareness of human rights among young people. She also worked closely with leading attorneys who were defending political activists, many of whom had been unfairly imprisoned. These were all important rule-of-law initiatives, and Elsa somehow carried them out while keeping below the regime's repressive radar.

As I mentioned in an earlier chapter, Bob Royal, a former *Time* magazine photojournalist, had a 1984 exhibit at the U.S. Cultural Center in Madrid when I was the director there. It included a photo of Equatorial Guinea that he'd taken when accompanying Spain's king and queen on their 1979 visit to Malabo. In 2013, Jane and I saw Bob in Madrid, and I proposed he do an exhibit in Malabo.

"Three Continents and One Photographer: The Vision of Robert Royal on Equatorial Guinea, the United States, and Spain" was the result. Cosponsored by the embassy of Spain at the Spanish Cultural Center in Malabo, it opened on May 15, 2015, with a largely young Equatoguinean audience in attendance. Bob's charming Polish-born wife, Grazyna, who'd never been to EG, traveled from Madrid to attend the opening.

Beyond the dozens of evocative photos in the exhibit, there was a section entitled "Civil Rights Icons" that once again carried a potent message on democracy. It featured shots of Julian Bond, John Lewis, Charles Evers, and Maynard Jackson as young civil rights activists with the following text:

"The sixties and the seventies were important times for the African American population in North America. Men and women, authentic heroes, fought to claim their legitimate rights to vote and live freely as North American citizens. The country's Constitution proclaims that all men are created equal and that the right to life, liberty, and the pursuit of happiness is guaranteed to all."

My Spanish counterpart and friend, Ambassador Arturo Spiegelberg, wrote in the catalogue's introduction: "Cultural diplomacy is undoubtedly one of the cornerstones of Spanish foreign policy." I could have said exactly the same thing about the use of soft power in U.S. diplomacy. It was only one of the cultural diplomacy programs I did in my final months.

While at the U.S.-Africa Leaders Summit, I learned about the State Department–sponsored tour of a hip-hop group called *Big Piph and Tomorrow Maybe*. Led by Epiphany "Big Piph" Morrow, the group was from Pine Bluff, Arkansas. They sang not only about life's disappointments but also about being strong to overcome life's challenges. Morrow saw himself as a "catalyst and innovator" who, with his seven-member band, offered young people messages of hope.

During their February 20–26 program, *Big Piph and Tomorrow Maybe* proved to be an enormous hit with Equatoguineans. Piph, a handsome, tall young man with a powerful voice and self-assured stage presence, was charismatic and engaging. Jane and I immediately liked him and his bandmates. The group gave standing-room-only concerts to enthusiastic young audiences at the Spanish and French Cultural Centers in Malabo as well as the Spanish Cultural Center in Bata.

But the concert with the most impact was in Rebola, a small, Bubi tribal town about four miles from Malabo. Rebola's people took great pride in their distinctive language, matrilineal societal beliefs, music, and dance. They resisted efforts by the ruling Fang patrilineal majority to strip them of their tribal identity and history. With no support from the government, they founded the Rebola Cultural Center, which offered classes for youngsters in the Bubi language, agricultural traditions, and tribal history. The center also had a large outdoor stage for cultural presentations.

The U.S. embassy did what it could to support Rebola's activities, but the government disapproved of this support, telling me I should have nothing to do with the town's "subversive youth." After someone at the Foreign Ministry learned we had arranged a concert there with Big Piph, I got a strange diplomatic note before the event. Written in uncharacteristically poor Spanish, it said it was too dangerous for me to travel the four miles from Malabo to see the group perform. The Foreign Ministry strongly recommended I not go to Rebola and took no responsibility "for anything that might happen to Ambassador Asquino" if I did.

I replied with a diplomatic note citing the Vienna Convention, which allowed diplomats unfettered freedom of movement in countries to which they were accredited. I had the right to attend the concert by a group sponsored by the U.S. embassy. If I were impeded from doing so, Equatoguinean diplomats in Washington would be barred from leaving the District of Colombia. Of course, this final flourish was far beyond my authority to impose, but I left it in anyway.

Shortly after my note was delivered, Minister Mba Mokuy called me, demanding to know what this was all about. I calmly explained that I was puzzled by being told by his ministry I should not attend a nearby concert for my own safety. He claimed to know nothing about the diplomatic note, which most likely was true, and said that of course I was free to go to the concert.

Jane and I arrived in Rebola early, and even before the concert started, there were close to a hundred children already near the stage. Soon, it seemed like the entire town had gathered. The concert began with several Bubi rappers energetically performing songs as a warm-up act for the visitors. Big Piph's performance was phenomenal. There were multiple encores during which he and the group directly engaged with the audience, inviting them to come on the stage. Dozens of young Bubis danced and sang with the group. The band performed at orphanages and vocational schools in both Malabo and Bata. During breaks at these events, they discussed the meaning of their lyrics and how music had helped them in their lives. Hip-hop proved to be an effective means to convey hopeful messages to the country's largely youthful population. Beyond that, it was lots of fun!

I couldn't have been happier with how well everything was going in early 2015. All of our outreach projects to the youth were accomplishing exactly what I thought would have long-term value. But I'd spent too much time in the country not to feel that everything was just a bit too smooth. And that proved to be right because I was headed for yet another difficult time with the regime. However, I never could have imagined this new dust-up would be over, of all things, the Africa Cup of Nations football tournament in Malabo.

The January–February tournament would determine the international men's football championship of Africa. It had been originally scheduled to take place in Morocco. But the government there demanded that the Africa Cup be postponed because of the Ebola virus epidemic in Africa. Equatorial Guinea stepped up to the plate and offered itself as the venue. But while no cases of Ebola had been detected in EG, the deadly virus was rapidly spreading in the nearby nations of Guinea, Liberia, and Sierra Leone.

The government's sudden decision to host the Africa Cup brought immediate condemnation from the opposition, particularly from Andres Esono, secretary general of the CPDS. He charged that the regime was endangering the health of its citizens by allowing hundreds of players, coaches, and fans from throughout Africa to enter the country during the Ebola pandemic. The CPDS, along with two unregistered parties, began a campaign calling on Equatoguineans to boycott the games. Others questioned how EG could possibly justify the enormous unbudgeted expense of hosting the tournament. They noted that in 2014 there had been a drastic downturn in the international price of oil and gas. The country was now facing tough economic times because of its near-total dependence on these resources.

In the days before the January 17 tournament began, Equatoguinean police arrested three opposition party members for handing out pamphlets and shirts in Bata, urging people not to attend the games. They were held on the vague charge of "destabilization" and denied the right to a hearing or bail until after the games ended. The government was also concerned that given all of the negative publicity about Ebola, few would be willing to attend the games. They were especially worried about this happening during the first match scheduled in Malabo's huge stadium. For this reason, hundreds of free tickets were distributed to youngsters from the city's slums. But much to the surprise of the authorities, there was a massive turnout of football fans on the day of the Malabo opener. When the kids showed up with their complimentary tickets for that game, they were told to go away.

Of course, this infuriated the mostly teenage boys who went on a rampage, breaking store windows and vandalizing cars. Marching to the ruling Democratic Party of Equatorial Guinea's (PDGE) lavish, modern headquarters, they began throwing rocks at its facade and chanting anti-government slogans. This was too much for the regime. National security police swooped in to arrest as many of the kids as they could collar. Dozens of them were then taken to the Ministry of National Security's infamous Guantanamo detention center and confined there. This, in turn, caused a public uproar, with many of their mothers wailing and protesting in front of the ministry as they saw their children unceremoniously hustled inside.

Photos of their protest were uploaded to social media and went viral on the Internet. International human rights organizations also protested the harsh treatment of children being imprisoned with hardened criminals. Days passed, and the youngsters remained in the center's holding area, with their mothers keeping a tearful vigil outside.

I decided it was time for me to make another visit to see my "friend," the minister of national security. In preparation, I downloaded some of the most heart-wrenching photos of the moms as well as Spanish language alerts from human rights groups calling attention to the kids' plight. After several delays, Minister Obama Nchama agreed to see me, but asked that I come alone and walk to the entrance with my car and driver discreetly waiting a few blocks away. My meeting with him reminded me of the very first time we'd seen each other. We sat at his small round table, and I began by saying how well EG's team was playing in the Africa Cup tournament. But I added there was a problem. Noting the children's rampage, I acknowledged their bad behavior, but I said imprisoning them at the minister's detention center was damaging EG's worldwide image during the games.

I gave the minister photos of the children being arrested. After glancing at them, he wanted to know where I'd found them and who had taken them. I told him these and other photos and videos were easily found in any Internet search. I then gave him articles that said the children had been arrested by his security forces and that he was detaining them at the ministry.

He exploded, almost hollering that the kids were criminals who had destroyed property. Even worse, they'd tried to storm the ruling PDGE party headquarters. Fortunately, he continued, his security forces had been there to stop them. Otherwise, who knew what they would have done if they had been able to enter the building? Lowering his voice, he then asked me exactly what it was I thought he should do. Was I telling him to let them go?

Here we go again, I thought. I replied that I understood the seriousness of some of the things the youngsters had done, but they were minors. It was wrong for them to be held in an adult detention center. I continued that certainly there were laws in EG regarding the treatment of alleged juvenile offenders. Whatever he might decide, detaining them for so long was harmful to the children and their families. It was also damaging to EG's international image at a time when it was in the CAN fifteen-minute spotlight. The minister thanked me for coming to see him. I'd spoken my piece and was now being shown the door.

I heard nothing from Obama Nchama that day, and I felt I'd failed as the youngsters were still jailed at Guantanamo. But the next morning, there was an official government announcement that the children would soon be released. Without the benefit of a trial, all had been convicted of criminal vandalism and disrespect toward the ruling party, both felonies. If they committed any future infractions, they would be returned to prison and sentenced as adults. I was relieved the children were no longer being detained but saddened they'd been dealt harsh justice for what other governments would have considered juvenile delinquency. Nevertheless, I'd done what I could, and I was only too happy when the Africa Cup of Nations ended. The fallout from the games, though, was just beginning.

The Obiang government had neither forgotten nor forgiven CPDS secretary general Andres Esono for bringing attention to the dangers of Ebola and calling for a national boycott of the tournament. They came up with a response that was as insidious as it was far-fetched. The regime claimed Esono's warnings about Ebola were really part of a plot to introduce the disease to EG. In April, state media began a steady drumbeat of stories suggesting that Andres had traveled before the games to Conakry, the capital of the West African nation of Guinea, to purchase vials with specimens of deadly Ebola. According to the reports, which lacked any factual basis, he would then return to EG, somehow "weaponize" the virus, and release it among crowds at the CAN games.

Of course, the allegations didn't make any sense. How could Esono and the CPDS possibly have the scientific know-how to use Ebola to infect others? And was it really credible that someone in an impoverished nation like Guinea would have isolated and marketed the Ebola virus in safe-to-travel-with vials? It sounded like pure science fiction, so a new story on Andres's "treachery" had to be created.

The government produced a Guinean who claimed Esono had gone to Conakry and contacted his brother, who was dying of Ebola. As the story went, Esono offered to pay the sick man's family €150,000 if the CPDS leader could bring him to Malabo. There, Esono would take the fatally ill Guinean to football games as a means of spreading Ebola. According to the government's "witness," his brother had perished in Guinea before the plot could be carried out. EG's television and radio networks soon began broadcasting these ridiculous new allegations.

By mid-April, the still-uncharged Esono was forbidden from traveling outside Malabo and subjected to repeated hours-long interrogations by the national security police. He vehemently denied the allegations. He pointed out there was no evidence he had ever traveled to Guinea, let alone had meetings there to bring someone with Ebola back to EG. How would he manage to get such a sick person past the strict medical inspections at the airports and border crossings? Once again, human rights organizations and international media pointed out the absurdity of the charges, arguing they were little more than an attempt to put Esono in jail. That would eliminate him, they pointed out, from running as a candidate against Obiang in the 2016 presidential elections.

Shortly after arriving as ambassador, I'd shared my personal cell phone number with Andres and a number of other opposition party and human rights leaders. I did so with the proviso they should use it only to contact me if they found themselves in some dire situation with the government. In such circumstances, I noted, there was probably not much I could do, but at least I'd be aware of what had happened. During my three years in Malabo, I received only a few such calls.

But on a Sunday afternoon in mid-May, I heard Andres's voice on the line, and I could tell he was upset. He told me that he'd been followed all weekend by an unmarked vehicle and assumed there were plainclothes security agents inside. He feared they were going to seize him in an extrajudicial kidnapping. He asked if he could please come right away to my residence on the embassy compound.

I didn't answer immediately as there was a lot to consider. If I allowed Andres to enter the embassy compound, he'd be on sovereign American territory and could claim political asylum. That was not something I wanted to happen, and neither did I think it would help him. The allegations against him were ludicrous, and what he needed to do was continue defending himself. Taking refuge at the U.S. embassy would make him a virtual prisoner there.

I told Andres that of course he could come to see me. However, I asked for his assurance that once on the compound. he would not ask for political asylum. I explained why. He said the meeting with me might make those in the unmarked vehicle think twice about kidnapping him. Andres arrived at the compound, and we talked for more than an hour before he left. I told him to inform me immediately if he was about to be arrested. I'm sure the security police reported to their supervisors that Andres had seen the U.S. ambassador. While it's hard to know for sure if the security detail was told to stop following Andres, that's what happened.

Through sheer serendipity during the coming week, I had a meeting scheduled with President Obiang. I decided to use the occasion to bring up with him Andres Esono's situation. As it turned out, it was the president who broached the issue with me by saying that Esono was a dangerous person whom I would do well to avoid. I assumed the warning stemmed from Obiang's being informed that Andres had come to see me. I told the president that respectfully I had to disagree with him. Neither Andres nor his fellow CPDS party members advocated violence. Rather, they were dedicated to policies that would benefit the country and its citizens.

Obiang then spoke at length about Esono's supposedly vile attempt to introduce the Ebola virus into the country. He noted that had his plot succeeded, hundreds, if not thousands, of Equatoguineans would have died from the terrible disease. Surely, I told the president that Andres Esono had no intention of smuggling someone with Ebola into EG. Had he done so, Esono and his immediate family members would have been the first to become infected and die from the virus. And if somehow, he'd become infected but not died, Esono and the sick man would certainly have been stopped at the stadium. As the president knew, everyone's temperature was taken before being allowed to attend a game. None of what had been said about the so-called plot had any scientific validity, as I was sure the president must realize. By having the national media and security police continue to make such charges against the CPDS leader, Equatorial Guinea risked being ridiculed by other nations. Unfortunately, I concluded, this was already happening.

Obiang listened to all of this, occasionally glancing at the foreign minister and other officials who were sitting in. But if he felt any emotion, he kept it to himself. I left the presidency with no idea of whether I'd persuaded him to call off the attacks on Esono. Gradually, the media reports about him all but stopped. And for whatever reason, by early summer, the infamous "CAN 2015 Ebola plot" disappeared as a subject of public discourse.

As my late-September departure date approached, I met and bade farewell to the ministers with whom I'd met the most often. These included Minister of National Security Nicolas Obama Nchama. During the Christmas season, I'd given all of the ministers a bottle of bourbon as a holiday present. Bourbon was hard to find and expensive in EG, and Nicolas had told me on frequent occasions how much he enjoyed it. I decided to bring a bottle for him at our last meeting. I told him the next ambassador might have different ideas about holiday gifts, and I wanted him to have the bourbon as a parting present from me. He was delighted but also flustered, saying that he wanted to give me a remembrance of our "friendship"—something small, he said. I replied this was totally unnecessary, but I would not refuse.

Several hours later, while I was in between other farewell calls, my cell phone rang. My staff said someone from the government had left a large package for me at the embassy's security entrance. What should they do with it? I answered they should open the package and leave it in my office. On my return to the embassy, I was appalled to see an unprocessed large ivory elephant tusk sitting on my desk and a card from Minister Nicolas.

I called him later in the day, thanking him profusely for his "thoughtful gift." I explained as diplomatically as I could, that there were strict laws against the importation of ivory into my country. In fact, it was a crime to kill elephants for their tusks because we regarded them as l animals that should be protected from poachers. I concluded that under these circumstances, I must return his gift but thanked him again. I'm sure the minister never understood why anyone would not want such a valuable "trophy" from his time in Africa.

My final farewell courtesy meeting was to be with President Obiang. In the preceding months, I clashed several times with him and his ministers on democracy and human rights issues. While the government sometimes decorated departing ambassadors from "friendly" countries like Cuba and Russia, I was sure I would not be so "honored," which was fine with me.

So, it came as an unpleasant surprise when the Foreign Ministry informed me that during my farewell call with the president, he would be giving me a medal. And this leads me to the question I posed in the first sentence of this memoir, what was I doing accepting the Order of the Grand Cross of Independence of the Republic of Equatorial Guinea from Africa's longest-serving dictator? There are a number of practical answers to this question. I certainly knew that my refusal to accept the medal would be deemed insulting to the government and make things harder for my successor. Having conferred with the State Department, I was also told it would be in the best interest of maintaining the U.S.-EG bilateral relationship to graciously accept the decoration. I was retiring and could have ignored such advice. Instead, I might have used my departure to issue a fiery denunciation of the regime as Ambassador John Bennet, with whom I'd become friends, had done decades earlier before he left the country.

But this was not how I wanted to end my diplomatic journey, and neither was what I thought was the right thing to do. On September 19, 2015, I went to the presidential palace with Jane and my new DCM, Petra Zabriskie, to participate reluctantly in the award ceremony. The government press release about the event noted that in presenting me with the medal, President Obiang said that I was someone who had successfully worked closely with his government. I replied in my remarks that I hoped to return someday to Equatorial Guinea to see progress in this country. Both were certainly true.

At the end of my career, I recognized that perhaps my greatest skill as a diplomat was being a chameleon but not in a pejorative sense. I'd learned long ago how to adapt myself to morally ambiguous circumstances. I was good at engaging with people who had values conflicting with those that I held dear, as well as with others with whom I had shared beliefs. I could appear as a friend and ally to both without ever fully satisfying either. While never losing a sense of my inner values, I was often perceived to be whatever different people thought they saw in me. That was how I felt on that day when I received the Order of the Grand Cross of Independence of the Republic of Equatorial Guinea. However, it would be far from my most enduring and certainly not the happiest memory at the journey's end.

During Jane's and my visit to Spain the previous June, I decided we should go to Oviedo, Asturias, where I'd been a Fulbright lecturer. It had been twenty-nine years since I'd last traveled to the city with Pilar as our marriage was drawing to an unceremonious end. As with much of the rest of Spain, Oviedo seemed transformed, having been significantly modernized. Despite how different the city looked, as I walked on the same streets I'd taken to the university forty years earlier, I was consumed with memories of my younger self. This was particularly true at the building where I'd taught. Standing in its deserted entry hall, I could almost see the students through a dense haze of acrid black tobacco and cigarette smoke and hear the din of their youthful voices. I felt as if I could touch them and draw back the curtain of time.

But I was now at the other end of my life. Having been twenty-six back then, I was now sixty-six years old. I had passed from youth to old age, and I was looking back at a time when I had been full of optimism and naively uncritical of Spain. The intervening years had led to maturity, disappointments, achievements, and, finally, the satisfaction of being a veteran diplomat about to retire. From tentative beginnings, I was now approaching a defined professional conclusion.

It had taken almost three decades for me to return to Oviedo, requiring that I put aside the often-bitter memories of my failed first marriage, struggles as a teacher, and so many uncertainties about the future. Here I was back again some forty years later with Jane by my side in our enduring, loving marriage. I returned to this beautiful Spanish city as the U.S. ambassador to Equatorial Guinea at the end of what had been a long purposeful career. This was something I could never have imagined in 1975 as a Fulbright lecturer. I also looked forward to retirement and the challenges and rewards it would soon offer.

I'd come full circle in my life from being that shy adolescent, fascinated by my mother's tale of a long-lost uncle who'd fought in the Spanish Civil War, to representing my country in Spain's only former colony in sub-Saharan Africa.

Along the way, I had experienced so many Spanish connections in what was an amazing, diplomatic journey.

INDEX

A

B

Baku, city of, 182
Baku-Tbilisi-Ceyhan (BTC), 182
Balkan shrug, 100, 114
Barajas Airport, 51
Basile (Joyce's husband), 292
Basilica of the Immaculate Conception, 257, 259
Basque terrorist group, 58
Bastille key, 93–95
Bata, city of, 257, 263, 307
Battle (ambassador), 279–80
Beaux Artes manse, 112
Bei, Hanul, 107
Belarus, 198
Bennet, John, 244, 273, 320
Berlin Conference, 239
Berlin Wall, fall of, 16
Berza, Maria, 126
Biblioteca Nacional. *See* National Library
billets, 227
bin Laden, Osama, 168, 170
Bioko Biodiversity Protection Program (BBPP), 245
Bioko Island, 238, 243–46, 259, 284. *See also* Fernando Po Island
Black Beach Prison, 242–43, 264–65, 267–69, 273, 286
Black Sea, 124, 181
Blanco, Luis Carrero, 58
Bocamandja, 294, 296
Bolivar, Simon, 47
Bolivarian Revolution, 52
Bond, Julian, 311
bourbon, 319
boyars, 101
Brancusi, Constantin, 102
Breadbasket of Europe. *See* Romania
breezeway, 1
Brion, Kathy, 143

British Reuters, 138
Brokaw, Jim, 236
Brown University, 5
Bubi tribe, 239
Bucharest, 98, 102, 105–7, 109, 117, 119, 122
Buftea, town of, 122
Bukhara, 154, 161, 177, 183
Bureau of Educational and Cultural Relations (CU), 29
Bureau of Examiners, 20
Bureau of Intelligence and Research (INR), 183
Bush, George W., 169, 173–74

C

Cacho (Juan Pablo's colleague), 136
Cadillac, 195
Calcutta, 46
Calvo-Sotelo, Leopoldo, 61
Cambodia, 33
Cameroon, xiv, 35, 38–41, 238, 244, 255, 257, 275
Campo Yaoundé, 277–78
Capitol Hill, 101
Caracas, 46, 48–49, 51–54
Careers in Business fellowship, 22–24, 27
Caribbean, 47
Carlos, Juan, 57–61
Carmen (Catalan woman), 80–81, 86
Carol I (king of Romania), 101
Carol II (Ferdinand's son), 102
Carpathian Mountains, 120
Carson, Johnnie, 230, 253
Carter, Jimmy, 28–29, 32, 75–76, 197, 225
Carter, Rosalyn, 75
Carter Center, 197, 225, 281
Casa Capşa, 102, 124
Casa de Campo Park, 72

Komsomol organization, 155
Kyrgyzstan, 144, 154, 160

L

La Concertation, 134
ladies, young, 12
LaGuardia Airport, 83
Lahue, Charles, 2–4
La Moneda, 133
La Movida Madrileña, 61–62, 71
Lange, Jessica, 118
La Paz Clinic, 278
Las Damas Diplomaticas, 55
Last Romantic, The (Pakula), 122
Latin America, 31, 43–44, 47–49, 52–
    53, 56, 134, 143–44
Leahy, Donald, 35–36, 38–41
Lenin Peace Prize, 103
Lewis, Jerry Lee, 70
Lewis, John, 311
Ligia (teacher), 103
Linda (Dick Virden's wife), 105, 131
Lipscani District, 107
Little Paris of Europe. *See* Bucharest
locally employed staff (LES), 39, 188
Locos por Cultura, 310
Louie (dad), 6, 30, 82–85, 148–49,
    231–32
Luers, William, 50–51
Lundberg, Richard, 98, 103, 106

M

Macias regime, 37–38, 41–42
Madrid, 3–4, 9, 11, 15, 56, 61–62, 71–
    72, 74, 77, 79, 89, 96, 239
Maidenform Bra Company, 25
Malabo, 35, 71, 78, 245–46, 257,
    277, 286
Malabo II, 247, 289
Malabo International Airport, 238
Mandela, Nelson, 293

Manene, Juan, 264
Mangue de Obiang, Constancia, 276
Mann, Simon, 285
Marathon Petroleum Corporation, 238
March 1969 coup, 37, 242
Marcia (American friends), 74
Maria Alexandrovna (duchess of
    Russia), 122
Marie (of Edinburgh), 122–23
Marley, Bob, 70
Marquis de Lafayette, 94
marriage, 3, 55, 71–74, 79–80, 123, 321
Mar-Sat, 91–92
Mary (American friends), 74
Mary-Alice (Jane's mother), 133
Maye, Ruben, 300–308
Mazar-i-Sharif, city of, 172
Mbaga Obiang Lima, Gabriel, 276
Mba Mokuy, Agapito, 248–49, 252–55,
    272–73, 275, 280, 300, 303–
    4, 312
McColm, R. Bruce, 282
Mekuy, Guillermina, 279
Memmott, Larry, 146–48, 152, 171–
    72, 184
Mennuti, Deborah, 194, 196–98
Michael (king of Romania), 102–3
Milam Tang, Ignacio, 293
Miller, Linda, 115
Ministry of National Security, 265, 268,
    273, 314
Mobil, 244
Moct Druzbie, 169
Moka, 245
money, 27, 30, 77, 86, 232, 285
Mongol invasion, 154
Mongomo, 78, 257–59
Mongomo Hotel, 259
Monsogo, Wenceslao, 258, 270
Montero, Rosa
    Te Trataré Como a Una Reina, 79

242–44, 249–53, 257–58, 270–73, 275, 281, 285–87, 296–97, 300, 302, 306–7, 309–11, 313–14, 319–21
revolution, information technology, 33
Rhode Island, xiii, 5, 8, 30–31, 43, 51, 53, 81, 83, 86–87, 147, 164–65
Rice, Condoleezza, 298
Rio Muni, xiii–xiv, 239–40, 243, 257
Rodica (assistant), 110, 114, 116, 128–30
Roman, Petre, 116
Romance languages, 97, 100
Romania, 97–98, 101–2, 116, 124
    foreign marriage in, 128
Romanian (language), 97–100
Romanian Athenaeum, 102
Romanian government, 118
Romanian United Principalities, 101
Romanian wine, 105, 124
Roosevelt, Teddy, 64
Rough Riders, 64
Royal, Grazyna, 311
Royal, Robert, 71, 310
Ruddy, Kateri, 76–78
Russell, McKinney, 56, 67, 74, 87
Russia, 154–55, 158
Russian (language), 100, 144–47, 150–53, 156, 158, 166, 185, 191
Russian Bear, 146
Russian Federation, 157, 182

S

Sahrawi Arab Democratic Republic, 297
Samal Towers, 184
Samarkand, 154, 161, 163, 183
Samarkand Institute of Foreign Languages (SIFL), 160
Sandock, Mollie, 236
San Juan Hill, 64
San Salvador, 44–45
Santa Isabel, xiii, 35, 38

Santiago, 127, 132–36, 141–43, 146, 158
Sarsenbayev, Altynbek, 190–93, 196–97, 199–201
Sarsenbayuly, Altynbek. See Sarsenbayev, Altynbek
School of Media and Public Affairs (SMPA), 227
Scramble for Africa, 239
Second Summit of the Americas, 143
Semipalatinsk, town of, 183
Semipalatinsk nuclear test site, 157
Senate Foreign Relations Committee, 8, 142
September 1968 State Department memorandum, 36
Sha Na Na, 24
Sharq building, 155
Sharq Troops, 156
Sherman, Wendy, 298–300
shipment, 94–95, 104–5, 247–50
Silk Road, 144, 154, 177, 183
Sipopo, 277
Slavic language, 126, 144–46
Smithsonian Museum of History, 94
Smithsonian Tropical Research Institute (STRI), 53
Socialist Party, 61–62, 75
Socialist Republics, 156
Sofitel Hotel, 277–78
soft power, 15, 142, 311
South Ossetia, 182
Soviet Socialist Republic (SSR), 154–55
Soviet Union, 15–16, 50, 62, 97, 103, 154, 156, 159, 178, 181–82, 185
    dissolution of, 16, 97, 154
Spain, xi, xiii, xvi–4, 9–11, 13–18, 51–52, 56–65, 67–68, 70–71, 73–79, 81, 86, 93, 95–96, 239–40, 310, 321–22
Spaniards, xiii, 1, 15, 44, 57, 59–60, 64, 68–69, 71, 73, 96, 241, 285

U

Ukraine, 198, 205
Ulaanbaatar, 189
Unique National Party, 242
United Airlines Flight 93, 168
United Nations Educational, Scientific and Cultural Organization (UNESCO), 254
United States, 5, 15–16, 37, 62, 73, 78, 96, 134, 158, 275
United States International Communication Agency (USICA), 28–30, 32, 44–45, 50
University of Bucharest and the Institute for Economic Studies (ASE), 113
University of Oviedo, 9–10, 13–14, 16, 18
US-Africa Leaders Summit, 311
US Agency for International Development (USAID), 110, 142, 155, 187
US Cultural Center, 11, 32, 52, 61–71, 74
US Embassy, 9, 11, 14, 35, 38–41, 46–47, 49, 53, 56, 74–77, 105–6, 132, 143–44, 157–58, 162, 171, 184–87, 189, 196, 244, 246–47, 253, 290, 294, 312
US Foreign Service, xv, 20, 31
US Government Public Diplomacy, 228
USIA officers, 16, 20–21, 29, 93, 134, 142, 157, 181
USIA Operations Center, 89, 91
US Information Agency (USIA), 15–16, 20, 28–30, 32, 70, 74, 89–90, 94, 98, 116–17, 126–27, 130, 142–43, 155–56, 179, 196, 228
US invasion of Cambodia, 7
US investment, xv
US-Spain Joint Committee for Cultural and Educational Cooperation, 96
US-Spain Joint Committee on Science and Technology, 96
Utembayev, Yerzhan, 200
Uzbek, 156–57
Uzbekistan, xv, 144, 146, 151, 154–62, 164–65, 169–73, 175–76, 178, 180, 183, 232–33
Uzbekistan., 175
Uzbekistan's 1991 Independence, 155

V

Venezuela, 46–49, 52, 55, 71, 135
Venezuelans, 47–48, 50, 52
Victor Animatograph Corporation, 33
Victoria (actress), 115–16
video cassette players, 33
Vietnam War, 5, 7
Virden, Dick, 98, 105, 127, 131
Virgin Lands campaign, 184–85
Voice of America, 228
Volkswagen Jetta, 105
volunteers, 4, 52, 118–21, 123, 218

W

Walker, Lannon, 39, 41
Warsaw, 43, 127, 131
watch officer, 89–93
Weil, Mark, 158–59
Wheatland, 133
Whitehead, Bob, 220, 230
White House, 91–92, 231, 234, 252
White Tomb, 185
Whitney, Jack, 188
Wick, Charles Z., 90–92
Wick, Mary Jane, 90
Widows and Orphans Friendly Society, The. See Prudential Insurance Company
winter of 1977, 20
Wonga Coup, 285
World Book Encyclopedia, 1

World Food Program, 175
WorldNet, 90
World War II, 5, 9, 29–30, 57, 112, 183, 228
Wyoming, 132, 164–65

Y

Yaoundé, 35, 39–40, 244
Young African Leaders Initiative (YALI), 296
Yugoslavia, 126

Z

Zaragoza, 63
Zaragoza Air Base, 62
zarzuela, 63
Zoroastrianism, 161